W9-AHU-631

SUPER HOROSCOPE
CANCER

2003

JUNE 21–JULY 20

BERKLEY BOOKS, NEW YORK

A Berkley Book
Published by The Berkley Publishing Group
A division of Penguin Putnam Inc.
375 Hudson Street
New York, New York 10014

2003 SUPER HOROSCOPE CANCER

The publishers regret that they cannot answer
individual letters requesting personal horoscope information.

Copyright © 1974, 1978, 1979, 1980, 1981, 1982
by Grosset & Dunlap, Inc.

Copyright © 1983, 1984 by Charter Communications, Inc.

Copyright © 1985, 1986, 1987, 1988, 1989, 1990, 1991, 1992, 1993, 1994, 1995,
1996, 1997, 1998, 1999, 2000, 2001, 2002
by The Berkley Publishing Group.

Cover design by Steven Ferlauto.

All rights reserved.
This book, or parts thereof, may not be reproduced
in any form without permission.
BERKLEY and the "B" design are
trademarks belonging to Penguin Putnam Inc.

PRINTING HISTORY
Berkley trade paperback edition / July 2002

Berkley trade paperback ISBN: 0-425-18483-8

ISSN: 1535-8933

Visit our website at
www.penguinputnam.com

PRINTED IN THE UNITED STATES OF AMERICA

10 9 8 7 6 5 4 3 2 1

CONTENTS

THE CUSP-BORN CANCER

Are you *really* a Cancer? If your birthday falls during the fourth week of June, at the beginning of Cancer, will you still retain the traits of Gemini, the sign of the Zodiac before Cancer? And what if you were born late in July—are you more Leo than Cancer? Many people born at the edge, or cusp, of a sign have difficulty determining exactly what sign they are. If you are one of these people, here's how you can figure it out, once and for all.

Consult the cusp table on the facing page, then locate the year of your birth. The table will tell you the precise days on which the Sun entered and left your sign for the year of your birth. In that way you can determine if you are a true Cancer—or whether you are a Gemini or Leo—according to the variations in cusp dates from year to year (see also page 17).

If you were born at the beginning or end of Cancer, yours is a lifetime reflecting a process of subtle transformation. Your life on Earth will symbolize a significant change in consciousness, for you are either about to enter a whole new way of living or are leaving one behind.

If you were born during the fourth week of June, you may want to read the Gemini book as well as Cancer. Because Gemini holds the keys to the more hidden sides of your personality, many of your dilemmas and uncertainties about the world and people around you can be revealed. You can tune in to your secret wishes, and your potential for cosmic unfoldment.

Although you feel you have a lot to say, you will often withdraw and remain silent. Sometimes, the more you say the more confused a situation can get. Talking can drain you, and you are vulnerable to gossip. You feel secure surrounded by intimates you can trust, but sometimes the neighbors—even your own relatives—seem to be talking behind your back and you sense a vague plot in the air.

You symbolize the birth of feeling, the silent but rich condition of a fertilized seed growing full with life. The family is always an issue. At best you are a "feeling" type whose power of sensing things remains a force behind everything you think and do.

If you were born the fourth week of July, you may want to read the horoscope book for Leo as well as Cancer, for Leo could be your greatest asset. You need a warm embrace, the comfort and safety of being cared for, protected, fed. You need strong ties to the past, to the family. Attachments are natural for you. You want to be your own person, yet you often find ties and attachments prohibiting you from the rebirth you are anticipating. You may find it hard to separate yourself from dependencies without being drawn backward again and again.

You symbolize the fullness of growth, the condition of being nearly ripe, the new life about to emerge from the shadows into the sunshine.

THE CUSPS OF CANCER

DATES SUN ENTERS CANCER (LEAVES GEMINI)

June 21 every year from 1900 to 2010, except for the following:

June 20	June 22		
1988	1902	1915	1931
1992	03	18	35
1996	06	19	39
2000	07	22	43
2004	10	23	47
2008	11	26	51
	14	27	55

DATES SUN LEAVES CANCER (ENTERS LEO)

July 23 every year from 1900 to 2010, except for the following:

July 22						
1928	1953	1968	1981	1992	2001	2010
32	56	69	84	93	2002	
36	57	72	85	94	2004	
40	60	73	86	96	2005	
44	61	76	88	97	2006	
48	64	77	89	98	2008	
52	65	80	90	2000	2009	

THE ASCENDANT: CANCER RISING

Could you be a "double" Cancer? That is, could you have Cancer as your Rising sign as well as your Sun sign? The tables on pages 8–9 will tell you Cancer people what your Rising sign happens to be. Just find the hour of your birth, then find the day of your birth, and you will see which sign of the Zodiac is your Ascendant, as the Rising sign is called. The Ascendant is called that because it is the sign rising on the eastern horizon at the time of your birth. For a more detailed discussion of the Rising sign and the twelve houses of the Zodiac, see pages 17–20.

The Ascendant, or Rising sign, is placed on the 1st house in a horoscope, of which there are twelve houses. The 1st house represents your response to the environment—your unique response. Call it identity, personality, ego, self-image, facade, come-on, body-mind-spirit—whatever term best conveys to you the meaning of the you that acts and reacts in the world. It is a you that is always changing, discovering a new you. Your identity started with birth and early environment, over which you had little conscious control, and continues to experience, to adjust, to express itself. The 1st house also represents how others see you. Has anyone ever guessed your sign to be your Rising sign? People may respond to that personality, that facade, that body type governed by your Rising sign.

Your Ascendant, or Rising sign, modifies your basic Sun sign personality, and it affects the way you act out the daily predictions for your Sun sign. If your Rising sign indeed is Cancer, what follows is a description of its effect on your horoscope. If your Rising sign is not Cancer, but some other sign of the Zodiac, you may wish to read the horoscope book for that sign as well.

With Cancer on the Ascendant, that is, in the 1st house, the ruling planet of the 1st house is the Moon. The Moon here gives you an especially keen ability to sense patterns and changes in the environment. The Moon in this position makes you more than just receptive; it makes you reactive and adaptive. You can integrate the most fleeting, irrational impressions received from the environment. There is, however, the danger that such sensory overload, so to speak, could inhibit your ability to act appropriately in a given situation.

Cancer in the 1st house accentuates your ambitiousness. Tenacity, a strong Cancer trait, is translated here into a highly developed power of focus. You can focus your energy on several levels at once—social, emotional, even psychic—in order to realize your aims. But always the scene of struggle and realization is personal rather than public, concrete rather than abstract. Your three basic loves—food, home, money—are all personal ones. Power is not a burning issue for you, but on the other hand, concepts of right and wrong are. You may also hide behind your concepts, posing as a more intellectual person than you really feel, whenever you become too timid to express your strongly emotional nature.

Sympathy and sensitivity are basic personality traits for Cancer Rising. That combination may lead to a subjective view of the world, one which has little in common with the views of other people. For that reason, you may appear to be shy, when in fact you are merely retiring from a possible occasion of misunderstanding or conflict. You prefer to protect yourself and those you love from any pain or suffering. You want to provide a comfortable haven for all the hurt creatures of the world. You can, therefore, be labeled a homebody or a mothering type.

Although the concept of home is central in your life, you are not a stick-in-the-mud; indeed, you do not necessarily like to be rooted in one place. You would like a family, to nurture and protect it, to develop and instill pervasive attitudes of right conduct. If you don't have a natural family, you will be happy serving a community cause, even if that service takes you far and wide and results in reversals of fortune along the way. There may be many travels and voyages in the lifetimes of those of you with Cancer Rising. Home is where your heart is. Possessions, too, have little meaning for you unless they are connected with a special person or intimate situation.

Supportiveness to others continually wars with inner insecurity, making you doubt the value and extent of your attachment. You need to feel appreciated by everyone in your immediate environment. Emotional satisfaction may be more compelling than honor and success. You could enter secret love affairs or alliances just for the personal gratification they provide, and despite the dangers they pose. There may be an aura of mystery surrounding you, inspired partly by your fondness for secrets, partly by your hidden, inaccessible, unsteady emotionality, partly by your success in isolation; some of you may engender enemies and long-standing rivals as a result.

Intuition and imagination are the key words for Cancer Rising. You can put them to use in the service of a fruitful lifestyle, or you can squander them in complaints. You are at your best when you are building something.

RISING SIGNS FOR CANCER

Hour of Birth*	Day of Birth		
	June 20–25	June 26–30	July 1–5
Midnight	Pisces; Aries 6/22	Aries	Aries
1 AM	Aries	Taurus	Taurus
2 AM	Taurus	Taurus	Taurus
3 AM	Gemini	Gemini	Gemini
4 AM	Gemini	Gemini	Gemini; Cancer 7/3
5 AM	Cancer	Cancer	Cancer
6 AM	Cancer	Cancer	Cancer
7 AM	Cancer; Leo 6/23	Leo	Leo
8 AM	Leo	Leo	Leo
9 AM	Leo	Leo; Virgo 6/30	Virgo
10 AM	Virgo	Virgo	Virgo
11 AM	Virgo	Virgo	Virgo
Noon	Virgo; Libra 6/24	Libra	Libra
1 PM	Libra	Libra	Libra
2 PM	Libra	Libra; Scorpio 6/29	Scorpio
3 PM	Scorpio	Scorpio	Scorpio
4 PM	Scorpio	Scorpio	Scorpio
5 PM	Scorpio; Sagittarius 6/23	Sagittarius	Sagittarius
6 PM	Sagittarius	Sagittarius	Sagittarius
7 PM	Sagittarius	Sagittarius; Capricorn 6/27	Capricorn
8 PM	Capricorn	Capricorn	Capricorn
9 PM	Capricorn	Aquarius	Aquarius
10 PM	Aquarius	Aquarius	Aquarius
11 PM	Pisces	Pisces	Pisces

*Hour of birth given here is for Standard Time in any time zone. If your hour of birth was recorded in Daylight Saving Time, subtract one hour from it and consult that hour in the table above. For example, if you were born at 9 AM D.S.T., see 8 AM above.

Hour of Birth*	Day of Birth		
	July 6–10	July 11–17	July 18–23
Midnight	Aries	Taurus	Taurus
1 AM	Taurus	Taurus	Taurus; Gemini 7/19
2 AM	Gemini	Gemini	Gemini
3 AM	Gemini	Gemini	Gemini
4 AM	Cancer	Cancer	Cancer
5 AM	Cancer	Cancer	Cancer; Leo 7/23
6 AM	Leo	Leo	Leo
7 AM	Leo	Leo	Leo
8 AM	Leo	Leo; Virgo 7/15	Virgo
9 AM	Virgo	Virgo	Virgo
10 AM	Virgo	Virgo	Virgo; Libra 7/23
11 AM	Libra	Libra	Libra
Noon	Libra	Libra	Libra
1 PM	Libra	Libra; Scorpio 7/15	Scorpio
2 PM	Scorpio	Scorpio	Scorpio
3 PM	Scorpio	Scorpio	Scorpio; Sagittarius 7/23
4 PM	Scorpio; Sagittarius 7/7	Sagittarius	Sagittarius
5 PM	Sagittarius	Sagittarius	Sagittarius
6 PM	Sagittarius	Capricorn	Capricorn
7 PM	Capricorn	Capricorn	Capricorn
8 PM	Capricorn	Aquarius	Aquarius
9 PM	Aquarius	Aquarius	Pisces
10 PM	Pisces	Pisces	Pisces; Aries 7/22
11 PM	Pisces; Aries 7/7	Aries	Aries

*See note on facing page.

THE PLACE OF ASTROLOGY IN TODAY'S WORLD

Does astrology have a place in the fast-moving, ultra-scientific world we live in today? Can it be justified in a sophisticated society whose outriders are already preparing to step off the moon into the deep space of the planets themselves? Or is it just a hangover of ancient superstition, a psychological dummy for neurotics and dreamers of every historical age?

These are the kind of questions that any inquiring person can be expected to ask when they approach a subject like astrology which goes beyond, but never excludes, the materialistic side of life.

The simple, single answer is that astrology works. It works for many millions of people in the western world alone. In the United States there are 10 million followers and in Europe, an estimated 25 million. America has more than 4000 practicing astrologers, Europe nearly three times as many. Even down-under Australia has its hundreds of thousands of adherents. In the eastern countries, astrology has enormous followings, again, because it has been proved to work. In India, for example, brides and grooms for centuries have been chosen on the basis of their astrological compatibility.

Astrology today is more vital than ever before, more practicable because all over the world the media devotes much space and time to it, more valid because science itself is confirming the precepts of astrological knowledge with every new exciting step. The ordinary person who daily applies astrology intelligently does not have to wonder whether it is true nor believe in it blindly. He can see it working for himself. And, if he can use it—and this book is designed to help the reader to do just that—he can make living a far richer experience, and become a more developed personality and a better person.

Astrology and Relationships

Astrology is the science of relationships. It is not just a study of planetary influences on man and his environment. It is the study of man himself.

We are at the center of our personal universe, of all our relationships. And our happiness or sadness depends on how we act, how we relate to the people and things that surround us. The emotions that we generate have a distinct effect—for better or worse—on the world around us. Our friends and our enemies will confirm this. Just look in the mirror the next time you are angry. In other words, each of us is a kind of sun or planet or star radiating our feelings on the environment around us. Our influence on our personal universe, whether loving, helpful, or destructive, varies with our changing moods, expressed through our individual character.

Our personal "radiations" are potent in the way they affect our moods and our ability to control them. But we usually are able to throw off our emotion in some sort of action—we have a good cry, walk it off, or tell someone our troubles—before it can build up too far and make us physically ill. Astrology helps us to understand the universal forces working on us, and through this understanding, we can become more properly adjusted to our surroundings so that we find ourselves coping where others may flounder.

The Challenge of Love

The challenge of love lies in recognizing the difference between infatuation, emotion, sex, and, sometimes, the intentional deceit of the other person. Mankind, with its record of broken marriages, despair, and disillusionment, is obviously not very good at making these distinctions.

Can astrology help?

Yes. In the same way that advance knowledge can usually help in any human situation. And there is probably no situation as human, as poignant, as pathetic and universal, as the failure of man's love.

Love, of course, is not just between man and woman. It involves love of children, parents, home, and friends. But the big problems usually involve the choice of partner.

Astrology has established degrees of compatibility that exist between people born under the various signs of the Zodiac. Because people are individuals, there are numerous variations and modifications. So the astrologer, when approached on mate and marriage matters, makes allowances for them. But the fact remains that some groups of people are suited for each other and some are not, and astrology has expressed this in terms of characteristics we all can study and use as a personal guide.

No matter how much enjoyment and pleasure we find in the different aspects of each other's character, if it is not an overall compatibility, the chances of our finding fulfillment or enduring happiness in each other are pretty hopeless. And astrology can help us to find someone compatible.

Astrology and Science

Closely related to our emotions is the "other side" of our personal universe, our physical welfare. Our body, of course, is largely influenced by things around us over which we have very little control. The phone rings, we hear it. The train runs late. We snag our stocking or cut our face shaving. Our body is under a constant bombardment of events that influence our daily lives to varying degrees.

The question that arises from all this is, what makes each of us act so that we have to involve other people and keep the ball of activity and evolution rolling? This is the question that both science and astrology are involved with. The scientists have attacked it from different angles: anthropology, the study of human evolution as body, mind and response to environment; anatomy, the study of bodily structure; psychology, the science of the human mind; and so on. These studies have produced very impressive classifications and valuable information, but because the approach to the problem is fragmented, so is the result. They remain "branches" of science. Science generally studies effects. It keeps turning up wonderful answers but no lasting solutions. Astrology, on the other hand, approaches the question from the broader viewpoint. Astrology began its inquiry with the totality of human experience and saw it as an effect. It then looked to find the cause, or at least the prime movers, and during thousands of years of observation of man and his *universal* environment came up with the extraordinary principle of planetary influence—or astrology, which, from the Greek, means the science of the stars.

Modern science, as we shall see, has confirmed much of astrology's foundations—most of it unintentionally, some of it reluctantly, but still, indisputably.

It is not difficult to imagine that there must be a connection between outer space and Earth. Even today, scientists are not too sure how our Earth was created, but it is generally agreed that it is only a tiny part of the universe. And as a part of the universe, people on Earth see and feel the influence of heavenly bodies in almost every aspect of our existence. There is no doubt that the Sun has the greatest influence on life on this planet. Without it there would be no life, for without it there would be no warmth, no division into day and night, no cycles of time or season at all. This is clear and easy to see. The influence of the Moon, on the other hand, is more subtle, though no less definite.

There are many ways in which the influence of the Moon manifests itself here on Earth, both on human and animal life. It is a well-known fact, for instance, that the large movements of water on our planet—that is the ebb and flow of the tides—are caused by the Moon's gravitational pull. Since this is so, it follows that these water movements do not occur only in the oceans, but that all bodies of water are affected, even down to the tiniest puddle.

The human body, too, which consists of about 70 percent water, falls within the scope of this lunar influence. For example the menstrual cycle of most women corresponds to the 28-day lunar month; the period of pregnancy in humans is 273 days, or equal to nine lunar months. Similarly, many illnesses reach a crisis at the change of the Moon, and statistics in many countries have shown that the crime rate is highest at the time of the Full Moon. Even human sexual desire has been associated with the phases of the Moon. But it is in the movement of the tides that we get the clearest demonstration of planetary influence, which leads to the irresistible correspondence between the so-called metaphysical and the physical.

Tide tables are prepared years in advance by calculating the future positions of the Moon. Science has known for a long time that the Moon is the main cause of tidal action. But only in the last few years has it begun to realize the possible extent of this influence on mankind. To begin with, the ocean tides do not rise and fall as we might imagine from our personal observations of them. The Moon as it orbits around Earth sets up a circular wave of attraction which pulls the oceans of the world after it, broadly in an east to west direction. This influence is like a phantom wave crest, a loop of power stretching from pole to pole which passes over and around the Earth like an invisible shadow. It travels with equal effect across the land masses and, as scientists were recently amazed to observe, caused oysters placed in the dark in the middle of the United States where there is no sea to open their shells to receive the nonexistent tide. If the land-locked oysters react to this invisible signal, what effect does it have on us who not so long ago in evolutionary time came out of the sea and still have its salt in our blood and sweat?

Less well known is the fact that the Moon is also the primary force behind the circulation of blood in human beings and animals, and the movement of sap in trees and plants. Agriculturists have established that the Moon has a distinct influence on crops, which explains why for centuries people have planted according to Moon cycles. The habits of many animals, too, are directed by the movement of the Moon. Migratory birds, for instance, depart only at or near the time of the Full Moon. And certain sea creatures, eels in particular, move only in accordance with certain phases of the Moon.

Know Thyself—Why?

In today's fast-changing world, everyone still longs to know what the future holds. It is the one thing that everyone has in common: rich and poor, famous and infamous, all are deeply concerned about tomorrow.

But the key to the future, as every historian knows, lies in the past. This is as true of individual people as it is of nations. You cannot understand your future without first understanding your past, which is simply another way of saying that you must first of all know yourself.

The motto "know thyself" seems obvious enough nowadays, but it was originally put forward as the foundation of wisdom by the ancient Greek philosophers. It was then adopted by the "mystery religions" of the ancient Middle East, Greece, Rome, and is still used in all genuine schools of mind training or mystical discipline, both in those of the East, based on yoga, and those of the West. So it is universally accepted now, and has been through the ages.

But how do you go about discovering what sort of person you are? The first step is usually classification into some sort of system of types. Astrology did this long before the birth of Christ. Psychology has also done it. So has modern medicine, in its way.

One system classifies people according to the source of the impulses they respond to most readily: the muscles, leading to direct bodily action; the digestive organs, resulting in emotion; or the brain and nerves, giving rise to thinking. Another such system says that character is determined by the endocrine glands, and gives us such labels as "pituitary," "thyroid," and "hyperthyroid" types. These different systems are neither contradictory nor mutually exclusive. In fact, they are very often different ways of saying the same thing.

Very popular, useful classifications were devised by Carl Jung, the eminent disciple of Freud. Jung observed among the different faculties of the mind, four which have a predominant influence on character. These four faculties exist in all of us without exception, but not in perfect balance. So when we say, for instance, that someone is a "thinking type," it means that in any situation he or she tries to be rational. Emotion, which may be the opposite of thinking, will be his or her weakest function. This thinking type can be sensible and reasonable, or calculating and unsympathetic. The emotional type, on the other hand, can often be recognized by exaggerated language—everything is either marvelous or terrible—and in extreme cases they even invent dramas and quarrels out of nothing just to make life more interesting.

The other two faculties are intuition and physical sensation. The sensation type does not only care for food and drink, nice clothes and furniture; he or she is also interested in all forms of physical experience. Many scientists are sensation types as are athletes and nature-lovers. Like sensation, intuition is a form of perception and we all possess it. But it works through that part of the mind which is not under conscious control—consequently it sees meanings and connections which are not obvious to thought or emotion. Inventors and original thinkers are always intuitive, but so, too, are superstitious people who see meanings where none exist.

Thus, sensation tells us what is going on in the world, feeling (that is, emotion) tells us how important it is to ourselves, thinking enables us to interpret it and work out what we should do about it, and intuition tells us what it means to ourselves and others. All four faculties are essential, and all are present in every one of us. But some people are guided chiefly by one, others by another. In addition, Jung also observed a division of the human personality into the extrovert and the introvert, which cuts across these four types.

A disadvantage of all these systems of classification is that one cannot tell very easily where to place oneself. Some people are reluctant to admit that they act to please their emotions. So they deceive themselves for years by trying to belong to whichever type they think is the "best." Of course, there is no best; each has its faults and each has its good points.

The advantage of the signs of the Zodiac is that they simplify classification. Not only that, but your date of birth is personal—it is unarguably yours. What better way to know yourself than by going back as far as possible to the very moment of your birth? And this is precisely what your horoscope is all about, as we shall see in the next section.

WHAT IS A HOROSCOPE?

If you had been able to take a picture of the skies at the moment of your birth, that photograph would be your horoscope. Lacking such a snapshot, it is still possible to recreate the picture—and this is at the basis of the astrologer's art. In other words, your horoscope is a representation of the skies with the planets in the exact positions they occupied at the time you were born.

The year of birth tells an astrologer the positions of the distant, slow-moving planets Jupiter, Saturn, Uranus, Neptune, and Pluto. The month of birth indicates the Sun sign, or birth sign as it is commonly called, as well as indicating the positions of the rapidly moving planets Venus, Mercury, and Mars. The day and time of birth will locate the position of our Moon. And the moment—the exact hour and minute—of birth determines the houses through what is called the Ascendant, or Rising sign.

With this information the astrologer consults various tables to calculate the specific positions of the Sun, Moon, and other planets relative to your birthplace at the moment you were born. Then he or she locates them by means of the Zodiac.

The Zodiac

The Zodiac is a band of stars (constellations) in the skies, centered on the Sun's apparent path around the Earth, and is divided into twelve equal segments, or signs. What we are actually dividing up is the Earth's path around the Sun. But from our point of view here on Earth, it seems as if the Sun is making a great circle around our planet in the sky, so we say it is the Sun's apparent path. This twelvefold division, the Zodiac, is a reference system for the astrologer. At any given moment the planets—and in astrology both the Sun and Moon are considered to be planets—can all be located at a specific point along this path.

Now where in all this are you, the subject of the horoscope? Your character is largely determined by the sign the Sun is in. So that is where the astrologer looks first in your horoscope, at your Sun sign.

The Sun Sign and the Cusp

There are twelve signs in the Zodiac, and the Sun spends approximately one month in each sign. But because of the motion of the Earth around the Sun—the Sun's apparent motion—the dates when the Sun enters and leaves each sign may change from year to year. Some people born near the cusp, or edge, of a sign have difficulty determining which is their Sun sign. But in this book a Table of Cusps is provided for the years 1900 to 2010 (page 5) so you can find out what your true Sun sign is.

Here are the twelve signs of the Zodiac, their ancient zodiacal symbol, and the dates when the Sun enters and leaves each sign for the year 2003. Remember, these dates may change from year to year.

ARIES	Ram	March 20–April 20
TAURUS	Bull	April 20–May 21
GEMINI	Twins	May 21–June 21
CANCER	Crab	June 21–July 23
LEO	Lion	July 23–August 23
VIRGO	Virgin	August 23–September 23
LIBRA	Scales	September 23–October 23
SCORPIO	Scorpion	October 23–November 22
SAGITTARIUS	Archer	November 22–December 22
CAPRICORN	Sea Goat	December 22–January 20
AQUARIUS	Water Bearer	January 20–February 18
PISCES	Fish	February 18–March 20

It is possible to draw significant conclusions and make meaningful predictions based simply on the Sun sign of a person. There are many people who have been amazed at the accuracy of the description of their own character based only on the Sun sign. But an astrologer needs more information than just your Sun sign to interpret the photograph that is your horoscope.

The Rising Sign and the Zodiacal Houses

An astrologer needs the exact time and place of your birth in order to construct and interpret your horoscope. The illustration on the next page shows the flat chart, or natural wheel, an astrologer uses. Note the inner circle of the wheel labeled 1 through 12. These 12 divisions are known as the houses of the Zodiac.

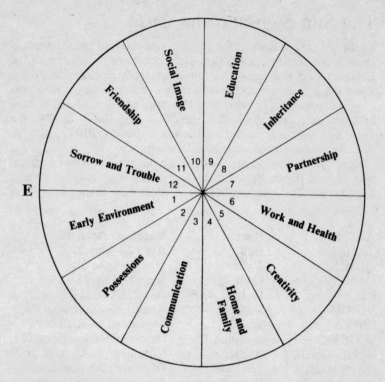

The 1st house always starts from the position marked E, which corresponds to the eastern horizon. The rest of the houses 2 through 12 follow around in a "counterclockwise" direction. The point where each house starts is known as a cusp, or edge.

The cusp, or edge, of the 1st house (point E) is where an astrologer would place your Rising sign, the Ascendant. And, as already noted, the exact time of your birth determines your Rising sign. Let's see how this works.

As the Earth rotates on its axis once every 24 hours, each one of the twelve signs of the Zodiac appears to be "rising" on the horizon, with a new one appearing about every 2 hours. Actually it is the turning of the Earth that exposes each sign to view, but in our astrological work we are discussing apparent motion. This Rising sign marks the Ascendant, and it colors the whole orientation of a horoscope. It indicates the sign governing the 1st house of the chart, and will thus determine which signs will govern all the other houses.

To visualize this idea, imagine two color wheels with twelve divisions superimposed upon each other. For just as the Zodiac is divided into twelve constellations that we identify as the signs, another twelvefold division is used to denote the houses. Now imagine one wheel (the signs) moving slowly while the other wheel (the houses) remains still. This analogy may help you see how the signs keep shifting the "color" of the houses as the Rising sign continues to change every two hours. To simplify things, a Table of Rising Signs has been provided (pages 8–9) for your specific Sun sign.

Once your Rising sign has been placed on the cusp of the 1st house, the signs that govern the rest of the 11 houses can be placed on the chart. In any individual's horoscope the signs do not necessarily correspond with the houses. For example, it could be that a sign covers part of two adjacent houses. It is the interpretation of such variations in an individual's horoscope that marks the professional astrologer.

But to gain a workable understanding of astrology, it is not necessary to go into great detail. In fact, we just need a description of the houses and their meanings, as is shown in the illustration above and in the table below.

THE 12 HOUSES OF THE ZODIAC

1st	Individuality, body appearance, general outlook on life	Personality house
2nd	Finance, possessions, ethical principles, gain or loss	Money house
3rd	Relatives, communication, short journeys, writing, education	Relatives house
4th	Family and home, parental ties, land and property, security	Home house
5th	Pleasure, children, creativity, entertainment, risk	Pleasure house
6th	Health, harvest, hygiene, work and service, employees	Health house
7th	Marriage and divorce, the law, partnerships and alliances	Marriage house
8th	Inheritance, secret deals, sex, death, regeneration	Inheritance house
9th	Travel, sports, study, philosophy and religion	Travel house
10th	Career, social standing, success and honor	Business house
11th	Friendship, social life, hopes and wishes	Friends house
12th	Troubles, illness, secret enemies, hidden agendas	Trouble house

The Planets in the Houses

An astrologer, knowing the exact time and place of your birth, will use tables of planetary motion in order to locate the planets in your horoscope chart. He or she will determine which planet or planets are in which sign and in which house. It is not uncommon, in an individual's horoscope, for there to be two or more planets in the same sign and in the same house.

The characteristics of the planets modify the influence of the Sun according to their natures and strengths.

Sun: Source of life. Basic temperament according to the Sun sign. The conscious will. Human potential.

Moon: Emotions. Moods. Customs. Habits. Changeable. Adaptive. Nurturing.

Mercury: Communication. Intellect. Reasoning power. Curiosity. Short travels.

Venus: Love. Delight. Charm. Harmony. Balance. Art. Beautiful possessions.

Mars: Energy. Initiative. War. Anger. Adventure. Courage. Daring. Impulse.

Jupiter: Luck. Optimism. Generous. Expansive. Opportunities. Protection.

Saturn: Pessimism. Privation. Obstacles. Delay. Hard work. Research. Lasting rewards after long struggle.

Uranus: Fashion. Electricity. Revolution. Independence. Freedom. Sudden changes. Modern science.

Neptune: Sensationalism. Theater. Dreams. Inspiration. Illusion. Deception.

Pluto: Creation and destruction. Total transformation. Lust for power. Strong obsessions.

Superimpose the characteristics of the planets on the functions of the house in which they appear. Express the result through the character of the Sun sign, and you will get the basic idea.

Of course, many other considerations have been taken into account in producing the carefully worked out predictions in this book: the aspects of the planets to each other; their strength according to position and sign; whether they are in a house of exaltation or decline; whether they are natural enemies or not; whether a planet occupies its own sign; the position of a planet in relation to its own house or sign; whether the sign is male or female; whether the sign is a fire, earth, water, or air sign. These are only a few of the colors on the astrologer's pallet which he or she must mix with the inspiration of the artist and the accuracy of the mathematician.

How To Use These Predictions

A person reading the predictions in this book should understand that they are produced from the daily position of the planets for a group of people and are not, of course, individually specialized. To get the full benefit of them our readers should relate the predictions to their own character and circumstances, coordinate them, and draw their own conclusions from them.

If you are a serious observer of your own life, you should find a definite pattern emerging that will be a helpful and reliable guide.

The point is that we always retain our free will. The stars indicate certain directional tendencies but we are not compelled to follow. We can do or not do, and wisdom must make the choice.

We all have our good and bad days. Sometimes they extend into cycles of weeks. It is therefore advisable to study daily predictions in a span ranging from the day before to several days ahead.

Daily predictions should be taken very generally. The word "difficult" does not necessarily indicate a whole day of obstruction or inconvenience. It is a warning to you to be cautious. Your caution will often see you around the difficulty before you are involved. This is the correct use of astrology.

In another section (pages 78–84), detailed information is given about the influence of the Moon as it passes through each of the twelve signs of the Zodiac. There are instructions on how to use the Moon Tables (pages 85–92), which provide Moon Sign Dates throughout the year as well as the Moon's role in health and daily affairs. This information should be used in conjunction with the daily forecasts to give a fuller picture of the astrological trends.

HISTORY OF ASTROLOGY

The origins of astrology have been lost far back in history, but we do know that reference is made to it as far back as the first written records of the human race. It is not hard to see why. Even in primitive times, people must have looked for an explanation for the various happenings in their lives. They must have wanted to know why people were different from one another. And in their search they turned to the regular movements of the Sun, Moon, and stars to see if they could provide an answer.

It is interesting to note that as soon as man learned to use his tools in any type of design, or his mind in any kind of calculation, he turned his attention to the heavens. Ancient cave dwellings reveal dim crescents and circles representative of the Sun and Moon, rulers of day and night. Mesopotamia and the civilization of Chaldea, in itself the foundation of those of Babylonia and Assyria, show a complete picture of astronomical observation and well-developed astrological interpretation.

Humanity has a natural instinct for order. The study of anthropology reveals that primitive people—even as far back as prehistoric times—were striving to achieve a certain order in their lives. They tried to organize the apparent chaos of the universe. They had the desire to attach meaning to things. This demand for order has persisted throughout the history of man. So that observing the regularity of the heavenly bodies made it logical that primitive peoples should turn heavenward in their search for an understanding of the world in which they found themselves so random and alone.

And they did find a significance in the movements of the stars. Shepherds tending their flocks, for instance, observed that when the cluster of stars now known as the constellation Aries was in sight, it was the time of fertility and they associated it with the Ram. And they noticed that the growth of plants and plant life corresponded with different phases of the Moon, so that certain times were favorable for the planting of crops, and other times were not. In this way, there grew up a tradition of seasons and causes connected with the passage of the Sun through the twelve signs of the Zodiac.

Astrology was valued so highly that the king was kept informed of the daily and monthly changes in the heavenly bodies, and the results of astrological studies regarding events of the future. Head astrologers were clearly men of great rank and position, and the office was said to be a hereditary one.

Omens were taken, not only from eclipses and conjunctions of the Moon or Sun with one of the planets, but also from storms and earthquakes. In the eastern civilizations, particularly, the reverence inspired by astrology appears to have remained unbroken since the very earliest days. In ancient China, astrology, astronomy, and religion went hand in hand. The astrologer, who was also an astronomer, was part of the official government service and had his own corner in the Imperial Palace. The duties of the Imperial astrologer, whose office was one of the most important in the land, were clearly defined, as this extract from early records shows:

> This exalted gentleman must concern himself with the stars in the heavens, keeping a record of the changes and movements of the Planets, the Sun and the Moon, in order to examine the movements of the terrestrial world with the object of prognosticating good and bad fortune. He divides the territories of the nine regions of the empire in accordance with their dependence on particular celestial bodies. All the fiefs and principalities are connected with the stars and from this their prosperity or misfortune should be ascertained. He makes prognostications according to the twelve years of the Jupiter cycle of good and evil of the terrestrial world. From the colors of the five kinds of clouds, he determines the coming of floods or droughts, abundance or famine. From the twelve winds, he draws conclusions about the state of harmony of heaven and earth, and takes note of good and bad signs that result from their accord or disaccord. In general, he concerns himself with five kinds of phenomena so as to warn the Emperor to come to the aid of the government and to allow for variations in the ceremonies according to their circumstances.

The Chinese were also keen observers of the fixed stars, giving them such unusual names as Ghost Vehicle, Sun of Imperial Concubine, Imperial Prince, Pivot of Heaven, Twinkling Brilliance, Weaving Girl. But, great astrologers though they may have been, the Chinese lacked one aspect of mathematics that the Greeks applied to astrology—deductive geometry. Deductive geometry was the basis of much classical astrology in and after the time of the Greeks, and this explains the different methods of prognostication used in the East and West.

Down through the ages the astrologer's art has depended, not so much on the uncovering of new facts, though this is important, as on the interpretation of the facts already known. This is the essence of the astrologer's skill.

But why should the signs of the Zodiac have any effect at all on the formation of human character? It is easy to see why people thought they did, and even now we constantly use astrological expressions in our everyday speech. The thoughts of "lucky star," "ill-fated," "star-crossed," "mooning around," are interwoven into the very structure of our language.

Wherever the concept of the Zodiac is understood and used, it could well appear to have an influence on the human character. Does this mean, then, that the human race, in whose civilization the idea of the twelve signs of the Zodiac has long been embedded, is divided into only twelve types? Can we honestly believe that it is really as simple as that? If so, there must be pretty wide ranges of variation within each type. And if, to explain the variation, we call in heredity and environment, experiences in early childhood, the thyroid and other glands, and also the four functions of the mind together with extroversion and introversion, then one begins to wonder if the original classification was worth making at all. No sensible person believes that his favorite system explains everything. But even so, he will not find the system much use at all if it does not even save him the trouble of bothering with the others.

In the same way, if we were to put every person under only one sign of the Zodiac, the system becomes too rigid and unlike life. Besides, it was never intended to be used like that. It may be convenient to have only twelve types, but we know that in practice there is every possible gradation between aggressiveness and timidity, or between conscientiousness and laziness. How, then, do we account for this?

A person born under any given Sun sign can be mainly influenced by one or two of the other signs that appear in their individual horoscope. For instance, famous persons born under the sign of Gemini include Henry VIII, whom nothing and no one could have induced to abdicate, and Edward VIII, who did just that. Obviously, then, the sign Gemini does not fully explain the complete character of either of them.

Again, under the opposite sign, Sagittarius, were both Stalin, who was totally consumed with the notion of power, and Charles V, who freely gave up an empire because he preferred to go into a monastery. And we find under Scorpio many uncompromising characters such as Luther, de Gaulle, Indira Gandhi, and Montgomery, but also Petain, a successful commander whose name later became synonymous with collaboration.

A single sign is therefore obviously inadequate to explain the differences between people; it can only explain resemblances, such as the combativeness of the Scorpio group, or the far-reaching devotion of Charles V and Stalin to their respective ideals—the Christian heaven and the Communist utopia.

But very few people have only one sign in their horoscope chart. In addition to the month of birth, the day and, even more, the hour to the nearest minute if possible, ought to be considered. Without this, it is impossible to have an actual horoscope, for the word horoscope literally means "a consideration of the hour."

The month of birth tells you only which sign of the Zodiac was occupied by the Sun. The day and hour tell you what sign was occupied by the Moon. And the minute tells you which sign was rising on the eastern horizon. This is called the Ascendant, and, as some astrologers believe, it is supposed to be the most important thing in the whole horoscope.

The Sun is said to signify one's heart, that is to say, one's deepest desires and inmost nature. This is quite different from the Moon, which signifies one's superficial way of behaving. When the ancient Romans referred to the Emperor Augustus as a Capricorn, they meant that he had the Moon in Capricorn. Or, to take another example, a modern astrologer would call Disraeli a Scorpion because he had Scorpio Rising, but most people would call him Sagittarius because he had the Sun there. The Romans would have called him Leo because his Moon was in Leo.

So if one does not seem to fit one's birth month, it is always worthwhile reading the other signs, for one may have been born at a time when any of them were rising or occupied by the Moon. It also seems to be the case that the influence of the Sun develops as life goes on, so that the month of birth is easier to guess in people over the age of forty. The young are supposed to be influenced mainly by their Ascendant, the Rising sign, which characterizes the body and physical personality as a whole.

It is nonsense to assume that all people born at a certain time will exhibit the same characteristics, or that they will even behave in the same manner. It is quite obvious that, from the very moment of its birth, a child is subject to the effects of its environment, and that this in turn will influence its character and heritage to a decisive extent. Also to be taken into account are education and economic conditions, which play a very important part in the formation of one's character as well.

People have, in general, certain character traits and qualities which, according to their environment, develop in either a positive or a negative manner. Therefore, selfishness (inherent selfishness, that is) might emerge as unselfishness; kindness and consideration as cruelty and lack of consideration toward others. In the same way, a naturally constructive person may, through frustration, become destructive, and so on. The latent characteristics with which people are born can, therefore, through environment and good or bad training, become something that would appear to be its opposite, and so give the lie to the astrologer's description of their character. But this is not the case. The true character is still there, but it is buried deep beneath these external superficialities.

Careful study of the character traits of various signs of the Zodiac are of immeasurable help, and can render beneficial service to the intelligent person. Undoubtedly, the reader will already have discovered that, while he is able to get on very well with some people, he just "cannot stand" others. The causes sometimes seem inexplicable. At times there is intense dislike, at other times immediate sympathy. And there is, too, the phenomenon of love at first sight, which is also apparently inexplicable. People appear to be either sympathetic or unsympathetic toward each other for no apparent reason.

Now if we look at this in the light of the Zodiac, we find that people born under different signs are either compatible or incompatible with each other. In other words, there are good and bad interrelating factors among the various signs. This does not, of course, mean that humanity can be divided into groups of hostile camps. It would be quite wrong to be hostile or indifferent toward people who happen to be born under an incompatible sign. There is no reason why everybody should not, or cannot, learn to control and adjust their feelings and actions, especially after they are aware of the positive qualities of other people by studying their character analyses, among other things.

Every person born under a certain sign has both positive and negative qualities, which are developed more or less according to our free will. Nobody is entirely good or entirely bad, and it is up to each of us to learn to control ourselves on the one hand and at the same time to endeavor to learn about ourselves and others.

It cannot be emphasized often enough that it is free will that determines whether we will make really good use of our talents and abilities. Using our free will, we can either overcome our failings or allow them to rule us. Our free will enables us to exert sufficient willpower to control our failings so that they do not harm ourselves or others.

Astrology can reveal our inclinations and tendencies. Astrology can tell us about ourselves so that we are able to use our free will to overcome our shortcomings. In this way astrology helps us do our best to become needed and valuable members of society as well as helpmates to our family and our friends. Astrology also can save us a great deal of unhappiness and remorse.

Yet it may seem absurd that an ancient philosophy could be a prop to modern men and women. But below the materialistic surface of modern life, there are hidden streams of feeling and thought. Symbology is reappearing as a study worthy of the scholar; the psychosomatic factor in illness has passed from the writings of the crank to those of the specialist; spiritual healing in all its forms is no longer a pious hope but an accepted phenomenon. And it is into this context that we consider astrology, in the sense that it is an analysis of human types.

Astrology and medicine had a long journey together, and only parted company a couple of centuries ago. There still remain in medical language such astrological terms as "saturnine," "choleric," and "mercurial," used in the diagnosis of physical tendencies. The herbalist, for long the handyman of the medical profession, has been dominated by astrology since the days of the Greeks. Certain herbs traditionally respond to certain planetary influences, and diseases must therefore be treated to ensure harmony between the medicine and the disease.

But the stars are expected to foretell and not only to diagnose.

Astrological forecasting has been remarkably accurate, but often it is wide of the mark. The brave person who cares to predict world events takes dangerous chances. Individual forecasting is less clear cut; it can be a help or a disillusionment. Then we come to the nagging question: if it is possible to foreknow, is it right to foretell? This is a point of ethics on which it is hard to pronounce judgment. The doctor faces the same dilemma if he finds that symptoms of a mortal disease are present in his patient and that he can only prognosticate a steady decline. How much to tell an individual in a crisis is a problem that has perplexed many distinguished scholars. Honest and conscientious astrologers in this modern world, where so many people are seeking guidance, face the same problem.

Five hundred years ago it was customary to call in a learned man who was an astrologer who was probably also a doctor and a philosopher. By his knowledge of astrology, his study of planetary influences, he felt himself qualified to guide those in distress. The world has moved forward at a fantastic rate since then, and yet people are still uncertain of themselves. At first sight it seems fantastic in the light of modern thinking that they turn to the most ancient of all studies, and get someone to calculate a horoscope for them. But is it *really* so fantastic if you take a second look? For astrology is concerned with tomorrow, with survival. And in a world such as ours, tomorrow and survival are the keywords for the twenty-first century.

ASTROLOGICAL BRIDGE TO THE 21st CENTURY

As the decade opens on a new century, indeed on a new millennium, the planets set the stage for change and challenge. Themes connecting past, present, and future are in play as new planetary cycles form the bridge to the twenty-first century and its broad horizons. The first few years of the new decade reveal hidden paths and personal hints for achieving your potential, for making the most of your message from the planets.

With the dawning of the twenty-first century look first to Jupiter, the planet of good fortune. Each new yearly Jupiter cycle follows the natural progression of the Zodiac. First is Jupiter in Aries and in Taurus through spring 2000, next Jupiter is in Gemini to summer 2001, then in Cancer to midsummer 2002, in Leo to late summer 2003, in Virgo to early autumn 2004, and so on through Jupiter in Pisces through June 2010. The beneficent planet Jupiter promotes your professional and educational goals while urging informed choice and deliberation. Jupiter sharpens your focus and hones your skills, providing a rich medium for creativity. Planet Jupiter's influence is protective, the generous helper that comes to the rescue just in the nick of time. And while safeguarding good luck, Jupiter can turn unusual risks into achievable aims.

In order to take advantage of luck and opportunity, to gain wisdom from experience, to persevere against adversity, look to beautiful planet Saturn. Saturn, planet of reason and responsibility, began a new cycle in earthy Taurus at the turn of the century. Saturn in Taurus until spring 2001 inspires industry and affection, blends practicality and imagination, all the while inviting caution and care. Persistence and planning can reverse setbacks and minimize risk. Saturn in Taurus lends beauty, order, and structure to your life. Then Saturn is in Gemini, the sign of mind and communication, until June 2003. Saturn in Gemini gives depth and inspiration to thought and feeling. Here, because of a lively intellectual capacity, the limits of creativity can be stretched and boundaries broken. Saturn in Gemini holds the promise of fruitful endeavor through sustained study, learning, and application. Saturn in Cancer from early June 2003 to mid-July 2005 poses issues of long-term security versus immediate gratification. Rely on deliberation and choice to make sense out of diversity and change. Saturn in Cancer can be a revealing cycle, leading to the desired outcomes of growth and maturity.

Uranus, planet of innovation and surprise, started an important new cycle in January of 1996. At that time Uranus entered its natural home in airy Aquarius. Uranus in Aquarius into the year 2003 has a profound effect on your personality and the lens through which you see the world. A basic change in the way you project yourself is just one impact of Uranus in Aquarius. More significantly, a whole new consciousness is evolving. Winds of change blowing your way emphasize movement and freedom. Uranus in Aquarius poses involvement in the larger community beyond self, family, friends, lovers, associates. Radical ideas and progressive thought signal a journey of liberation. As the new century begins, follow Uranus on the path of humanitarianism. A new Uranus cycle begins March 2003 when Uranus visits Pisces, briefly revisits Aquarius, then returns late in 2003 to Pisces where it will stay into May 2010. Uranus in Pisces, a strongly intuitive force, urges work and service for the good of humankind to make the world a better place for all people.

Neptune, planet of vision and mystery, is enjoying a long cycle that excites creativity and imaginative thinking. Neptune is in airy Aquarius from November 1998 to February of 2012. Neptune in Aquarius, the sign of the Water Bearer, represents two sides of the coin of wisdom: inspiration and reason. Here Neptune stirs powerful currents bearing a rich and varied harvest, the fertile breeding ground for idealistic aims and practical considerations. Neptune's fine intuition tunes in to your dreams, your imagination, your spirituality. You can never turn your back on the mysteries of life. Uranus and Neptune, the planets of enlightenment and idealism, give you glimpses into the future, letting you peek through secret doorways into the twenty-first century.

Pluto, planet of beginnings and endings, began a new cycle of growth and learning late in 1995. Pluto entered fiery Sagittarius and remains there into the year 2008. Pluto in Sagittarius during its long stay over twelve years can create significant change. The great power of Pluto in Sagittarius is already starting its transformation of your character and lifestyle. Pluto in Sagittarius takes you on a new journey of exploration and learning. The awakening you experience on intellectual and artistic levels heralds a new cycle of growth. Uncompromising Pluto, seeker of truth, challenges your identity, persona, and self-expression. Uncovering the real you, Pluto holds the key to understanding and meaningful communication. Pluto in Sagittarius can be the guiding light illuminating the first decade of the twenty-first century. Good luck is riding on the waves of change.

THE SIGNS OF THE ZODIAC

Dominant Characteristics

Aries: March 21–April 20

The Positive Side of Aries

The Aries has many positive points to his character. People born under this first sign of the Zodiac are often quite strong and enthusiastic. On the whole, they are forward-looking people who are not easily discouraged by temporary setbacks. They know what they want out of life and they go out after it. Their personalities are strong. Others are usually quite impressed by the Ram's way of doing things. Quite often they are sources of inspiration for others traveling the same route. Aries men and women have a special zest for life that can be contagious; for others, they are a fine example of how life should be lived.

The Aries person usually has a quick and active mind. He is imaginative and inventive. He enjoys keeping busy and active. He generally gets along well with all kinds of people. He is interested in mankind, as a whole. He likes to be challenged. Some would say he thrives on opposition, for it is when he is set against that he often does his best. Getting over or around obstacles is a challenge he generally enjoys. All in all, Aries is quite positive and young-thinking. He likes to keep abreast of new things that are happening in the world. Aries are often fond of speed. They like things to be done quickly, and this sometimes aggravates their slower colleagues and associates.

The Aries man or woman always seems to remain young. Their whole approach to life is youthful and optimistic. They never say die, no matter what the odds. They may have an occasional setback, but it is not long before they are back on their feet again.

The Negative Side of Aries

Everybody has his less positive qualities—and Aries is no exception. Sometimes the Aries man or woman is not very tactful in communicating with others; in his hurry to get things done he is apt to be a little callous or inconsiderate. Sensitive people are likely to find him somewhat sharp-tongued in some situations. Often in his eagerness to get the show on the road, he misses the mark altogether and cannot achieve his aims.

At times Aries can be too impulsive. He can occasionally be stubborn and refuse to listen to reason. If things do not move quickly enough to suit the Aries man or woman, he or she is apt to become rather nervous or irritable. The uncultivated Aries is not unfamiliar with moments of doubt and fear. He is capable of being destructive if he does not get his way. He can overcome some of his emotional problems by steadily trying to express himself as he really is, but this requires effort.

Taurus: April 21–May 20

The Positive Side of Taurus

The Taurus person is known for his ability to concentrate and for his tenacity. These are perhaps his strongest qualities. The Taurus man or woman generally has very little trouble in getting along with others; it's his nature to be helpful toward people in need. He can always be depended on by his friends, especially those in trouble.

Taurus generally achieves what he wants through his ability to persevere. He never leaves anything unfinished but works on something until it has been completed. People can usually take him at his word; he is honest and forthright in most of his dealings. The Taurus person has a good chance to make a success of his life because of his many positive qualities. The Taurus who aims high seldom falls short of his mark. He learns well by experience. He is thorough and does not believe in shortcuts of any kind. The Bull's thoroughness pays off in the end, for through his deliberateness he learns how to rely on himself and what he has learned. The Taurus person tries to get along with others, as a rule. He is not overly critical and likes people to be themselves. He is a tolerant person and enjoys peace and harmony—especially in his home life.

Taurus is usually cautious in all that he does. He is not a person who believes in taking unnecessary risks. Before adopting any one line of action, he will weigh all of the pros and cons. The Taurus person is steadfast. Once his mind is made up it seldom changes. The person born under this sign usually is a good family person— reliable and loving.

The Negative Side of Taurus

Sometimes the Taurus man or woman is a bit too stubborn. He won't listen to other points of view if his mind is set on something. To others, this can be quite annoying. Taurus also does not like to be told what to do. He becomes rather angry if others think him not too bright. He does not like to be told he is wrong, even when he is. He dislikes being contradicted.

Some people who are born under this sign are very suspicious of others—even of those persons close to them. They find it difficult to trust people fully. They are often afraid of being deceived or taken advantage of. The Bull often finds it difficult to forget or forgive. His love of material things sometimes makes him rather avaricious and petty.

Gemini: May 21–June 20

The Positive Side of Gemini

The person born under this sign of the Heavenly Twins is usually quite bright and quick-witted. Some of them are capable of doing many different things. The Gemini person very often has many different interests. He keeps an open mind and is always anxious to learn new things.

Gemini is often an analytical person. He is a person who enjoys making use of his intellect. He is governed more by his mind than by his emotions. He is a person who is not confined to one view; he can often understand both sides to a problem or question. He knows how to reason, how to make rapid decisions if need be.

He is an adaptable person and can make himself at home almost anywhere. There are all kinds of situations he can adapt to. He is a person who seldom doubts himself; he is sure of his talents and his ability to think and reason. Gemini is generally most satisfied

when he is in a situation where he can make use of his intellect. Never short of imagination, he often has strong talents for invention. He is rather a modern person when it comes to life; Gemini almost always moves along with the times—perhaps that is why he remains so youthful throughout most of his life.

Literature and art appeal to the person born under this sign. Creativity in almost any form will interest and intrigue the Gemini man or woman.

The Gemini is often quite charming. A good talker, he often is the center of attraction at any gathering. People find it easy to like a person born under this sign because he can appear easygoing and usually has a good sense of humor.

The Negative Side of Gemini

Sometimes the Gemini person tries to do too many things at one time—and as a result, winds up finishing nothing. Some Twins are easily distracted and find it rather difficult to concentrate on one thing for too long a time. Sometimes they give in to trifling fancies and find it rather boring to become too serious about any one thing. Some of them are never dependable, no matter what they promise.

Although the Gemini man or woman often appears to be well-versed on many subjects, this is sometimes just a veneer. His knowledge may be only superficial, but because he speaks so well he gives people the impression of erudition. Some Geminis are sharp-tongued and inconsiderate; they think only of themselves and their own pleasure.

Cancer: June 21–July 20

The Positive Side of Cancer

The Moon Child's most positive point is his understanding nature. On the whole, he is a loving and sympathetic person. He would never go out of his way to hurt anyone. The Cancer man or woman is often very kind and tender; they give what they can to others. They hate to see others suffering and will do what they can to help someone in less fortunate circumstances than themselves. They are often very concerned about the world. Their interest in people generally goes beyond that of just their own families and close friends; they have a deep sense of community and respect humanitarian values. The Moon Child means what he says, as a rule; he is honest about his feelings.

The Cancer man or woman is a person who knows the art of patience. When something seems difficult, he is willing to wait until the situation becomes manageable again. He is a person who knows how to bide his time. Cancer knows how to concentrate on one thing at a time. When he has made his mind up he generally sticks with what he does, seeing it through to the end.

Cancer is a person who loves his home. He enjoys being surrounded by familiar things and the people he loves. Of all the signs, Cancer is the most maternal. Even the men born under this sign often have a motherly or protective quality about them. They like to take care of people in their family—to see that they are well loved and well provided for. They are usually loyal and faithful. Family ties mean a lot to the Cancer man or woman. Parents and in-laws are respected and loved. Young Cancer responds very well to adults who show faith in him. The Moon Child has a strong sense of tradition. He is very sensitive to the moods of others.

The Negative Side of Cancer

Sometimes Cancer finds it rather hard to face life. It becomes too much for him. He can be a little timid and retiring, when things don't go too well. When unfortunate things happen, he is apt to just shrug and say, "Whatever will be will be." He can be fatalistic to a fault. The uncultivated Cancer is a bit lazy. He doesn't have very much ambition. Anything that seems a bit difficult he'll gladly leave to others. He may be lacking in initiative. Too sensitive, when he feels he's been injured, he'll crawl back into his shell and nurse his imaginary wounds. The immature Moon Child often is given to crying when the smallest thing goes wrong.

Some Cancers find it difficult to enjoy themselves in environments outside their homes. They make heavy demands on others, and need to be constantly reassured that they are loved. Lacking such reassurance, they may resort to sulking in silence.

Leo: July 21–August 21

The Positive Side of Leo

Often Leos make good leaders. They seem to be good organizers and administrators. Usually they are quite popular with others. Whatever group it is that they belong to, the Leo man or woman is almost sure to be or become the leader. Loyalty, one of the Lion's noblest traits, enables him or her to maintain this leadership position.

Leo is generous most of the time. It is his best characteristic. He or she likes to give gifts and presents. In making others happy, the Leo person becomes happy himself. He likes to splurge when spending money on others. In some instances it may seem that the Lion's generosity knows no boundaries. A hospitable person, the Leo man or woman is very fond of welcoming people to his house and entertaining them. He is never short of company.

Leo has plenty of energy and drive. He enjoys working toward some specific goal. When he applies himself correctly, he gets what he wants most often. The Leo person is almost never unsure of himself. He has plenty of confidence and aplomb. He is a person who is direct in almost everything he does. He has a quick mind and can make a decision in a very short time.

He usually sets a good example for others because of his ambitious manner and positive ways. He knows how to stick to something once he's started. Although Leo may be good at making a joke, he is not superficial or glib. He is a loving person, kind and thoughtful.

There is generally nothing small or petty about the Leo man or woman. He does what he can for those who are deserving. He is a person others can rely upon at all times. He means what he says. An honest person, generally speaking, he is a friend who is valued and sought out.

The Negative Side of Leo

Leo, however, does have his faults. At times, he can be just a bit too arrogant. He thinks that no one deserves a leadership position except him. Only he is capable of doing things well. His opinion of himself is often much too high. Because of his conceit, he is

sometimes rather unpopular with a good many people. Some Leos are too materialistic; they can only think in terms of money and profit.

Some Leos enjoy lording it over others—at home or at their place of business. What is more, they feel they have the right to. Egocentric to an impossible degree, this sort of Leo cares little about how others think or feel. He can be rude and cutting.

Virgo: August 22–September 22

The Positive Side of Virgo

The person born under the sign of Virgo is generally a busy person. He knows how to arrange and organize things. He is a good planner. Above all, he is practical and is not afraid of hard work.

Often called the sign of the Harvester, Virgo knows how to attain what he desires. He sticks with something until it is finished. He never shirks his duties, and can always be depended upon. The Virgo person can be thoroughly trusted at all times.

The man or woman born under this sign tries to do everything to perfection. He doesn't believe in doing anything halfway. He always aims for the top. He is the sort of a person who is always learning and constantly striving to better himself—not because he wants more money or glory, but because it gives him a feeling of accomplishment.

The Virgo man or woman is a very observant person. He is sensitive to how others feel, and can see things below the surface of a situation. He usually puts this talent to constructive use.

It is not difficult for the Virgo to be open and earnest. He believes in putting his cards on the table. He is never secretive or underhanded. He's as good as his word. The Virgo person is generally plainspoken and down to earth. He has no trouble in expressing himself.

The Virgo person likes to keep up to date on new developments in his particular field. Well-informed, generally, he sometimes has a keen interest in the arts or literature. What he knows, he knows well. His ability to use his critical faculties is well-developed and sometimes startles others because of its accuracy.

Virgos adhere to a moderate way of life; they avoid excesses. Virgo is a responsible person and enjoys being of service.

The Negative Side of Virgo

Sometimes a Virgo person is too critical. He thinks that only he can do something the way it should be done. Whatever anyone else does is inferior. He can be rather annoying in the way he quibbles over insignificant details. In telling others how things should be done, he can be rather tactless and mean.

Some Virgos seem rather emotionless and cool. They feel emotional involvement is beneath them. They are sometimes too tidy, too neat. With money they can be rather miserly. Some Virgos try to force their opinions and ideas on others.

Libra: September 23–October 22

The Positive Side of Libra

Libras love harmony. It is one of their most outstanding character traits. They are interested in achieving balance; they admire beauty and grace in things as well as in people. Generally speaking, they are kind and considerate people. Libras are usually very sympathetic. They go out of their way not to hurt another person's feelings. They are outgoing and do what they can to help those in need.

People born under the sign of Libra almost always make good friends. They are loyal and amiable. They enjoy the company of others. Many of them are rather moderate in their views; they believe in keeping an open mind, however, and weighing both sides of an issue fairly before making a decision.

Alert and intelligent, Libra, often known as the Lawgiver, is always fair-minded and tries to put himself in the position of the other person. They are against injustice; quite often they take up for the underdog. In most of their social dealings, they try to be tactful and kind. They dislike discord and bickering, and most Libras strive for peace and harmony in all their relationships.

The Libra man or woman has a keen sense of beauty. They appreciate handsome furnishings and clothes. Many of them are artistically inclined. Their taste is usually impeccable. They know how to use color. Their homes are almost always attractively arranged and inviting. They enjoy entertaining people and see to it that their guests always feel at home and welcome.

Libra gets along with almost everyone. He is well-liked and socially much in demand.

The Negative Side of Libra

Some people born under this sign tend to be rather insincere. So eager are they to achieve harmony in all relationships that they will even go so far as to lie. Many of them are escapists. They find facing the truth an ordeal and prefer living in a world of make-believe.

In a serious argument, some Libras give in rather easily even when they know they are right. Arguing, even about something they believe in, is too unsettling for some of them.

Libras sometimes care too much for material things. They enjoy possessions and luxuries. Some are vain and tend to be jealous.

Scorpio: October 23–November 22

The Positive Side of Scorpio

The Scorpio man or woman generally knows what he or she wants out of life. He is a determined person. He sees something through to the end. Scorpio is quite sincere, and seldom says anything he doesn't mean. When he sets a goal for himself he tries to go about achieving it in a very direct way.

The Scorpion is brave and courageous. They are not afraid of hard work. Obstacles do not frighten them. They forge ahead until they achieve what they set out for. The Scorpio man or woman has a strong will.

Although Scorpio may seem rather fixed and determined, inside he is often quite tender and loving. He can care very much for others. He believes in sincerity in all relationships. His feelings about someone tend to last; they are profound and not superficial.

The Scorpio person is someone who adheres to his principles no matter what happens. He will not be deterred from a path he believes to be right.

Because of his many positive strengths, the Scorpion can often achieve happiness for himself and for those that he loves.

He is a constructive person by nature. He often has a deep understanding of people and of life, in general. He is perceptive and unafraid. Obstacles often seem to spur him on. He is a positive person who enjoys winning. He has many strengths and resources; challenge of any sort often brings out the best in him.

The Negative Side of Scorpio

The Scorpio person is sometimes hypersensitive. Often he imagines injury when there is none. He feels that others do not bother to recognize him for his true worth. Sometimes he is given to excessive boasting in order to compensate for what he feels is neglect.

Scorpio can be proud, arrogant, and competitive. They can be sly when they put their minds to it and they enjoy outwitting persons or institutions noted for their cleverness.

Their tactics for getting what they want are sometimes devious and ruthless. They don't care too much about what others may think. If they feel others have done them an injustice, they will do their best to seek revenge. The Scorpion often has a sudden, violent temper; and this person's interest in sex is sometimes quite unbalanced or excessive.

Sagittarius: November 23–December 20

The Positive Side of Sagittarius

People born under this sign are honest and forthright. Their approach to life is earnest and open. Sagittarius is often quite adult in his way of seeing things. They are broad-minded and tolerant people. When dealing with others the person born under the sign of the Archer is almost always open and forthright. He doesn't believe in deceit or pretension. His standards are high. People who associate with Sagittarius generally admire and respect his tolerant viewpoint.

The Archer trusts others easily and expects them to trust him. He is never suspicious or envious and almost always thinks well of others. People always enjoy his company because he is so friendly and easygoing. The Sagittarius man or woman is often good-humored. He can always be depended upon by his friends, family, and co-workers.

The person born under this sign of the Zodiac likes a good joke every now and then. Sagittarius is eager for fun and laughs, which makes him very popular with others.

A lively person, he enjoys sports and outdoor life. The Archer is fond of animals. Intelligent and interesting, he can begin an

animated conversation with ease. He likes exchanging ideas and discussing various views.

He is not selfish or proud. If someone proposes an idea or plan that is better than his, he will immediately adopt it. Imaginative yet practical, he knows how to put ideas into practice.

The Archer enjoys sport and games, and it doesn't matter if he wins or loses. He is a forgiving person, and never sulks over something that has not worked out in his favor.

He is seldom critical, and is almost always generous.

The Negative Side of Sagittarius

Some Sagittarius are restless. They take foolish risks and seldom learn from the mistakes they make. They don't have heads for money and are often mismanaging their finances. Some of them devote much of their time to gambling.

Some are too outspoken and tactless, always putting their feet in their mouths. They hurt others carelessly by being honest at the wrong time. Sometimes they make promises which they don't keep. They don't stick close enough to their plans and go from one failure to another. They are undisciplined and waste a lot of energy.

Capricorn: December 21–January 19

The Positive Side of Capricorn

The person born under the sign of Capricorn, known variously as the Mountain Goat or Sea Goat, is usually very stable and patient. He sticks to whatever tasks he has and sees them through. He can always be relied upon and he is not averse to work.

An honest person, Capricorn is generally serious about whatever he does. He does not take his duties lightly. He is a practical person and believes in keeping his feet on the ground.

Quite often the person born under this sign is ambitious and knows how to get what he wants out of life. The Goat forges ahead and never gives up his goal. When he is determined about something, he almost always wins. He is a good worker—a hard worker. Although things may not come easy to him, he will not complain, but continue working until his chores are finished.

He is usually good at business matters and knows the value of money. He is not a spendthrift and knows how to put something away for a rainy day; he dislikes waste and unnecessary loss.

Capricorn knows how to make use of his self-control. He can apply himself to almost anything once he puts his mind to it. His ability to concentrate sometimes astounds others. He is diligent and does well when involved in detail work.

The Capricorn man or woman is charitable, generally speaking, and will do what is possible to help others less fortunate. As a friend, he is loyal and trustworthy. He never shirks his duties or responsibilities. He is self-reliant and never expects too much of the other fellow. He does what he can on his own. If someone does him a good turn, then he will do his best to return the favor.

The Negative Side of Capricorn

Like everyone, Capricorn, too, has faults. At times, the Goat can be overcritical of others. He expects others to live up to his own high standards. He thinks highly of himself and tends to look down on others.

His interest in material things may be exaggerated. The Capricorn man or woman thinks too much about getting on in the world and having something to show for it. He may even be a little greedy.

He sometimes thinks he knows what's best for everyone. He is too bossy. He is always trying to organize and correct others. He may be a little narrow in his thinking.

Aquarius: January 20–February 18

The Positive Side of Aquarius

The Aquarius man or woman is usually very honest and forthright. These are his two greatest qualities. His standards for himself are generally very high. He can always be relied upon by others. His word is his bond.

Aquarius is perhaps the most tolerant of all the Zodiac personalities. He respects other people's beliefs and feels that everyone is entitled to his own approach to life.

He would never do anything to injure another's feelings. He is never unkind or cruel. Always considerate of others, the Water

Bearer is always willing to help a person in need. He feels a very strong tie between himself and all the other members of mankind.

The person born under this sign, called the Water Bearer, is almost always an individualist. He does not believe in teaming up with the masses, but prefers going his own way. His ideas about life and mankind are often quite advanced. There is a saying to the effect that the average Aquarius is fifty years ahead of his time.

Aquarius is community-minded. The problems of the world concern him greatly. He is interested in helping others no matter what part of the globe they live in. He is truly a humanitarian sort. He likes to be of service to others.

Giving, considerate, and without prejudice, Aquarius have no trouble getting along with others.

The Negative Side of Aquarius

Aquarius may be too much of a dreamer. He makes plans but seldom carries them out. He is rather unrealistic. His imagination has a tendency to run away with him. Because many of his plans are impractical, he is always in some sort of a dither.

Others may not approve of him at all times because of his unconventional behavior. He may be a bit eccentric. Sometimes he is so busy with his own thoughts that he loses touch with the realities of existence.

Some Aquarius feel they are more clever and intelligent than others. They seldom admit to their own faults, even when they are quite apparent. Some become rather fanatic in their views. Their criticism of others is sometimes destructive and negative.

Pisces: February 19–March 20

The Positive Side of Pisces

Known as the sign of the Fishes, Pisces has a sympathetic nature. Kindly, he is often dedicated in the way he goes about helping others. The sick and the troubled often turn to him for advice and assistance. Possessing keen intuition, Pisces can easily understand people's deepest problems.

He is very broad-minded and does not criticize others for their faults. He knows how to accept people for what they are. On the whole, he is a trustworthy and earnest person. He is loyal to his friends and will do what he can to help them in time of need. Generous and good-natured, he is a lover of peace; he is often willing to help others solve their differences. People who have taken a wrong turn in life often interest him and he will do what he can to persuade them to rehabilitate themselves.

He has a strong intuitive sense and most of the time he knows how to make it work for him. Pisces is unusually perceptive and often knows what is bothering someone before that person, himself, is aware of it. The Pisces man or woman is an idealistic person, basically, and is interested in making the world a better place in which to live. Pisces believes that everyone should help each other. He is willing to do more than his share in order to achieve cooperation with others.

The person born under this sign often is talented in music or art. He is a receptive person; he is able to take the ups and downs of life with philosophic calm.

The Negative Side of Pisces

Some Pisces are often depressed; their outlook on life is rather glum. They may feel that they have been given a bad deal in life and that others are always taking unfair advantage of them. Pisces sometimes feel that the world is a cold and cruel place. The Fishes can be easily discouraged. The Pisces man or woman may even withdraw from the harshness of reality into a secret shell of his own where he dreams and idles away a good deal of his time.

Pisces can be lazy. He lets things happen without giving the least bit of resistance. He drifts along, whether on the high road or on the low. He can be lacking in willpower.

Some Pisces people seek escape through drugs or alcohol. When temptation comes along they find it hard to resist. In matters of sex, they can be rather permissive.

Sun Sign Personalities

ARIES: Hans Christian Andersen, Pearl Bailey, Marlon Brando, Wernher Von Braun, Charlie Chaplin, Joan Crawford, Da Vinci, Bette Davis, Doris Day, W. C. Fields, Alec Guinness, Adolf Hitler, William Holden, Thomas Jefferson, Nikita Khrushchev, Elton John, Arturo Toscanini, J. P. Morgan, Paul Robeson, Gloria Steinem, Sarah Vaughn, Vincent van Gogh, Tennessee Williams

TAURUS: Fred Astaire, Charlotte Brontë, Carol Burnett, Irving Berlin, Bing Crosby, Salvador Dali, Tchaikovsky, Queen Elizabeth II, Duke Ellington, Ella Fitzgerald, Henry Fonda, Sigmund Freud, Orson Welles, Joe Louis, Lenin, Karl Marx, Golda Meir, Eva Peron, Bertrand Russell, Shakespeare, Kate Smith, Benjamin Spock, Barbra Streisand, Shirley Temple, Harry Truman

GEMINI: Ruth Benedict, Josephine Baker, Rachel Carson, Carlos Chavez, Walt Whitman, Bob Dylan, Ralph Waldo Emerson, Judy Garland, Paul Gauguin, Allen Ginsberg, Benny Goodman, Bob Hope, Burl Ives, John F. Kennedy, Peggy Lee, Marilyn Monroe, Joe Namath, Cole Porter, Laurence Olivier, Harriet Beecher Stowe, Queen Victoria, John Wayne, Frank Lloyd Wright

CANCER: "Dear Abby," Lizzie Borden, David Brinkley, Yul Brynner, Pearl Buck, Marc Chagall, Princess Diana, Babe Didrikson, Mary Baker Eddy, Henry VIII, John Glenn, Ernest Hemingway, Lena Horne, Oscar Hammerstein, Helen Keller, Ann Landers, George Orwell, Nancy Reagan, Rembrandt, Richard Rodgers, Ginger Rogers, Rubens, Jean-Paul Sartre, O. J. Simpson

LEO: Neil Armstrong, James Baldwin, Lucille Ball, Emily Brontë, Wilt Chamberlain, Julia Child, William J. Clinton, Cecil B. De Mille, Ogden Nash, Amelia Earhart, Edna Ferber, Arthur Goldberg, Alfred Hitchcock, Mick Jagger, George Meany, Annie Oakley, George Bernard Shaw, Napoleon, Jacqueline Onassis, Henry Ford, Francis Scott Key, Andy Warhol, Mae West, Orville Wright

VIRGO: Ingrid Bergman, Warren Burger, Maurice Chevalier, Agatha Christie, Sean Connery, Lafayette, Peter Falk, Greta Garbo, Althea Gibson, Arthur Godfrey, Goethe, Buddy Hackett, Michael Jackson, Lyndon Johnson, D. H. Lawrence, Sophia Loren, Grandma Moses, Arnold Palmer, Queen Elizabeth I, Walter Reuther, Peter Sellers, Lily Tomlin, George Wallace

LIBRA: Brigitte Bardot, Art Buchwald, Truman Capote, Dwight D. Eisenhower, William Faulkner, F. Scott Fitzgerald, Gandhi, George Gershwin, Micky Mantle, Helen Hayes, Vladimir Horowitz, Doris Lessing, Martina Navratalova, Eugene O'Neill, Luciano Pavarotti, Emily Post, Eleanor Roosevelt, Bruce Springsteen, Margaret Thatcher, Gore Vidal, Barbara Walters, Oscar Wilde

SCORPIO: Vivien Leigh, Richard Burton, Art Carney, Johnny Carson, Billy Graham, Grace Kelly, Walter Cronkite, Marie Curie, Charles de Gaulle, Linda Evans, Indira Gandhi, Theodore Roosevelt, Rock Hudson, Katherine Hepburn, Robert F. Kennedy, Billie Jean King, Martin Luther, Georgia O'Keeffe, Pablo Picasso, Jonas Salk, Alan Shepard, Robert Louis Stevenson

SAGITTARIUS: Jane Austen, Louisa May Alcott, Woody Allen, Beethoven, Willy Brandt, Mary Martin, William F. Buckley, Maria Callas, Winston Churchill, Noel Coward, Emily Dickinson, Walt Disney, Benjamin Disraeli, James Doolittle, Kirk Douglas, Chet Huntley, Jane Fonda, Chris Evert Lloyd, Margaret Mead, Charles Schulz, John Milton, Frank Sinatra, Steven Spielberg

CAPRICORN: Muhammad Ali, Isaac Asimov, Pablo Casals, Dizzy Dean, Marlene Dietrich, James Farmer, Ava Gardner, Barry Goldwater, Cary Grant, J. Edgar Hoover, Howard Hughes, Joan of Arc, Gypsy Rose Lee, Martin Luther King, Jr., Rudyard Kipling, Mao Tse-tung, Richard Nixon, Gamal Nasser, Louis Pasteur, Albert Schweitzer, Stalin, Benjamin Franklin, Elvis Presley

AQUARIUS: Marian Anderson, Susan B. Anthony, Jack Benny, John Barrymore, Mikhail Baryshnikov, Charles Darwin, Charles Dickens, Thomas Edison, , Clark Gable, Jascha Heifetz, Abraham Lincoln, Yehudi Menuhin, Mozart, Jack Nicklaus, Ronald Reagan, Jackie Robinson, Norman Rockwell, Franklin D. Roosevelt, Gertrude Stein, Charles Lindbergh, Margaret Truman

PISCES: Edward Albee, Harry Belafonte, Alexander Graham Bell, Chopin, Adelle Davis, Albert Einstein, Golda Meir, Jackie Gleason, Winslow Homer, Edward M. Kennedy, Victor Hugo, Mike Mansfield, Michelangelo, Edna St. Vincent Millay, Liza Minelli, John Steinbeck, Linus Pauling, Ravel, Renoir, Diana Ross, William Shirer, Elizabeth Taylor, George Washington

The Signs and Their Key Words

		POSITIVE	NEGATIVE
ARIES	self	courage, initiative, pioneer instinct	brash rudeness, selfish impetuosity
TAURUS	money	endurance, loyalty, wealth	obstinacy, gluttony
GEMINI	mind	versatility	capriciousness, unreliability
CANCER	family	sympathy, homing instinct	clannishness, childishness
LEO	children	love, authority, integrity	egotism, force
VIRGO	work	purity, industry, analysis	faultfinding, cynicism
LIBRA	marriage	harmony, justice	vacillation, superficiality
SCORPIO	sex	survival, regeneration	vengeance, discord
SAGITTARIUS	travel	optimism, higher learning	lawlessness
CAPRICORN	career	depth	narrowness, gloom
AQUARIUS	friends	human fellowship, genius	perverse unpredictability
PISCES	confinement	spiritual love, universality	diffusion, escapism

The Elements and Qualities of The Signs

Every sign has both an *element* and a *quality* associated with it. The element indicates the basic makeup of the sign, and the quality describes the kind of activity associated with each.

Element	Sign	Quality	Sign
FIRE	ARIES LEO SAGITTARIUS	CARDINAL	ARIES LIBRA CANCER CAPRICORN
EARTH	TAURUS VIRGO CAPRICORN	FIXED	TAURUS LEO SCORPIO AQUARIUS
AIR.........	GEMINI LIBRA AQUARIUS	MUTABLE	GEMINI VIRGO SAGITTARIUS PISCES
WATER....	CANCER SCORPIO PISCES		

Signs can be grouped together according to their element and quality. Signs of the same element share many basic traits in common. They tend to form stable configurations and ultimately harmonious relationships. Signs of the same quality are often less harmonious, but they share many dynamic potentials for growth as well as profound fulfillment.

Further discussion of each of these sign groupings is provided on the following pages.

The Fire Signs

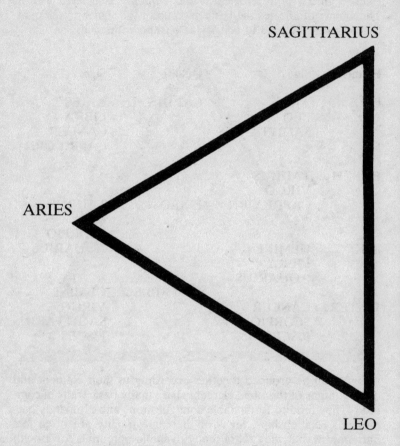

This is the fire group. On the whole these are emotional, volatile types, quick to anger, quick to forgive. They are adventurous, powerful people and act as a source of inspiration for everyone. They spark into action with immediate exuberant impulses. They are intelligent, self-involved, creative, and idealistic. They all share a certain vibrancy and glow that outwardly reflects an inner flame and passion for living.

The Earth Signs

CAPRICORN

TAURUS   VIRGO

This is the earth group. They are in constant touch with the material world and tend to be conservative. Although they are all capable of spartan self-discipline, they are earthy, sensual people who are stimulated by the tangible, elegant, and luxurious. The thread of their lives is always practical, but they do fantasize and are often attracted to dark, mysterious, emotional people. They are like great cliffs overhanging the sea, forever married to the ocean but always resisting erosion from the dark, emotional forces that thunder at their feet.

The Air Signs

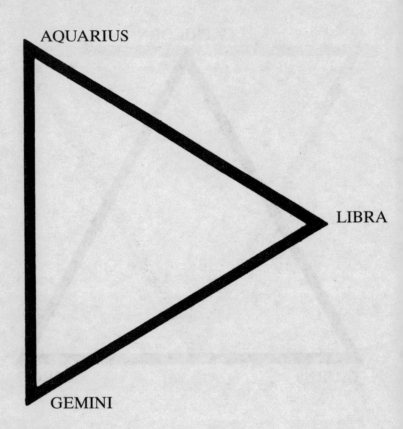

This is the air group. They are light, mental creatures desirous of contact, communication, and relationship. They are involved with people and the forming of ties on many levels. Original thinkers, they are the bearers of human news. Their language is their sense of word, color, style, and beauty. They provide an atmosphere suitable and pleasant for living. They add change and versatility to the scene, and it is through them that we can explore new territory of human intelligence and experience.

The Water Signs

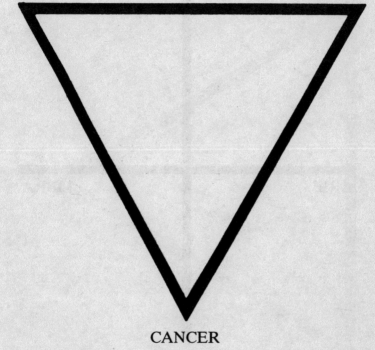

PISCES

SCORPIO

CANCER

This is the water group. Through the water people, we are all joined together on emotional, nonverbal levels. They are silent, mysterious types whose magic hypnotizes even the most determined realist. They have uncanny perceptions about people and are as rich as the oceans when it comes to feeling, emotion, or imagination. They are sensitive, mystical creatures with memories that go back beyond time. Through water, life is sustained. These people have the potential for the depths of darkness or the heights of mysticism and art.

The Cardinal Signs

CAPRICORN

ARIES   LIBRA

CANCER

Put together, this is a clear-cut picture of dynamism, activity, tre-
mendous stress, and remarkable achievement. These people know
the meaning of great change since their lives are often characterized by significant crises and major successes. This combination is
like a simultaneous storm of summer, fall, winter, and spring. The
danger is chaotic diffusion of energy; the potential is irrepressible
growth and victory.

The Fixed Signs

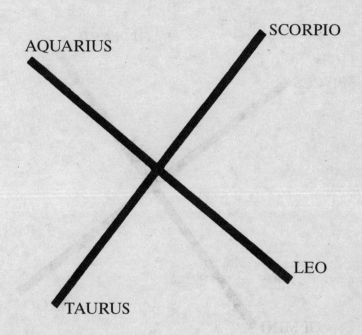

Fixed signs are always establishing themselves in a given place or area of experience. Like explorers who arrive and plant a flag, these people claim a position from which they do not enjoy being deposed. They are staunch, stalwart, upright, trusty, honorable people, although their obstinacy is well-known. Their contribution is fixity, and they are the angels who support our visible world.

The Mutable Signs

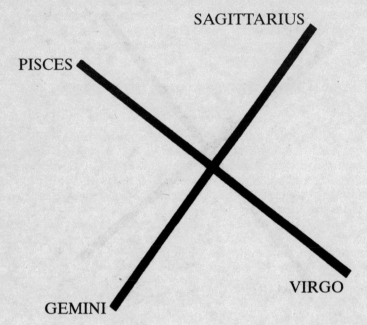

Mutable people are versatile, sensitive, intelligent, nervous, and deeply curious about life. They are the translators of all energy. They often carry out or complete tasks initiated by others. Combinations of these signs have highly developed minds; they are imaginative and jumpy and think and talk a lot. At worst their lives are a Tower of Babel. At best they are adaptable and ready creatures who can assimilate one kind of experience and enjoy it while anticipating coming changes.

THE PLANETS
OF THE SOLAR SYSTEM

This section describes the planets of the solar system. In astrology, both the Sun and the Moon are considered to be planets. Because of the Moon's influence in our day-to-day lives, the Moon is described in a separate section following this one.

The Planets and the Signs They Rule

The signs of the Zodiac are linked to the planets in the following way. Each sign is governed or ruled by one or more planets. No matter where the planets are located in the sky at any given moment, they still rule their respective signs, and when they travel through the signs they rule, they have special dignity and their effects are stronger.

Following is a list of the planets and the signs they rule. After looking at the list, read the definitions of the planets and see if you can determine how the planet ruling *your* Sun sign has affected your life.

SIGNS	RULING PLANETS
Aries	Mars, Pluto
Taurus	Venus
Gemini	Mercury
Cancer	Moon
Leo	Sun
Virgo	Mercury
Libra	Venus
Scorpio	Mars, Pluto
Sagittarius	Jupiter
Capricorn	Saturn
Aquarius	Saturn, Uranus
Pisces	Jupiter, Neptune

Characteristics of the Planets

The following pages give the meaning and characteristics of the planets of the solar system. They all travel around the Sun at different speeds and different distances. Taken with the Sun, they all distribute individual intelligence and ability throughout the entire chart.

The planets modify the influence of the Sun in a chart according to their own particular natures, strengths, and positions. Their positions must be calculated for each year and day, and their function and expression in a horoscope will change as they move from one area of the Zodiac to another.

We start with a description of the sun.

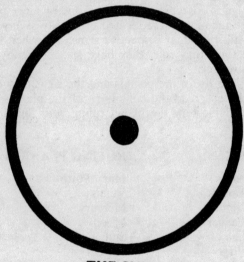

THE SUN

SUN

This is the center of existence. Around this flaming sphere all the planets revolve in endless orbits. Our star is constantly sending out its beams of light and energy without which no life on Earth would be possible. In astrology it symbolizes everything we are trying to become, the center around which all of our activity in life will always revolve. It is the symbol of our basic nature and describes the natural and constant thread that runs through everything that we do from birth to death on this planet.

To early astrologers, the Sun seemed to be another planet because it crossed the heavens every day, just like the rest of the bodies in the sky.

It is the only star near enough to be seen well—it is, in fact, a dwarf star. Approximately 860,000 miles in diameter, it is about ten times as wide as the giant planet Jupiter. The next nearest star is nearly 300,000 times as far away, and if the Sun were located as far away as most of the bright stars, it would be too faint to be seen without a telescope.

Everything in the horoscope ultimately revolves around this singular body. Although other forces may be prominent in the charts of some individuals, still the Sun is the total nucleus of being and symbolizes the complete potential of every human being alive. It is vitality and the life force. Your whole essence comes from the position of the Sun.

You are always trying to express the Sun according to its position by house and sign. Possibility for all development is found in the Sun, and it marks the fundamental character of your personal radiations all around you.

It is the symbol of strength, vigor, wisdom, dignity, ardor, and generosity, and the ability for a person to function as a mature individual. It is also a creative force in society. It is consciousness of the gift of life.

The underdeveloped solar nature is arrogant, pushy, undependable, and proud, and is constantly using force.

MERCURY

Mercury is the planet closest to the Sun. It races around our star, gathering information and translating it to the rest of the system. Mercury represents your capacity to understand the desires of your own will and to translate those desires into action.

In other words it is the planet of mind and the power of communication. Through Mercury we develop an ability to think, write, speak, and observe—to become aware of the world around us. It colors our attitudes and vision of the world, as well as our capacity to communicate our inner responses to the outside world. Some people who have serious disabilities in their power of verbal communication have often wrongly been described as people lacking intelligence.

Although this planet (and its position in the horoscope) indicates your power to communicate your thoughts and perceptions to the world, intelligence is something deeper. Intelligence is distributed throughout all the planets. It is the relationship of the planets to each other that truly describes what we call intelligence. Mercury rules speaking, language, mathematics, draft and design, students, messengers, young people, offices, teachers, and any pursuits where the mind of man has wings.

VENUS

Venus is beauty. It symbolizes the harmony and radiance of a rare and elusive quality: beauty itself. It is refinement and delicacy, softness and charm. In astrology it indicates grace, balance, and the aesthetic sense. Where Venus is we see beauty, a gentle drawing in of energy and the need for satisfaction and completion. It is a special touch that finishes off rough edges. It is sensitivity, and affection, and it is always the place for that other elusive phenomenon: love. Venus describes our sense of what is beautiful and loving. Poorly developed, it is vulgar, tasteless, and self-indulgent. But its ideal is the flame of spiritual love—Aphrodite, goddess of love, and the sweetness and power of personal beauty.

MARS

Mars is raw, crude energy. The planet next to Earth but outward from the Sun is a fiery red sphere that charges through the horoscope with force and fury. It represents the way you reach out for new adventure and new experience. It is energy and drive, initiative, courage, and daring. It is the power to start something and see it through. It can be thoughtless, cruel and wild, angry and hostile, causing cuts, burns, scalds, and wounds. It can stab its way through a chart, or it can be the symbol of healthy spirited adventure, well-channeled constructive power to begin and keep up the drive. If you have trouble starting things, if you lack the get-up-and-go to start the ball rolling, if you lack aggressiveness and self-confidence, chances are there's another planet influencing your Mars. Mars rules soldiers, butchers, surgeons, salesmen—any field that requires daring, bold skill, operational technique, or self-promotion.

JUPITER

This is the largest planet of the solar system. Scientists have recently learned that Jupiter reflects more light than it receives from the Sun. In a sense it is like a star itself. In astrology it rules good luck and good cheer, health, wealth, optimism, happiness, success, and joy. It is the symbol of opportunity and always opens the way for new possibilities in your life. It rules exuberance, enthusiasm, wisdom, knowledge, generosity, and all forms of expansion in general. It rules actors, statesmen, clerics, professional people, religion, publishing, and the distribution of many people over large areas.

Sometimes Jupiter makes you think you deserve everything, and you become sloppy, wasteful, careless and rude, prodigal and lawless, in the illusion that nothing can ever go wrong. Then there is the danger of overconfidence, exaggeration, undependability, and overindulgence.

Jupiter is the minimization of limitation and the emphasis on spirituality and potential. It is the thirst for knowledge and higher learning.

SATURN

Saturn circles our system in dark splendor with its mysterious rings, forcing us to be awakened to whatever we have neglected in the past. It will present real puzzles and problems to be solved, causing delays, obstacles, and hindrances. By doing so, Saturn stirs our own sensitivity to those areas where we are laziest.

Here we must patiently develop *method*, and only through painstaking effort can our ends be achieved. It brings order to a horoscope and imposes reason just where we are feeling least reasonable. By creating limitations and boundary, Saturn shows the consequences of being human and demands that we accept the changing cycles inevitable in human life. Saturn rules time, old age, and sobriety. It can bring depression, gloom, jealousy, and greed, or serious acceptance of responsibilities out of which success will develop. With Saturn there is nothing to do but face facts. It rules laborers, stones, granite, rocks, and crystals of all kinds.

THE OUTER PLANETS:
URANUS, NEPTUNE, PLUTO

Uranus, Neptune, Pluto are the outer planets. They liberate human beings from cultural conditioning, and in that sense are the lawbreakers. In early times it was thought that Saturn was the last planet of the system—the outer limit beyond which we could never go. The discovery of the next three planets ushered in new phases of human history, revolution, and technology.

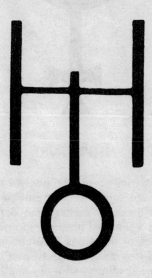

URANUS

Uranus rules unexpected change, upheaval, revolution. It is the symbol of total independence and asserts the freedom of an individual from all restriction and restraint. It is a breakthrough planet and indicates talent, originality, and genius in a horoscope. It usually causes last-minute reversals and changes of plan, unwanted separations, accidents, catastrophes, and eccentric behavior. It can add irrational rebelliousness and perverse bohemianism to a personality or a streak of unaffected brilliance in science and art. It rules technology, aviation, and all forms of electrical and electronic advancement. It governs great leaps forward and topsy-turvy situations, and *always* turns things around at the last minute. Its effects are difficult to predict, since it rules sudden last-minute decisions and events that come like lightning out of the blue.

NEPTUNE

Neptune dissolves existing reality the way the sea erodes the cliffs beside it. Its effects are subtle like the ringing of a buoy's bell in the fog. It suggests a reality higher than definition can usually describe. It awakens a sense of higher responsibility often causing guilt, worry, anxieties, or delusions. Neptune is associated with all forms of escape and can make things seem a certain way so convincingly that you are absolutely sure of something that eventually turns out to be quite different.

It is the planet of illusion and therefore governs the invisible realms that lie beyond our ordinary minds, beyond our simple factual ability to prove what is "real." Treachery, deceit, disillusionment, and disappointment are linked to Neptune. It describes a vague reality that promises eternity and the divine, yet in a manner so complex that we cannot really fathom it at all. At its worst Neptune is a cheap intoxicant; at its best it is the poetry, music, and inspiration of the higher planes of spiritual love. It has dominion over movies, photographs, and much of the arts.

PLUTO

Pluto lies at the outpost of our system and therefore rules finality in a horoscope—the final closing of chapters in your life, the passing of major milestones and points of development from which there is no return. It is a final wipeout, a closeout, an evacuation. It is a distant, subtle but powerful catalyst in all transformations that occur. It creates, destroys, then recreates. Sometimes Pluto starts its influence with a minor event or insignificant incident that might even go unnoticed. Slowly but surely, little by little, everything changes, until at last there has been a total transformation in the area of your life where Pluto has been operating. It rules mass thinking and the trends that society first rejects, then adopts, and finally outgrows.

Pluto rules the dead and the underworld—all the powerful forces of creation and destruction that go on all the time beneath, around, and above us. It can bring a lust for power with strong obsessions.

It is the planet that rules the metamorphosis of the caterpillar into a butterfly, for it symbolizes the capacity to change totally and forever a person's lifestyle, way of thought, and behavior.

THE MOON IN EACH SIGN

The Moon is the nearest planet to the Earth. It exerts more observable influence on us from day to day than any other planet. The effect is very personal, very intimate, and if we are not aware of how it works it can make us quite unstable in our ideas. And the annoying thing is that at these times we often see our own instability but can do nothing about it. A knowledge of what can be expected may help considerably. We can then be prepared to stand strong against the Moon's negative influences and use its positive ones to help us to get ahead. Who has not heard of going with the tide?

The Moon reflects, has no light of its own. It reflects the Sun—the life giver—in the form of vital movement. The Moon controls the tides, the blood rhythm, the movement of sap in trees and plants. Its nature is inconstancy and change so it signifies our moods, our superficial behavior—walking, talking, and especially thinking. Being a true reflector of other forces, the Moon is cold, watery like the surface of a still lake, brilliant and scintillating at times, but easily ruffled and disturbed by the winds of change.

The Moon takes about 27⅓ days to make a complete transit of the Zodiac. It spends just over 2¼ days in each sign. During that time it reflects the qualities, energies, and characteristics of the sign and, to a degree, the planet which rules the sign. When the Moon in its transit occupies a sign incompatible with our own birth sign, we can expect to feel a vague uneasiness, perhaps a touch of irritableness. We should not be discouraged nor let the feeling get us down, or, worse still, allow ourselves to take the discomfort out on others. Try to remember that the Moon has to change signs within 55 hours and, provided you are not physically ill, your mood will probably change with it. It is amazing how frequently depression lifts with the shift in the Moon's position. And, of course, when the Moon is transiting a sign compatible or sympathetic to yours, you will probably feel some sort of stimulation or just be plain happy to be alive.

In the horoscope, the Moon is such a powerful indicator that competent astrologers often use the sign it occupied at birth as the birth sign of the person. This is done particularly when the Sun is on the cusp, or edge, of two signs. Most experienced astrologers, however, coordinate both Sun and Moon signs by reading and confirming from one to the other and secure a far more accurate and personalized analysis.

For these reasons, the Moon tables which follow this section (see pages 86–92) are of great importance to the individual. They show the days and the exact times the Moon will enter each sign of the Zodiac for the year. Remember, you have to adjust the indicated times to local time. The corrections, already calculated for most of the main cities, are at the beginning of the tables. What follows now is a guide to the influences that will be reflected to the Earth by the Moon while it transits each of the twelve signs. The influence is at its peak about 26 hours after the Moon enters a sign. As you read the daily forecast, check the Moon sign for any given day and glance back at this guide.

MOON IN ARIES

This is a time for action, for reaching out beyond the usual self-imposed limitations and faint-hearted cautions. If you have plans in your head or on your desk, put them into practice. New ventures, applications, new jobs, new starts of any kind—all have a good chance of success. This is the period when original and dynamic impulses are being reflected onto Earth. Such energies are extremely vital and favor the pursuit of pleasure and adventure in practically every form. Sick people should feel an improvement. Those who are well will probably find themselves exuding confidence and optimism. People fond of physical exercise should find their bodies growing with tone and well-being. Boldness, strength, determination should characterize most of your activities with a readiness to face up to old challenges. Yesterday's problems may seem petty and exaggerated—so deal with them. Strike out alone. Self-reliance will attract others to you. This is a good time for making friends. Business and marriage partners are more likely to be impressed with the man and woman of action. Opposition will be overcome or thrown aside with much less effort than usual. CAUTION: Be dominant but not domineering.

MOON IN TAURUS

The spontaneous, action-packed person of yesterday gives way to the cautious, diligent, hardworking "thinker." In this period ideas will probably be concentrated on ways of improving finances. A great deal of time may be spent figuring out and going over schemes and plans. It is the right time to be careful with detail. People will find themselves working longer than usual at their desks. Or devoting more time to serious thought about the future. A strong desire to put order into business and financial arrangements may cause extra work. Loved ones may complain of being neglected and may fail to appreciate that your efforts are for their ultimate benefit. Your desire for system may extend to criticism of arrangements in the home and lead to minor upsets. Health may be affected through overwork. Try to secure a reasonable amount of rest and relaxation, although the tendency will be to "keep going" despite good advice. Work done conscientiously in this period should result in a solid contribution to your future security. CAUTION: Try not to be as serious with people as the work you are engaged in.

MOON IN GEMINI
The humdrum of routine and too much work should suddenly end. You are likely to find yourself in an expansive, quicksilver world of change and self-expression. Urges to write, to paint, to experience the freedom of some sort of artistic outpouring, may be very strong. Take full advantage of them. You may find yourself finishing something you began and put aside long ago. Or embarking on something new which could easily be prompted by a chance meeting, a new acquaintance, or even an advertisement. There may be a yearning for a change of scenery, the feeling to visit another country (not too far away), or at least to get away for a few days. This may result in short, quick journeys. Or, if you are planning a single visit, there may be some unexpected changes or detours on the way. Familiar activities will seem to give little satisfaction unless they contain a fresh element of excitement or expectation. The inclination will be toward untried pursuits, particularly those that allow you to express your inner nature. The accent is on new faces, new places. CAUTION: Do not be too quick to commit yourself emotionally.

MOON IN CANCER
Feelings of uncertainty and vague insecurity are likely to cause problems while the Moon is in Cancer. Thoughts may turn frequently to the warmth of the home and the comfort of loved ones. Nostalgic impulses could cause you to bring out old photographs and letters and reflect on the days when your life seemed to be much more rewarding and less demanding. The love and understanding of parents and family may be important, and, if it is not forthcoming, you may have to fight against bouts of self-pity. The cordiality of friends and the thought of good times with them that

are sure to be repeated will help to restore you to a happier frame of mind. The desire to be alone may follow minor setbacks or rebuffs at this time, but solitude is unlikely to help. Better to get on the telephone or visit someone. This period often causes peculiar dreams and upsurges of imaginative thinking which can be helpful to authors of occult and mystical works. Preoccupation with the personal world of simple human needs can overshadow any material strivings. CAUTION: Do not spend too much time thinking—seek the company of loved ones or close friends.

MOON IN LEO

New horizons of exciting and rather extravagant activity open up. This is the time for exhilarating entertainment, glamorous and lavish parties, and expensive shopping sprees. Any merrymaking that relies upon your generosity as a host has every chance of being a spectacular success. You should find yourself right in the center of the fun, either as the life of the party or simply as a person whom happy people like to be with. Romance thrives in this heady atmosphere and friendships are likely to explode unexpectedly into serious attachments. Children and younger people should be attracted to you and you may find yourself organizing a picnic or a visit to a fun-fair, the movies, or the beach. The sunny company and vitality of youthful companions should help you to find some unsuspected energy. In career, you could find an opening for promotion or advancement. This should be the time to make a direct approach. The period favors those engaged in original research. CAUTION: Bask in popularity, not in flattery.

MOON IN VIRGO

Off comes the party cap and out steps the busy, practical worker. He wants to get his personal affairs straight, to rearrange them, if necessary, for more efficiency, so he will have more time for more work. He clears up his correspondence, pays outstanding bills, makes numerous phone calls. He is likely to make inquiries, or sign up for some new insurance and put money into gilt-edged investment. Thoughts probably revolve around the need for future security—to tie up loose ends and clear the decks. There may be a tendency to be "finicky," to interfere in the routine of others, particularly friends and family members. The motive may be a genuine desire to help with suggestions for updating or streamlining their affairs, but these will probably not be welcomed. Sympathy may be felt for less fortunate sections of the community and a flurry of some sort of voluntary service is likely. This may be accompanied by strong feelings of responsibility on several fronts and health may suffer from extra efforts made. CAUTION: Everyone may not want your help or advice.

MOON IN LIBRA

These are days of harmony and agreement and you should find yourself at peace with most others. Relationships tend to be smooth and sweet-flowing. Friends may become closer and bonds deepen in mutual understanding. Hopes will be shared. Progress by cooperation could be the secret of success in every sphere. In business, established partnerships may flourish and new ones get off to a good start. Acquaintances could discover similar interests that lead to congenial discussions and rewarding exchanges of some sort. Love, as a unifying force, reaches its optimum. Marriage partners should find accord. Those who wed at this time face the prospect of a happy union. Cooperation and tolerance are felt to be stronger than dissension and impatience. The argumentative are not quite so loud in their bellowings, nor as inflexible in their attitudes. In the home, there should be a greater recognition of the other point of view and a readiness to put the wishes of the group before selfish insistence. This is a favorable time to join an art group. CAUTION: Do not be too independent—let others help you if they want to.

MOON IN SCORPIO

Driving impulses to make money and to economize are likely to cause upsets all around. No area of expenditure is likely to be spared the ax, including the household budget. This is a time when the desire to cut down on extravagance can become near fanatical. Care must be exercised to try to keep the aim in reasonable perspective. Others may not feel the same urgent need to save and may retaliate. There is a danger that possessions of sentimental value will be sold to realize cash for investment. Buying and selling of stock for quick profit is also likely. The attention turns to organizing, reorganizing, tidying up at home and at work. Neglected jobs could suddenly be done with great bursts of energy. The desire for solitude may intervene. Self-searching thoughts could disturb. The sense of invisible and mysterious energies in play could cause some excitability. The reassurance of loves ones may help. CAUTION: Be kind to the people you love.

MOON IN SAGITTARIUS

These are days when you are likely to be stirred and elevated by discussions and reflections of a religious and philosophical nature. Ideas of faraway places may cause unusual response and excitement. A decision may be made to visit someone overseas, perhaps a person whose influence was important to your earlier character development. There could be a strong resolution to get away from present intellectual patterns, to learn new subjects, and to meet more interesting people. The superficial may be rejected in all its forms. An impatience with old ideas and unimaginative contacts could lead to a change of companions and interests. There may be an upsurge of religious feeling and metaphysical inquiry. Even a new insight into the significance of astrology and other occult studies is likely under the curious stimulus of the Moon in Sagittarius. Physically, you may express this need for fundamental change by spending more time outdoors: sports, gardening, long walks appeal. CAUTION: Try to channel any restlessness into worthwhile study.

MOON IN CAPRICORN

Life in these hours may seem to pivot around the importance of gaining prestige and honor in the career, as well as maintaining a spotless reputation. Ambitious urges may be excessive and could be accompanied by quite acquisitive drives for money. Effort should be directed along strictly ethical lines where there is no possibility of reproach or scandal. All endeavors are likely to be characterized by great earnestness, and an air of authority and purpose which should impress those who are looking for leadership or reliability. The desire to conform to accepted standards may extend to sharp criticism of family members. Frivolity and unconventional actions are unlikely to amuse while the Moon is in Capricorn. Moderation and seriousness are the orders of the day. Achievement and recognition in this period could come through community work or organizing for the benefit of some amateur group. CAUTION: Dignity and esteem are not always self-awarded.

MOON IN AQUARIUS

Moon in Aquarius is in the second last sign of the Zodiac where ideas can become disturbingly fine and subtle. The result is often a mental "no-man's land" where imagination cannot be trusted with the same certitude as other times. The dangers for the individual are the extremes of optimism and pessimism. Unless the imagination is held in check, situations are likely to be misread, and rosy conclusions drawn where they do not exist. Consequences for the unwary can be costly in career and business. Best to think twice and not speak or act until you think again. Pessimism can be a cruel self-inflicted penalty for delusion at this time. Between the two extremes are strange areas of self-deception which, for example, can make the selfish person think he is actually being generous. Eerie dreams which resemble the reality and even seem to continue into the waking state are also possible. CAUTION: Look for the fact and not just for the image in your mind.

MOON IN PISCES

Everything seems to come to the surface now. Memory may be crystal clear, throwing up long-forgotten information which could be valuable in the career or business. Flashes of clairvoyance and intuition are possible along with sudden realizations of one's own nature, which may be used for self-improvement. A talent, never before suspected, may be discovered. Qualities not evident before in friends and marriage partners are likely to be noticed. As this is a period in which the truth seems to emerge, the discovery of false characteristics is likely to lead to disenchantment or a shift in attachments. However, when qualities are accepted, it should lead to happiness and deeper feeling. Surprise solutions could bob up for old problems. There may be a public announcement of the solving of a crime or mystery. People with secrets may find someone has "guessed" correctly. The secrets of the soul or the inner self also tend to reveal themselves. Religious and philosophical groups may make some interesting discoveries. CAUTION: Not a time for activities that depend on secrecy.

NOTE: When you read your daily forecasts, use the Moon Sign Dates that are provided in the following section of Moon Tables. Then you may want to glance back here for the Moon's influence in a given sign.

MOON TABLES

CORRECTION FOR NEW YORK TIME, FIVE HOURS WEST OF GREENWICH

Atlanta, Boston, Detroit, Miami, Washington, Montreal,
Ottawa, Quebec, Bogota,
Havana, Lima, Santiago...............................Same time
Chicago, New Orleans, Houston, Winnipeg, Churchill,
Mexico City.. Deduct 1 hour
Albuquerque, Denver, Phoenix, El Paso, Edmonton,
Helena .... Deduct 2 hours
Los Angeles, San Francisco, Reno, Portland,
Seattle, Vancouver .... Deduct 3 hours
Honolulu, Anchorage, Fairbanks, Kodiak .... Deduct 5 hours
Nome, Samoa, Tonga, Midway.................... Deduct 6 hours
Halifax, Bermuda, San Juan, Caracas, La Paz,
Barbados...Add 1 hour
St. John's, Brasilia, Rio de Janeiro, Sao Paulo,
Buenos Aires, Montevideo..........................Add 2 hours
Azores, Cape Verde Islands...........................Add 3 hours
Canary Islands, Madeira, Reykjavik ....Add 4 hours
London, Paris, Amsterdam, Madrid, Lisbon,
Gibraltar, Belfast, Rabat ....Add 5 hours
Frankfurt, Rome, Oslo, Stockholm, Prague,
Belgrade..Add 6 hours
Bucharest, Beirut, Tel Aviv, Athens, Istanbul, Cairo,
Alexandria, Cape Town, Johannesburg ....Add 7 hours
Moscow, Leningrad, Baghdad, Dhahran,
Addis Ababa, Nairobi, Teheran, Zanzibar.........Add 8 hours
Bombay, Calcutta, Sri Lanka..................... Add 10 ½ hours
Hong Kong, Shanghai, Manila, Peking, Perth...... Add 13 hours
Tokyo, Okinawa, Darwin, Pusan.................... Add 14 hours
Sydney, Melbourne, Port Moresby, Guam.......... Add 15 hours
Auckland, Wellington, Suva, Wake................. Add 17 hours

2003 MOON SIGN DATES—
NEW YORK TIME

JANUARY		FEBRUARY		MARCH	
Day Moon Enters		**Day Moon Enters**		**Day Moon Enters**	
1. Capric.	6:44 pm	1. Aquar.		1. Pisces	10:27 pm
2. Capric.		2. Pisces	2:56 pm	2. Pisces	
3. Aquar.	10:58 pm	3. Pisces		3. Pisces	
4. Aquar.		4. Pisces		4. Aries	8:31 am
5. Aquar.		5. Aries	12:45 am	5. Aries	
6. Pisces	5:58 am	6. Aries		6. Taurus	8:37 pm
7. Pisces		7. Taurus	1:00 pm	7. Taurus	
8. Aries	4:16 pm	8. Taurus		8. Taurus	
9. Aries		9. Taurus		9. Gemini	9:39 am
10. Aries		10. Gemini	1:46 am	10. Gemini	
11. Taurus	4:49 am	11. Gemini		11. Cancer	9:13 pm
12. Taurus		12. Cancer	12:20 pm	12. Cancer	
13. Gemini	5:09 pm	13. Cancer		13. Cancer	
14. Gemini		14. Leo	7:05 pm	14. Leo	5:07 am
15. Gemini		15. Leo		15. Leo	
16. Cancer	2:57 am	16. Virgo	10:24 pm	16. Virgo	8:54 am
17. Cancer		17. Virgo		17. Virgo	
18. Leo	9:30 am	18. Libra	11:49 pm	18. Libra	9:44 am
19. Leo		19. Libra		19. Libra	
20. Virgo	1:33 pm	20. Libra		20. Scorp.	9:39 am
21. Virgo		21. Scorp.	1:10 am	21. Scorp.	
22. Libra	4:24 pm	22. Scorp.		22. Sagitt.	10:34 am
23. Libra		23. Sagitt.	3:47 am	23. Sagitt.	
24. Scorp.	7:10 pm	24. Sagitt.		24. Capric.	1:49 pm
25. Scorp.		25. Capric.	8:12 am	25. Capric.	
26. Sagitt.	10:27 pm	26. Capric.		26. Aquar.	7:52 pm
27. Sagitt.		27. Aquar.	2:26 pm	27. Aquar.	
28. Sagitt.		28. Aquar.		28. Aquar.	
29. Capric.	2:31 am			29. Pisces	4:27 am
30. Capric.				30. Pisces	
31. Aquar.	7:45 am			31. Aries	3:06 pm

Summer time to be considered where applicable.

2003 MOON SIGN DATES—
NEW YORK TIME

APRIL Day Moon Enters		MAY Day Moon Enters		JUNE Day Moon Enters	
1. Aries		1. Taurus		1. Cancer	4:28 pm
2. Aries		2. Gemini	10:28 pm	2. Cancer	
3. Taurus	3:21 am	3. Gemini		3. Cancer	
4. Taurus		4. Gemini		4. Leo	2:26 am
5. Gemini	4:25 pm	5. Cancer	10:43 am	5. Leo	
6. Gemini		6. Cancer		6. Virgo	9:52 am
7. Gemini		7. Leo	8:47 pm	7. Virgo	
8. Cancer	4:37 am	8. Leo		8. Libra	2:31 pm
9. Cancer		9. Leo		9. Libra	
10. Leo	1:55 pm	10. Virgo	3:32 am	10. Scorp.	4:40 pm
11. Leo		11. Virgo		11. Scorp.	
12. Virgo	7:08 pm	12. Libra	6:43 am	12. Sagitt.	5:13 pm
13. Virgo		13. Libra		13. Sagitt.	
14. Libra	8:43 pm	14. Scorp.	7:15 am	14. Capric.	5:39 pm
15. Libra		15. Scorp.		15. Capric.	
16. Scorp.	8:17 pm	16. Sagitt.	6:44 am	16. Aquar.	7:42 pm
17. Scorp.		17. Sagitt.		17. Aquar.	
18. Sagitt.	7:53 pm	18. Capric.	7:04 am	18. Aquar.	
19. Sagitt.		19. Capric.		19. Pisces	12:58 am
20. Capric.	9:21 pm	20. Aquar.	10:02 am	20. Pisces	
21. Capric.		21. Aquar.		21. Aries	10:07 am
22. Capric.		22. Pisces	4:42 pm	22. Aries	
23. Aquar.	1:59 am	23. Pisces		23. Taurus	10:16 pm
24. Aquar.		24. Pisces		24. Taurus	
25. Pisces	10:03 am	25. Aries	3:00 am	25. Taurus	
26. Pisces		26. Aries		26. Gemini	11:14 am
27. Aries	8:55 pm	27. Taurus	3:33 pm	27. Gemini	
28. Aries		28. Taurus		28. Cancer	10:53 pm
29. Aries		29. Taurus		29. Cancer	
30. Taurus	9:27 am	30. Gemini	4:33 am	30. Cancer	
		31. Gemini			

Summer time to be considered where applicable.

2003 MOON SIGN DATES—
NEW YORK TIME

JULY Day Moon Enters		AUGUST Day Moon Enters		SEPTEMBER Day Moon Enters	
1. Leo	8:14 am	1. Virgo		1. Scorp.	
2. Leo		2. Libra	1:49 am	2. Sagitt.	1:33 pm
3. Virgo	3:17 pm	3. Libra		3. Sagitt.	
4. Virgo		4. Scorp.	5:13 am	4. Capric.	4:52 pm
5. Libra	8:21 pm	5. Scorp.		5. Capric.	
6. Libra		6. Sagitt.	8:12 am	6. Aquar.	9:16 pm
7. Scorp.	11:45 pm	7. Sagitt.		7. Aquar.	
8. Scorp.		8. Capric.	11:03 am	8. Aquar.	
9. Scorp.		9. Capric.		9. Pisces	3:08 am
10. Sagitt.	1:49 am	10. Aquar.	2:25 pm	10. Pisces	
11. Sagitt.		11. Aquar.		11. Aries	11:10 am
12. Capric.	3:22 am	12. Pisces	7:20 pm	12. Aries	
13. Capric.		13. Pisces		13. Taurus	9:51 pm
14. Aquar.	5:39 am	14. Pisces		14. Taurus	
15. Aquar.		15. Aries	3:01 am	15. Taurus	
16. Pisces	10:15 am	16. Aries		16. Gemini	10:33 am
17. Pisces		17. Taurus	1:53 pm	17. Gemini	
18. Aries	6:21 pm	18. Taurus		18. Cancer	11:08 pm
19. Aries		19. Taurus		19. Cancer	
20. Aries		20. Gemini	2:42 am	20. Cancer	
21. Taurus	5:49 am	21. Gemini		21. Leo	9:04 am
22. Taurus		22. Cancer	2:45 pm	22. Leo	
23. Gemini	6:43 pm	23. Cancer		23. Virgo	3:06 pm
24. Gemini		24. Leo	11:49 pm	24. Virgo	
25. Gemini		25. Leo		25. Libra	5:50 pm
26. Cancer	6:24 am	26. Leo		26. Libra	
27. Cancer		27. Virgo	5:28 am	27. Scorp.	6:53 pm
28. Leo	3:18 pm	28. Virgo		28. Scorp.	
29. Leo		29. Libra	8:42 am	29. Sagitt.	7:58 pm
30. Virgo	9:28 pm	30. Libra		30. Sagitt.	
31. Virgo		31. Scorp.	11:01 am		

Summer time to be considered where applicable.

2003 MOON SIGN DATES—
NEW YORK TIME

OCTOBER		NOVEMBER		DECEMBER	
Day Moon Enters		**Day Moon Enters**		**Day Moon Enters**	
1. Capric.	10:22 pm	1. Aquar.		1. Pisces	
2. Capric.		2. Pisces	2:53 pm	2. Aries	5:57 am
3. Capric.		3. Pisces		3. Aries	
4. Aquar.	2:46 am	4. Pisces		4. Taurus	5:31 pm
5. Aquar.		5. Aries	12:04 am	5. Taurus	
6. Pisces	9:21 am	6. Aries		6. Taurus	
7. Pisces		7. Taurus	11:30 am	7. Gemini	6:27 am
8. Aries	6:09 pm	8. Taurus		8. Gemini	
9. Aries		9. Taurus		9. Cancer	7:12 pm
10. Aries		10. Gemini	12:15 am	10. Cancer	
11. Taurus	5:06 am	11. Gemini		11. Cancer	
12. Taurus		12. Cancer	1:11 pm	12. Leo	6:41 am
13. Gemini	5:46 pm	13. Cancer		13. Leo	
14. Gemini		14. Cancer		14. Virgo	4:08 pm
15. Gemini		15. Leo	12:49 am	15. Virgo	
16. Cancer	6:42 am	16. Leo		16. Libra	10:48 pm
17. Cancer		17. Virgo	9:37 am	17. Libra	
18. Leo	5:42 pm	18. Virgo		18. Libra	
19. Leo		19. Libra	2:43 pm	19. Scorp.	2:21 am
20. Leo		20. Libra		20. Scorp.	
21. Virgo	1:02 am	21. Scorp.	4:25 pm	21. Sagitt.	3:17 am
22. Virgo		22. Scorp.		22. Sagitt.	
23. Libra	4:28 am	23. Sagitt.	4:04 pm	23. Capric.	2:56 am
24. Libra		24. Sagitt.		24. Capric.	
25. Scorp.	5:10 am	25. Capric.	3:32 pm	25. Aquar.	3:14 am
26. Scorp.		26. Capric.		26. Aquar.	
27. Sagitt.	4:56 am	27. Aquar.	4:49 pm	27. Pisces	6:11 am
28. Sagitt.		28. Aquar.		28. Pisces	
29. Capric.	5:38 am	29. Pisces	9:26 pm	29. Aries	1:09 pm
30. Capric.		30. Pisces		30. Aries	
31. Aquar.	8:42 am			31. Aries	

Summer time to be considered where applicable.

2003 PHASES OF THE MOON—
NEW YORK TIME

New Moon	First Quarter	Full Moon	Last Quarter
Jan. 2	Jan. 10	Jan. 18	Jan. 25
Feb. 1	Feb. 9	Feb. 16	Feb. 23
March 2	March 11	March 18	March 24
April 1	April 9	April 16	April 23
May 1	May 9	May 15	May 22
May 30	June 7	June 14	June 21
June 29	July 6	July 13	July 21
July 29	Aug. 5	Aug. 11	Aug. 19
Aug. 27	Sept. 3	Sept. 10	Sept. 18
Sept. 25	Oct. 2	Oct. 10	Oct. 18
Oct. 25	Oct. 31	Nov. 8	Nov. 16
Nov. 23	Nov. 30	Dec. 8	Dec. 16
Dec. 23	Dec. 30	Jan. 7 ('04)	Jan. 15 ('04)

Each phase of the Moon lasts approximately seven to eight days, during which the Moon's shape gradually changes as it comes out of one phase and goes into the next.

There will be a solar eclipse during the New Moon phase on May 30 and November 23.

There will be a lunar eclipse during the Full Moon phase on May 15 and November 8.

2003 FISHING GUIDE

	Good	Best
January	10-15-18-19-20-21	2-16-17-25
February	1-15-16-17-18-23	9-13-14-19
March	11-15-16-17-18	3-19-20-21-25
April	1-13-14-19-23	9-15-16-17-18
May	1-9-16-17-18-31	13-14-15-19-23
June	7-13-14-17-21	11-12-15-16-29
July	10-11-14-15-16-21-29	7-12-13
August	10-11-12-15-20-27	5-9-13-14
September	3-7-8-11-12-13-18	9-10-26
October	9-10-11	2-7-8-12-13-18-25
November	1-6-7-10-11-12-17-23	8-9-30
December	7-8-9-16-30	5-6-10-11-23

2003 PLANTING GUIDE

	Aboveground Crops	Root Crops
January	3-7-11-12-13-16-17	23-24-25-26-29-30
February	3-4-8-9-13-14	19-20-21-22-26
March	3-7-8-12-13	2-19-20-21-25-26-29-30
April	3-4-8-9-15	17-18-21-22-26-27
May	2-6-7-13-14-15	19-23-24-28-29
June	2-3-9-10-11-12-30	15-16-19-20-24-25
July	6-7-8-9-12	17-18-22-23-27
August	2-3-4-5-9-30-31	13-14-18-19-23-24
September	1-5-6-9-26-27-28-29	14-15-19-20
October	2-3-7-8-26-30	12-13-17-18-23-24
November	3-4-8-26-30	9-13-14-20-21-22
December	1-5-6-23-24-28	10-11-17-18-19-20

	Pruning	Weeds and Pests
January	25-26	1-19-20-21-27-28
February	21-22	17-18-23-24-28
March	2-21-29-30	1-23-27-28
April	17-18-26-27	19-20-23-24-28-29
May	23-24	17-21-25-26-30
June	19-20	17-18-22-23-27-28
July	17-18-27	15-19-20-24-25
August	13-14-23-24	12-15-16-20-21-25-26
September	19-20	12-13-17-18-22-23-24-25
October	17-18	10-14-15-19-20-21-22
November	13-14-22	10-11-15-16-17-18
December	10-11-19-20	9-13-14-15-16-21-22

MOON'S INFLUENCE OVER PLANTS

Centuries ago it was established that seeds planted when the Moon is in signs and phases called Fruitful will produce more growth than seeds planted when the Moon is in a Barren sign.

Fruitful Signs: Taurus, Cancer, Libra, Scorpio, Capricorn, Pisces
Barren Signs: Aries, Gemini, Leo, Virgo, Sagittarius, Aquarius
Dry Signs: Aries, Gemini, Sagittarius, Aquarius

Activity	Moon In
Mow lawn, trim plants	**Fruitful sign:** 1st & 2nd quarter
Plant flowers	**Fruitful sign:** 2nd quarter; best in Cancer and Libra
Prune	**Fruitful sign:** 3rd & 4th quarter
Destroy pests; spray	**Barren sign:** 4th quarter
Harvest potatoes, root crops	**Dry sign:** 3rd & 4th quarter; Taurus, Leo, and Aquarius

MOON'S INFLUENCE OVER YOUR HEALTH

ARIES   Head, brain, face, upper jaw
TAURUS   Throat, neck, lower jaw
GEMINI   Hands, arms, lungs, shoulders, nervous system
CANCER   Esophagus, stomach, breasts, womb, liver
LEO   Heart, spine
VIRGO   Intestines, liver
LIBRA   Kidneys, lower back
SCORPIO   Sex and eliminative organs
SAGITTARIUS   Hips, thighs, liver
CAPRICORN   Skin, bones, teeth, knees
AQUARIUS   Circulatory system, lower legs
PISCES   Feet, tone of being

Try to avoid work being done on that part of the body when the
Moon is in the sign governing that part.

MOON'S INFLUENCE OVER DAILY AFFAIRS

The Moon makes a complete transit of the Zodiac every 27 days
7 hours and 43 minutes. In making this transit the Moon forms
different aspects with the planets and consequently has favorable
or unfavorable bearings on affairs and events for persons according to the sign of the Zodiac under which they were born.

When the Moon is in conjunction with the Sun it is called a
New Moon; when the Moon and Sun are in opposition it is called
a Full Moon. From New Moon to Full Moon, first and second
quarter—which takes about two weeks—the Moon is increasing
or waxing. From Full Moon to New Moon, third and fourth quarter, the Moon is decreasing or waning.

Activity	Moon In
Business: buying and selling new, requiring public support	Sagittarius, Aries, Gemini, Virgo 1st and 2nd quarter
meant to be kept quiet	3rd and 4th quarter
Investigation	3rd and 4th quarter
Signing documents	1st & 2nd quarter, Cancer, Scorpio, Pisces
Advertising	2nd quarter, Sagittarius
Journeys and trips	1st & 2nd quarter, Gemini, Virgo
Renting offices, etc.	Taurus, Leo, Scorpio, Aquarius
Painting of house/apartment	3rd & 4th quarter, Taurus, Scorpio, Aquarius
Decorating	Gemini, Libra, Aquarius
Buying clothes and accessories	Taurus, Virgo
Beauty salon or barber shop visit	1st & 2nd quarter, Taurus, Leo, Libra, Scorpio, Aquarius
Weddings	1st & 2nd quarter

Cancer

CANCER

Character Analysis

Cancer is generally rather sensitive. He or she is quite often a generous person by nature, and is willing to help almost anyone in need. He is emotional and often feels sorry for people less fortunate than he. He could never refuse to answer someone's call for help. It is because of his sympathetic nature that others take advantage of him now and again.

In spite of his willingness to help others, the Cancer man or woman may seem difficult to approach by anyone not well acquainted with their character. On the whole, he seems subdued and reserved. Others may feel there is a wall between them and Cancer, although this may not be the case at all. The person born under this sign, which is ruled by the Moon, is careful not to let others hurt him. He has learned through hard experience that protection of some sort is necessary in order to get along in life. The person who wins his confidence and is able to get beyond this barrier will find the Moon Child a warm and loving person.

With his family and close friends, he is a very faithful and dependable person. In his quiet way, he can be affectionate and loving. He is generally not one given to demonstrative behavior. He can be fond of someone without telling them so a dozen times a day. With people he is close to, Cancer is more open about his own need for affection, and he enjoys being pampered by his loved ones. He likes to feel wanted and protected.

When he has made up his mind about something, he sticks to it, and is generally a very constant person. He knows how to hold his ground. He never wavers. People who don't know him may think him weak and easily managed, because he is so quiet and modest, but this is far from true. He can take a lot of punishment for an idea or a cause he believes in. For Cancer, right is right. In order to protect himself, the person born under this sign will sometimes put up a pose as someone bossy and domineering. Sometimes he is successful in fooling others with his brash front. People who have known him for a while, however, are seldom taken in.

Many people born under this sign of the Crab are shy and seemingly lacking in confidence. They know their own minds, though, even if they do not seem to. He responds to kindness and encouragement. He will be himself with people he trusts. A good person can bring out the best in the Crab. Disagreeable or unfeeling people can send him scurrying back into his shell. He is a person who does not appreciate sharp criticism. Some Crabs are worriers. They are very concerned about what others may think of them. This may bother them so much that they develop a deep feeling of inferiority. Sometimes this reaches the point where he is so unsure of himself in some matters that he allows himself to be influenced by someone who has a stronger personality. Also, some Crabs may be afraid that people will talk behind his back if he doesn't comply with their wishes. However, this does not stop him from doing what he feels is right. The cultivated Cancer learns to think for himself and has no fear of disapproval.

The Cancer man or woman is most himself at home. The person born under this sign is a real lover of domesticity. He likes a place where he can relax and feel properly sheltered. Cancers like things to stay as they are; they are not fond of changes of any sort. They are not very adaptable people. When visiting others or going to unfamiliar places, they are not likely to feel very comfortable. They are not the most talkative people at a party. In the comfort of their own homes, however, they blossom and bloom.

The Cancer man or woman sticks by the rules, whatever the game. He is not a person who would ever think of going against an established grain. He is conventional and moderate in almost all things. In a way he likes the old-fashioned things. However, in spite of this, he is interested in new things and does what he can to keep up with the times. In a way, he has two sides to his character. He is seldom forgetful. He has a memory like an elephant and can pick out any detail from the past with no trouble at all. He often reflects on things that have happened. He prefers the past to the future, which sometimes fills him with a feeling of apprehension.

This fourth sign of the Zodiac is a motherly one. Even the Cancer man has something maternal about him. He is usually kind and considerate, ready to help and protect. Others are drawn to Cancer because of these gentle qualities. People in trouble often turn to him for advice and sympathy. People find him easy to confide in.

The Cancer person in general is very forgiving. He almost never holds a grudge. Still, it would not be wise to anger him. Treat him fairly and he will treat you the same. He does not appreciate people who lose patience with him. Cancer is usually proud of his mind and does not like to be considered unintelligent. Even if others feel that he is somewhat slow in some areas, he would rather not have this opinion expressed in his presence. He's not a person to be played with; he can tell when someone is treating him like a fool.

Quite often people born under this sign are musically inclined. Some of them have a deep interest in religious matters. They are apt to be interested in mystical matters, as well. Although they are fascinated by these things, they may be somewhat afraid of being overwhelmed if they go into them too deeply. In spite of this feeling of apprehension, Moon Children try to satisfy their curiosity in these matters.

Health

For the person born under the sign of Cancer, the stomach is the weak point. Chances are that Cancer is easily susceptible to infection. Sometimes his health is affected by nervousness. He can be quite a worrier. Even little things eat at him from time to time, which is apt to lower his resistance to infectious illnesses. He is often upset by small matters.

A Cancer as a child is sometimes sickly and weak. His physique during this period of growth can be described in most cases as fragile. Some develop into physically strong adults, others may have the remnants of childhood ailments with them for a good part of their adult lives. They are frightened of being sick. Illness is a word they would rather not mention. Pain is also a thing they fear.

They are given to quick-changing moods at times, which often has an effect on their overall health. Worry or depression can have a subliminal effect on their general health. Usually their illnesses are not as serious as they imagine them to be. They sometimes find it easy to feel sorry for themselves.

On the whole, the Cancer man or woman is a quiet person. He is not one to brag or push his weight around. However, let it not be thought that he lacks the force that others have. He can be quite purposeful and energetic when the situation calls for it. However, when it comes to tooting their own horn, they can be somewhat shy and reticent. They may lack the get-up-and-go that others have when it comes to pushing their personal interests ahead.

Some Cancers are quite aware of the fact that they are not what one would call sturdy in physique or temperament. Some may go through life rather painfully trying to cover up the weak side of their nature.

Sons and daughters of the Moon may not be very vigorous or active. As a rule, they are not too fond of physical exercise, and they have a weakness for rich and heavy foods. As a result, in later life they could end up overweight. Some Cancers have trouble with their kidneys and intestines. Others digest their food poorly. The wise Cancer man or woman, however, adheres to a strict and well-balanced diet with plenty of fresh fruit and vegetables. Moreover, they see to it that they properly exercise daily. The Cancer man or woman who learns to cut down on rich foods and worry often lives to a ripe old age.

Occupation

Cancer generally has no trouble at all establishing himself in the business world. He has all those qualities that make one a success professionally. He is careful with his equipment as well as his money. He is patient and he knows how to persevere. Any job where he has a chance to use his mind instead of his body is usually a job in which he has no trouble succeeding. He can work well with people—especially people situated in dire straits. Welfare work is the kind of occupation in which he usually excels. He can really be quite a driving person if his job calls for it. Cancer is surprisingly resourceful. In spite of his retiring disposition, he is capable of accomplishing some very difficult tasks.

Cancer can put on an aggressive front, and in some cases it can carry him far. Quite often he is able to develop leadership qualities and make good use of them. He knows how to direct his energy so that he never becomes immediately exhausted. He'll work away at a difficult chore gradually, seldom approaching anything head-on. By working at something obliquely he often finds advantages along the way that are not apparent to others. In spite of his cautious approach, Cancer is often taxed by work that is too demanding of his energy. He may put up a good front of being strong and courageous while actually he is at the end of his emotional rope. Risks sometimes frighten the Crab. It is often fear that exhausts him. The possible dangers in the world of business set him to worrying.

Cancer does not boast about what he is going to do. He or she just quietly goes ahead and does it. Quite often he accomplishes more than others in this quiet way.

The person born under this sign enjoys helping others. By nature, he is quite a sympathetic individual. He does not like to see others suffer or do without. He is willing to make sacrifices for someone he trusts and cares for. Cancer's maternal streak works wonders with children. People born under the fourth sign of the Zodiac often make excellent teachers. They understand young people well and do what they can to help them grow up properly.

Cancers also are fairly intuitive. In business or financial matters, they often make an important strike by playing a strong hunch. In some cases they are able to rely almost entirely on their feelings rather than on reason.

Water attracts the Cancer person. Often they have connections with the oceans through their professions. Cancer homemakers experimenting in the kitchen often are very successful creating new drinks and blending liquid recipes. Overseas trade and commerce also appeal.

The average Cancer has many choices as far as a career is concerned. There are many things that he can do well once he puts his mind to it. In the arts he is quite likely to do well. The Cancer man or woman has a way with beauty, harmony, and creativity. Basically, he is a very capable person in many things; it depends on which of his talents he wants to develop to a professional point. He has a rich imagination and sometimes can make use of it in the area of painting, music, or sculpture.

When working for someone else, Cancer can always be depended upon. He makes a loyal and conscientious employee.

It is important for Cancer to select a job that is well suited to his talents and temperament. Although he may feel that earning money is important, Cancer eventually comes to the point where he realizes that it is even more important to enjoy the work he is doing. He should have a position that allows him to explore the recesses of his personality and to develop. When placed in the wrong job, the Cancer man or woman might wish they were somewhere else.

Cancers know the value of money. They are not the sort of people who go throwing money around recklessly. Cancer is honest and expects others to be the same. He is quite modest in most things and deplores unnecessary display. Cancers have a genius for making money and for investing or saving it.

Security is important to the person born under this sign. He'll always see to it that he has something put away for that inevitable rainy day. He is also a hard worker and is willing to put in long hours for the money it brings him. Financial success is usually the result of his own perseverance and industry. Through his own need for security, it is often easy for Cancer to sympathize with those of like dispositions. He is a helpful person. If he sees someone trying to do his best to get ahead—and still not succeeding—he is quite apt to put aside his own interests temporarily to help another.

Sometimes Cancer worries about money even when he has it. Even the wealthy Cancer can never be too secure. It would be better for him to learn how to relax and not to let his worries undermine his health. Financial matters often cause him considerable concern—even when it is not necessary.

Home and Family

Cancers are usually great home lovers. They are very domestic by nature; home for them spells security. Cancer is a family person. He respects those who are related to him. He feels a great responsibility toward all the members of his family. There is usually a very strong tie between Cancer and his mother that lasts through his whole life. Something a Cancer will not tolerate is for someone to speak ill of a member of his family. This for him is a painful and deep insult. He has a great respect for his family and family traditions. Quite often Cancer is well-acquainted with his family tree. If he happens to have a relative who has been quite successful in life, he is proud of the fact. Once he is home for the weekend, he generally stays there.

Cancer is sentimental about old things and habits. He is apt to have many things stored away from years ago. Something that was dear to his parents will probably be dear to him as well.

Many Cancers travel near and far from time to time. But no matter what their destination, they are always glad to be back where they feel they belong.

The home of a Cancer is usually quite comfortable and tastefully furnished. Cancer men and women are romantic, which is usually reflected in the way their house is arranged.

The Cancer child is always attached to his home and family. He may not care to go out and play with other children very much but enjoys it when his friends come to his house.

The maternal nature of the Cancer person comes out when he gives a party. He is a very attentive host and worries over a guest like a mother hen—anxious to see that they are comfortable and lack nothing. He does his best to make others happy and at home, and he is admired and loved for that. People who visit are usually deeply impressed by their outgoing ways. The Cancer host prepares unusual and delicious snacks for visitors. Cancer is very concerned about them and sees to it that they are well-fed while visiting.

Homebodies that they are, Cancers generally do what they can to make their home a comfortable and interesting place for themselves as well as for others. They feel very flattered when a visitor pays them a compliment on their home.

Children play a very important part in the lives of people born under this sign. Cancers fuss over their youngsters and give them the things they feel that they need. They generally like to have large families. They see to it that their children are well provided for and that they have the chances in life that their parents never had. The best mother of the Zodiac is usually someone born under the sign of Cancer. They have a strong protective nature. They usually have a strong sense of duty, and when their children are in difficulty they do everything they can to set matters right. Children, needless to say, are fond of their Cancer parent, and respond lovingly to make the parent-child relationship a harmonious one.

Social Relationships

Cancer may seem rather retiring and quiet, and this gives people the impression that he is not too warm or sympathetic. However, most Moon Children are very sensitive and loving. Their ability to understand and sympathize with others is great. Cancer likes to have close friends—people who love and understand him as well as he tries to love and understand them. He wants to be well-liked—to be noticed by people who he feels should like him. If he does not get the attention and affection he feels he is entitled to, he is apt to become sullen and difficult to deal with.

The Cancer man or woman has strong powers of intuition and can generally sense when he has met a person who is likely to turn into a good friend. Cancer suffers greatly if ever he should lose a friend. To him friendships are sacred. Sometimes Cancer sets friends on too high a pedestal. He or she is apt to feel crest-fallen when he discovers that they have feet of clay. He is often romantic in his approach to friendship and is likely to seek people out for sentimental reasons rather than for practical ones.

Cancer is a very sensitive person and sometimes this contributes to making a friendship unsatisfactory. He sometimes makes the wrong interpretation of a remark that is made by a friend or acquaintance. He imagines something injurious behind a very innocent remark. He sometimes feels that people who profess to be his friends laugh at him cruelly behind his back. He has to be constantly reassured of a friend's sincerity, especially in the beginning of a relationship. If he wants to have the wide circle of friends he desires, Cancer must learn to curb these persecution fantasies.

Love and Marriage

The Cancer man or woman has to have love in their life, otherwise their existence is a dull and humdrum affair. When they love someone, Cancer will do everything in their power to make a lover happy. They are not afraid to sacrifice in order to make an important relationship work. To his loved one he is likely to seem uncertain and moody. Cancer is usually very influenced by the impression he has of his lover. They may even be content to let their romance partner have his or her own way in the relationship. He may not make many demands but be willing to follow those of his loved one. At times he may feel that he is not really loved, and draw away somewhat from the relationship. Sometimes it takes a lot of coaxing before he can be won over to the fact that he is indeed loved for himself alone.

Cancer is often possessive about people as well as material objects. This often makes the relationship difficult to accept for his partner.

His standards are sometimes impossibly high and because of this he is difficult to please. The Cancer man or woman is interested in finding someone with whom he can spend the rest of his life. He or she is not interested in any fly-by-night romance.

Romance and the Cancer Woman

The Cancer woman is sincere in her approach to love. Her feelings run deep. Still, she's moody, tempestuous, and changeable. She is so sensitive in romance that her lover may find her difficult to understand at times. The Moon Child knows exactly the sort of man she is looking for. If she can find him, she'll never let him go.

The trouble is she frequently goes through a lot of men in her search for the perfect lover. She surrenders completely to her emotions. She can experience the whole melodrama of falling in love, longing to be with her man, then being desolate when parted from him. If she does find her ideal mate, she will take to marriage for the rest of her life without looking back or even at another man. If she can't marry the man of her dreams, or even live with him, she might carry a torch for the rest of her days. That is the tenacity of the Cancer woman's pure devotion to the man she loves.

Marriage is a union suited to the Crab's temperament, which needs a safe haven in which her feelings can be nurtured. She longs for permanence in a relationship, and usually is not fond of flings or meaningless romantic adventures. Because her emotions are so deep, she can easily feel wronged by a minor slight. Once she imagines she has been hurt, she can retreat rapidly and withdraw deep within herself to brood. It may be quite a while before she comes out of her shell. She desires a man who is protective and affectionate, someone who can understand and cope with her moods so that she does not feel threatened.

As a Moon Child, Cancer is very temperamental. She'll soar to the heights of ecstasy, then plunge into the depths of despondency all with dazzling speed. She'll sparkle like champagne, then fizzle out before the high wears off. Such marked changes of personality can be bewildering to a lover who may have done nothing to provoke them. Reason and logic will not coax her out of a bad mood. Only patient love will work. And if do you not have staying power or refined sensibilities, then you don't stand the ghost of a chance with the Cancer woman.

Cancer's intuition is usually right on. She can size up a situation instinctively, and more times than not she is right. What her gut feelings tell her can be the cause of many a quarrel and the occasion for nagging her mate about a myriad of things. Because she is possessive, there can be discord. And she more she loves, the more possessive and jealous she can become. The demands she is likely to make can be overbearing at times. But as long as she is reassured and appreciated, all will be well.

The Cancer woman makes a devoted wife and mother who will do everything to keep her family together. The only danger is that she may transfer all her love to the children, making her man feel useless and left out. As long as her man participates fully in family life, there will be harmony and affection.

Romance and the Cancer Man

The Cancer man may come on as the reserved type. It can be difficult for some women to understand him. Generally, he is a very loving person, but sometimes he will not let his sensitive side show. He is afraid of being rejected or hurt, so he tries to keep his true feelings hidden until he knows that the intended object of his affections is capable of taking him seriously.

For him, love is a serious business. And he is so serious about love that you might say he lives for love—to give it and to receive it. True to the symbol of the sign of Cancer, which is the Crab, he feels his way very carefully in any romantic alliance. He is not going to make any rash mistakes. But even if it's only a brief affair, the Cancer man will treat his lover as the only woman in the world. When he is convinced that you, too, are serious, then this sensuous idealist is all yours.

You must never play around with his feelings. Like the Crab, the Cancer man pretends to be tough and invulnerable on the outside, but on the inside he is so soft it hurts. He is perhaps the most sensitive person you have ever met. Your Moon Child is highly emotive and moody, reflecting the Moon's quick changeability and shifts of temperament. And, like his ruler the Moon, he is terribly responsive to the vibes coming from his lover. It's all or nothing with him, so jealousy and possessiveness can become a problem. He needs to be constantly reassured that you love him.

If you love him, tell him so often. And show him that you love him, not only with physical love but also with thoughtfully chosen fine gifts no matter how small. He is sentimental. He will treasure everything you give him. He will keep mementos of your happy moments together, especially souvenirs of the occasion when he became sure you would be the love his life.

When deeply in love, the Cancer man does everything in his power to hold the woman of his choice. He is very affectionate and may be extravagant from time to time with the woman he loves. He will lavish gifts upon you and will see that you never lack anything you desire to make your home life together warm and cozy.

Marriage is something the Cancer man sets as a goal early in his life. He wants to settle down with someone who will mother him to some extent. Often he looks for a woman who has the same qualities as his mother, especially if his early childhood revolved around his mother's central role in the family. The remembrance of things maternal makes him feel truly loved and secure.

The Cancer man is an attentive father. He is fond of large families. Sometimes his love for the children may be too possessive, and he can stifle their independence with smothering ways.

Woman—Man

CANCER WOMAN
ARIES MAN

Although it's possible that you could find happiness with a man born under the sign of the Ram, it's uncertain as to how long that happiness would last.

An Aries who has made his mark in the world and is somewhat steadfast in his outlooks and attitudes could be quite a catch for you. On the other hand, men under this sign are often swift-footed and quick-minded. Their industrious mannerisms may fail to impress you, especially if you feel that much of their get-up-and-go often leads nowhere.

When it comes to a fine romance, you want someone with a nice, broad shoulder to lean on. You are likely to find a relationship with someone who doesn't like to stay put for too long somewhat upsetting.

Aries may have a little trouble in understanding you, too, at least in the beginning of the relationship. He may find you too shy and moody. Aries speak their minds and can criticize at the drop of a hat.

You may find a Ram too demanding. He may give you the impression that he expects you to be at his beck and call. You have a barrelful of patience at your disposal and he may try every last bit of it. He is apt not to be as thorough as you are in everything that he does. In order to achieve success or a goal quickly, he will overlook small but important details—and regret it when it is far too late.

Being married to an Aries does not mean that you'll have a secure and safe life as far as finances are concerned. Not all Aries are rash with cash, but they lack that sound head you have for putting away something for that inevitable rainy day. He'll do his best, however, to see that you're adequately provided for, even though his efforts may leave something to be desired as far as you're concerned.

With an Aries mate, you'll find yourself constantly among people. Aries generally have many friends—and you may not heartily approve of them all. Rams are more interested in interesting people than they are in influential ones. Although there can be a family squabble from time to time, you are stable enough to take it all in your stride. Your love of permanence and a harmonious home life will help you to take the bitter with the sweet.

Aries men love children. They make wonderful fathers. Kids take to them like ducks to water. Their quick minds and behavior appeal to the young.

CANCER WOMAN
TAURUS MAN

Some Taurus men are strong and silent. They do all they can to protect and provide for the women they love. The Taurus man will never let you down. He's steady, sturdy, and reliable. He's pretty honest and practical, too. He says what he means and means what he says. He never indulges in deceit and will always put his cards on the table.

Taurus is very affectionate. Being loved, appreciated, and understood is very important for his well-being. Like you, he is also looking for peace, harmony, and security in his life. If you both work toward these goals together, they are easily attained.

If you should marry a Taurus, you can be sure that the wolf will never darken your door. They are notoriously good providers and do everything they can to make their families comfortable and happy.

He'll appreciate the way you have of making a home warm and inviting. Good meals and the evening papers are essential ingredients in making your Taurus husband happy at the end of the workday. Although he may be a big lug of a guy, he's fond of gentleness and soft things. If you puff up his pillow and tuck him in at night, he won't complain.

You probably won't complain about his friends. Taurus tends to seek out friends who are successful or prominent. You admire people, too, who work hard and achieve what they set out for. It helps to reassure your way of life and the way you look at things.

The Taurus man doesn't care too much for change. He's a stay-at-home of the first degree. Chances are that the house you move into after you're married will be the house you'll live in for the rest of your life.

You'll find that the man born under the sign of the Bull is easy to get along with. It's unlikely that you'll have many quarrels or arguments.

Although he'll be gentle and tender with you, your Taurus man is far from being a sensitive type. He's a man's man. Chances are he loves sports like fishing and football. He can be earthy as well as down to earth.

Taurus love their children very much but try hard not to spoil them. They believe in children staying in their places. They make excellent disciplinarians. Your children will be polite and respectful. They may find their Taurus father a little gruff, but as they grow older they'll learn to understand him.

CANCER WOMAN
GEMINI MAN

Gemini men, in spite of their charm and dashing manner, may unnerve you. They seem to lack the common sense you set so much store in. Their tendency to start something, then out of boredom never finish it, may exasperate you.

You may be inclined to interpret a Gemini's jumping from here to there as childish or neurotic. A man born under the sign of the Twins will seldom stay put. If you should take it upon yourself to try and make him sit still, he will resent it.

On the other hand, the Gemini man may think you're a slow-poke, someone far too interested in security and material things. He's attracted to things that sparkle and dazzle. You, with your practical way of looking at things, are likely to seem a little dull and uninteresting to this gadabout. If you're looking for a life of security and permanence—and what Cancer isn't—then you'd better look elsewhere for your Mr. Right.

Chances are you'll be taken in by his charming ways and facile wit—few women can resist Gemini magic. But after you've seen through his live-for-today, gossamer facade, you'll most likely be very happy to turn your attention to someone more stable, even if he is not as interesting. You want a man who is there when you need him. You need someone on whom you can fully rely. Keeping track of a Gemini's movements will make you dizzy. Still, you are a patient woman, most of the time, and you are able to put up with something contrary if you feel that in the end it will prove well worth the effort.

A successful and serious Gemini could make you a very happy woman, perhaps, if you gave him half a chance. Although you may think that he has holes in his head, the Gemini man generally has a good brain and can make good use of it when he wants. Some Geminis who have learned the importance of being consistent have risen to great heights professionally. Once you can convince yourself that not all Twins are witless grasshoppers, you'll find you've come a long way in trying to understand them.

Life with a Gemini man can be more fun than a barrel of clowns. You'll never have a chance to experience a dull moment. He lacks your sense when it comes to money, however. You should see to it that you handle the budgeting and bookkeeping.

In ways, Gemini is like a child himself. Perhaps that is why a Gemini father can get along so well with his own children, indeed with most of the younger generation.

CANCER WOMAN
CANCER MAN
You'll find the man born under the same sign as you easy to get along with. You're both sensitive and sensible people. You'll see eye-to-eye on most things. He'll share your interest in security and practicality.

Cancer men are always hard workers. They are very interested in making successes of themselves in business and socially. Like you, he's a conservative person who has a great deal of respect for tradition. He's a man you can depend on come rain or come shine. He'll never shirk his responsibilities as provider and will always see to it that you never want.

The Cancer man is not the type that rushes headlong into romance. Neither are you, for that matter. Courtship between the two of you will be a sensible and thorough affair. It may take months before you even get to that holding-hands stage of romance. One thing you can be sure of: he'll always treat you like a lady. He'll have great respect and consideration for your feelings. Only when he is sure that you approve of him as someone to love, will he reveal the warmer side of his nature. His coolness, like yours, is just a front. Beneath it lies a very affectionate heart.

Although he may seem restless or moody at times, on the whole the Cancer man is very considerate and kind. His standards are extremely high. He is looking for a partner who can measure up to his ideals—a partner like you.

Marriage means a lot to the Cancer male. He's very interested in settling down with someone who has the same attitudes and outlooks as he has. He's a man who loves being at home. He'll be a faithful husband. Cancers never pussyfoot around after they have made their marriage vows. They do not take their marriage responsibilities lightly. They see to it that everything in this relationship is just the way it should be. Between the two of you, your home will be well managed, bills will be paid on time, there will be adequate insurance on everything of value, and there will be money in the bank. When retirement time rolls around, you both should be very well off.

The Cancer man has a great respect for family. You'll most likely be seeing a lot of his mother during your marriage, just as he'll probably be seeing a lot of yours. He'll do his best to get along with your relatives; he'll treat them with the kindness and concern you think they deserve. He'll expect you to be just as considerate with his relatives.

Cancer is a very good father. He's very patient and understanding, especially when the children are young and dependent and need his protection.

CANCER WOMAN
LEO MAN

To know a man born under the sign of the Lion is not necessarily to love him—even though the temptation may be great. When he fixes most women with his leonine double-whammy, it causes their hearts to throb and their minds to soar.

But with you, the sensible Cancer, it takes more than a regal strut and roar to win you over. There is no denying that Leo has a way with women, even practical Cancers. If he sweeps you off your feet, it may be hard for you to scramble upright again. Still, you are no pushover for romantic charm when you feel there may be no security behind it.

He'll wine you and dine you in the fanciest places. He'll croon to you under the moon and shower you with diamonds if he can get ahold of them. Still, it would be wise to find out just how long that shower is going to last before consenting to be his wife.

Lions in love are hard to ignore, let alone brush off. Once mesmerized by this romantic powerhouse, you may find yourself doing things you never dreamed of. Leos can be vain pussycats when involved romantically. They like to be cuddled and petted, tickled under the chin, and told how wonderful they are. This may not be your cup of tea. Still, when you're romantically dealing with a Lion, you'll instinctively do the things that make him purr.

Although he may be big and magnanimous while trying to win you, he'll let out a blood-curdling roar if he thinks he's not getting the tender love and care he feels is his due. If you keep him well supplied with affection, you can be sure his eyes will never stray and his heart will never wander.

Leo men often tend to be authoritarian. They are born to lord it over others in one way or another, it seems. If he is the top banana of his firm, he'll most likely do everything he can to stay on top. If he's not number one, he's most likely working on it and will be sitting on the throne before long. You'll have more security than you can use if he is in a position to support you in the manner to which he feels you should be accustomed. He's apt to be too lavish, though, at least by your standards.

You'll always have plenty of friends when you have a Leo for a mate. He's a natural born friend-maker and entertainer. He loves to kick up his heels at a party.

As fathers, Leos may go from one extreme to another with their children. Leos either lavish too much attention on the youngsters or demand too much from them.

CANCER WOMAN
VIRGO MAN

The Virgo man is often a quiet, respectable type who sets great store in conservative behavior and levelheadedness. He'll admire you for your practicality and tenacity—perhaps even more than for your good looks. The Virgo man is seldom bowled over by glamour. When looking for someone to love, he always turns to a serious, reliable woman.

He'll be far from a Valentino while dating. In fact, you may wind up making all the passes. Once he gets his motor running, however, he can be warm and wonderful to the right lover.

The Virgo man is gradual about love. Chances are your romance with him will start out looking like an ordinary friendship. Once he's sure that you are no fly-by-night flirt and have no plans of taking him for a ride, he'll open up and rain sunshine all over your heart.

The Virgo man takes his time about romance. It may be many years before he seriously considers settling down. Virgos are often middle-aged when they make their first marriage vows. They hold out as long as they can for the woman who perfectly measures up to their ideals.

He may not have many names in his little black book; in fact, he may not even have a little black book. He's not interested in playing the field; leave that to the more flamboyant signs. The Virgo man is so particular that he may remain romantically inactive for a long period of time. The mate he chooses has to be perfect or it's no go.

With your surefire perseverance, you'll be able to make him listen to reason, as far as romance is concerned. Before long, you'll find him returning your love. He's no block of ice and will respond to what he considers to be the right feminine flame.

Once your love life with Virgo starts to bubble, don't give it a chance to die down. The Virgo man will never give a woman a second chance at winning his heart. If there should ever be a bad break between you, forget about picking up the pieces. With him, it's one strike and you're out.

Once married, he'll stay that way—even if it hurts. He's too conscientious to back out of a legal deal of any sort. He'll always be faithful and considerate. He's as neat as a pin and will expect you to be the same.

If you marry a Virgo man, keep your kids spic-and-span, at least by the time he gets home from work. He likes children to be clean and polite.

CANCER WOMAN
LIBRA MAN

Cancers are apt to find Libra men too wrapped up in their own private dreams to be romantically interesting. He's a difficult man to bring back down to earth, at times. Although he may be very careful about weighing both sides of an argument, he may never really come to a reasonable decision about anything. Decisions, large and small, are capable of giving Libra the willies. Don't ask him why. He probably doesn't know.

If you are looking for permanence and constancy in a love relationship, you may find him a puzzlement. One moment he comes on hard and strong with declarations of his love; the next moment you find he's left you like yesterday's mashed potatoes. It does no good to wonder what went wrong. Chances are nothing, really. It's just one of Libra's strange ways.

On the other hand, you'll probably admire his way with harmony and beauty. If you're all decked out in your fanciest gown, you'll receive a ready compliment and one that's really deserved. Libras don't pass out compliments to all and sundry. If something strikes him as distasteful, he'll remain silent. He's tactful.

He may not seem as ambitious as you would like your lover or husband to be. Where you have a great interest in getting ahead, Libra is often content just to drift along. It is not that he is lazy or shiftless. Material gain generally means little to him. He is more interested in aesthetic matters. If he is in love with you, however, he'll do everything in his power to make you happy.

You may have to give him a good nudge now and again to get him to recognize the light of reality. On the whole, he'll enjoy the company of his artistic dreams when you're not around. If you love your Libra, don't be too harsh or impatient with him. Try to understand him.

Libras are peace-loving people. They hate any kind of confrontation that might lead to an argument. Some of them will do almost anything to keep the peace—even tell a little lie.

If you find yourself involved with a man born under this sign, either temporarily or permanently, you'd better take over the task of managing his money. It's for his own good. Money will never interest a Libra as much as it should. He often has a tendency to be generous when he shouldn't be.

Don't let him see the materialistic side of your nature too often. It might frighten him off.

Libra makes a gentle and understanding father. He's careful not to spoil children or to demand too much from them. He believes that discipline should be a matter of gentle guidance.

CANCER WOMAN
SCORPIO MAN

Some people have a hard time understanding the man born under the sign of Scorpio. Few, however, are able to resist his fiery charm. When angered, he can act like an overturned wasps' nest; his sting can leave an almost permanent mark. If you find yourself interested in a Scorpion, you'd better learn how to keep on his good side.

The Scorpio man can be quite blunt when he chooses; at times, he'll seem like a brute to you. He's touchy—more so than you— and it can get on your nerves after a while. When you feel like you can't take it anymore, you'd better tiptoe away from the scene rather than chance an explosive confrontation. He's capable of giving you a sounding-out that will make you pack your bags and go back to Mother for good.

If he finds fault with you, he'll let you know. He might misinterpret your patience and think it a sign of indifference. Still and all, you are the kind of woman who can adapt to almost any sort of relationship or circumstance if you put your heart and mind to it.

Scorpio men are perceptive and intelligent. In some respects, they know how to use their brains more effectively than most. They believe in winning in whatever they do; second place holds no interest for them. In business, they usually achieve the position they want through drive and use of intellect.

Your interest in home life is not likely to be shared by him. No matter how comfortable you've managed to make the house, it will have little influence on making him aware of his family responsibilities. He does not like to be tied down, generally, and would rather be out on the battlefield of life, belting away for what he feels is a just and worthy cause. Don't try to keep the home fires burning too brightly while you wait for him to come home from work; you may run out of firewood.

The Scorpio man is passionate in all things—including love. Most women are easily attracted to him, and the Cancer woman is no exception, at least before she knows what she might be getting into. If you are swept off your feet by a Scorpio man, soon you find you are dealing with a carton of romantic fireworks. The Scorpio man is passionate with a capital P, make no mistake about that.

Scorpio men are straight to the point. They can be as sharp as a razor blade and just as cutting. Always manage to stay out of his line of fire; if you don't, it could cost you your love life.

Scorpio men like large families. They love children but they do not always live up to the role of the responsible, nurturing father.

CANCER WOMAN
SAGITTARIUS MAN

Sagittarius men are not easy to catch. They get cold feet whenever visions of the altar enter the romance. You'll most likely be attracted to Sagittarius because of his exuberant nature. He's lots of laughs and easy to get along with. But as soon as the relationship begins to take on a serious hue, you may feel let down.

Sagittarius are full of bounce, perhaps too much bounce to suit you. They are often hard to pin down; they dislike staying put. If he ever has a chance to be on the move, he'll go without so much as a how-do-you-do. Archers are quick people both in mind and spirit. If ever they do make mistakes, it's because of their zip. They leap before they look.

If you offer him good advice, he probably will not follow it. Sagittarius like to rely on their own wits and ways whenever possible.

His up-and-at-'em manner about most things is likely to drive you up the wall at times. And your cautious, deliberate manner is likely to make him seem impatient. He will tease when you're accompanying him on a hike or jogging through the park. He can't abide a slowpoke.

At times you'll find him too much like a kid—too breezy. Don't mistake his youthful zest for premature senility. Sagittarius are equipped with first-class brainpower and know how to use it well. They are often full of good ideas and drive. Generally, they are very broad-minded people and very much concerned with fair play and equality.

In the romance department, he's quite capable of loving you wholeheartedly while treating you like a good buddy. His hail-fellow-well-met manner in the arena of love is likely to scare off a dainty damsel. However, a woman who knows that his heart is in the right place won't mind it too much if, once in a while, he pats her on the back instead of giving her a gentle embrace.

He's not very much of a homebody. He's got ants in his pants and enjoys being on the move. Humdrum routine, especially at home, bores him silly. At the drop of a hat, he may ask you to dine out for a change. He's a past master in the instant-surprise department. He'll love keeping you guessing. His friendly, candid nature will win him many friends. He'll expect his friends to be yours, and vice versa.

Sagittarius is a good father when youngsters are old enough for rough-and-tumble sports. But with infants, Sagittarius may be all thumbs and feel helpless.

CANCER WOMAN
CAPRICORN MAN

The Capricorn man is often not the romantic lover that attracts most women. Still, with his reserve and calm, he is capable of giving his heart completely once he has found the right partner. The Cancer woman who is thorough and deliberate can appreciate these same qualities in the average Capricorn man. He is slow and sure about most things—love included.

He doesn't believe in flirting and would never lead a heart on a merry chase just for the game of it. If you win his trust, he'll give you his heart on a platter. Quite often, it is the woman who has to take the lead when romance is in the air. As long as he knows you're making the advances in earnest, he won't mind—in fact, he'll probably be grateful. Don't get to thinking he's all cold fish; he isn't. While some Capricorns are indeed quite capable of expressing passion, others often have difficulty displaying affection. He should have no trouble in this area, however, once he has found a patient and understanding mate.

The Capricorn man is very interested in getting ahead. He's ambitious and usually knows how to apply himself well to whatever task he undertakes. He's far from being a spendthrift. Like you, he knows how to handle money with extreme care. You, with your knack for putting pennies away for that rainy day, should have no difficulty in understanding his way with money. Capricorn thinks in terms of future security. He saves to make sure that he and his wife have something to fall back on when they reach retirement age. There's nothing wrong with that; in fact, it's a plus quality.

The Capricorn man will want to handle household matters efficiently. Most Cancers have no trouble in doing this. If he should check up on you from time to time, don't let it irritate you. Once you assure him that you can handle this area to his liking, he'll leave it all up to you.

Although he's a hard man to catch when it comes to marriage, once he's made that serious step, he's likely to become possessive. Capricorns need to know that they have the support of their women in whatever they do, every step of the way.

The Capricorn man likes to be liked. He may seem like a dull, reserved person. But underneath it all, he's often got an adventurous nature that has never had the chance to express itself. He may be a real daredevil in his heart of hearts. The right woman, the affectionate and adoring woman, can bring out that hidden zest in his nature.

Although he may not understand his children fully, Capricon will be a loving and dutiful father, raising his children with strong codes of honor and allegiance.

CANCER WOMAN
AQUARIUS MAN

You may find the Aquarius man the most broad-minded man you have ever met. On the other hand, you may find him the most impractical. Oftentimes, he's more of a dreamer than a doer. If you don't mind putting up with a man whose heart and mind are as wide as the universe and whose head is almost always up in the clouds, then start dating that Aquarius who has somehow captured your fancy. Maybe you, with your good sense, can bring him back down to earth when he gets too starry-eyed.

He's no dope, make no mistake about that. He can be busy making some very complicated and idealistic plans when he's got that out-to-lunch look in his eyes. But more than likely, he'll never execute them. After he's shared one or two of his progressive ideas with you, you'll think he's a nut. But don't go jumping to conclusions. There's a saying that Aquarius are a half-century ahead of everybody else in the thinking department.

If you decide to say yes to his will you marry me, you'll find out how right his zany whims are on or about your 50th anniversary. Maybe the waiting will be worth it. Could be that you have an Einstein on your hands—and heart.

Life with an Aquarius won't be one of total despair if you can learn to temper his airiness with your down-to-earth practicality. He won't gripe if you do. The Aquarius man always maintains an open mind. He'll entertain the ideas and opinions of everybody, though he may not agree with all of them.

Don't go tearing your hair out when you find that it's almost impossible to hold a normal conversation with your Aquarius friend at times. He's capable of answering a casual question with an imposing intellectual response. But always try to keep in mind that he means well.

His broad-mindedness doesn't stop when it comes to you and your personal freedom. You won't have to give up any of your hobbies or projects after you're married. In fact, he'll encourage you to continue your interests.

He'll be a kind and generous husband. He'll never quibble over petty things. Keep track of the money you both spend. He can't. Money burns a hole in his pocket.

You'll have plenty of chances to put your legendary patience to good use during your relationship with an Aquarius. At times, you may feel like tossing in the towel, but you'll never call it quits.

Aquarius is a good family man and father. He understands children as much as he loves them.

CANCER WOMAN
PISCES MAN
The Pisces man is perhaps the man you've been looking all over for, high and low—the man you thought didn't exist. As a lover, he'll be attentive and faithful.

The Pisces man is very sensitive and very romantic. Still, he is a reasonable person. He may wish on the moon, yet he's got enough good sense to know that it isn't made of green cheese.

He'll be very considerate of your every wish and whim. He will do his best to be a very compatible mate. The Pisces man is great for showering the object of his affection with all kinds of little gifts and tokens of his affection. He's just the right mixture of dreamer and realist that pleases most women.

When it comes to earning bread and butter, the strong Pisces man will do all right in the world. Quite often they are capable of rising to very high positions. Some do very well as writers or psychiatrists. He'll be as patient and understanding with you as you are with him.

One thing a Pisces man dislikes is pettiness. Anyone who delights in running another into the ground is almost immediately crossed off his list of possible mates. If you have even small grievances with any of your friends, don't tell him about them. He will be quite disappointed in you if you complain and criticize.

If you fall in love with a weak Pisces man, don't give up your job at the office before you get married. Better still: hang onto it a good while after the honeymoon; you may need it.

A funny thing about the man born under the sign of the Fishes is that he can be content almost anywhere. This is perhaps because he is inner-directed and places little value on some exterior things. In a shack or a palace, the Pisces man is capable of making the best of all possible adjustments. He won't kick up a fuss if the roof leaks or if the fence is in sad need of repair. He's got more important things on his mind. Still and all, the Pisces man is not lazy or aimless. It's important to understand that material gain is never a direct goal for him.

Pisces men have a way with the sick and troubled. He'll offer his shoulder to anyone in the mood for a good cry. He can listen to one hard-luck story after another without seeming to tire. Quite often he knows what is bothering someone before that person, himself, realizes what it is. It's almost intuitive with Pisces, it seems.

Children are often delighted with Pisces men. As fathers, they are never strict or faultfinding. They are encouraging and always permissive with their youngsters.

Man—Woman

CANCER MAN
ARIES WOMAN

The Aries woman may be too bossy and busy for you. Aries are ambitious creatures. They can become impatient with people who are more thorough and deliberate than they are, especially if they feel such people are taking too much time. The Aries woman is a fast worker. Sometimes she's so fast she forgets to look where she's going. When she stumbles or falls, it would be nice if you were there to grab her.

Aries are proud women. They don't like to be told "I told you so" when they err. Criticism can turn them into blocks of ice. Don't begin to think that the Aries woman frequently gets tripped up in her plans. Quite often they are capable of taking aim and hitting the bull's-eye. You'll be flabbergasted at times by their accuracy as well as by their ambition. On the other hand, because of your interest in being sure and safe, you're apt to spot a flaw in your Aries' plans before she does.

You are somewhat slower than Aries in attaining what you have your sights set on. Still, you don't make any mistakes along the way; you're almost always well-prepared.

The Aries woman is sensitive at times. She likes to be handled with gentleness and respect. Let her know that you love her for her brains as well as for her good looks. Never give her cause to become jealous. When your Aries date sees green, you'd better forget about sharing a rosy future together. Handle her with tender love and care and she's yours.

The Aries woman can be giving if she feels her partner is deserving. She is no iceberg; she responds to the proper flame. She needs a man she can look up to and feel proud of. If the shoe fits, put it on. If not, better put your sneakers back on and quietly tiptoe out of her sight. She can cause you heartache if you've made up your mind about her but she hasn't made up hers about you. Aries women are very demanding at times. Some of them are high-strung. They can be difficult if they feel their independence is being hampered.

The cultivated Aries woman makes a wonderful homemaker and hostess. She's clever in decorating and color use. Your house will be tastefully furnished. She'll see to it that it radiates harmony. Friends and acquaintances will love your Aries wife. She knows how to make everyone feel at home and welcome.

Although the Aries woman may not be keen on the responsibilities of motherhood, she is fond of children and the joy they bring.

CANCER MAN
TAURUS WOMAN

A Taurus woman could perhaps understand you better than most women. She is very considerate and loving. She is methodical and thorough in whatever she does. She knows how to take her time in doing things; she is anxious to avoid mistakes. Like you, she is a careful person. She never skips over things that may seem unimportant; she goes over everything with a fine-tooth comb.

Home is very important to the Taurus woman. She is an excellent homemaker. Although your home may not be a palace, it will become, under her care, a comfortable and happy abode. She'll love it when friends drop by for the evening. She is a good cook and enjoys feeding people well. No one will ever go away from your house with an empty stomach.

The Taurus woman is serious about love and affection. When she has taken a tumble for someone, she'll stay by him—for good, if possible. She will try to be practical in romance, to some extent. When she sets her cap for a man, she keeps after him until he's won her. Generally, the Taurus woman is a passionate lover, even though she may appear otherwise at first glance. She is on the lookout for someone who can return her affection fully. Taurus are sometimes given to fits of jealousy and possessiveness. They expect fair play in the area of marriage. When it doesn't happen, they can be bitingly sarcastic and mean.

The Taurus woman is easygoing. She's fond of keeping peace. She won't argue unless she has to. She'll do her best to keep a love relationship on even keel.

Marriage is generally a one-time thing for Taurus. Once they've made the serious step, they seldom try to back out of it. Marriage is for keeps. They are fond of love and warmth. With the right man, they turn out to be ideal wives.

The Taurus woman will respect you for your steady ways; she'll have confidence in your common sense.

Taurus women seldom put up with nonsense from their children. They are not so much strict as concerned. They like their children to be well-behaved and dutiful. Nothing pleases a Taurus mother more than a compliment from a neighbor or teacher about her child's behavior. Although children may inwardly resent the iron hand of a Taurus woman, in later life they are often thankful that they were brought up in such an orderly and conscientious way.

CANCER MAN
GEMINI WOMAN

The Gemini woman may be too much of a flirt ever to take your heart too seriously. Then again, it depends on what kind of mood she's in. Gemini women can change from hot to cold quicker than a cat can wink its eye. Chances are her fluctuations will tire you after a time, and you'll pick up your heart—if it's not already broken into small pieces—and go elsewhere. Women born under the sign of the Twins have the talent of being able to change their moods and attitudes as frequently as they change their party dresses.

Sometimes, Geminis like to whoop it up. Some of them are good-time gals who love burning the candle to the wick. You'll always see them at parties and gatherings, surrounded by men of all types, laughing gaily or kicking up their heels at every opportunity. Wallflowers, they're not. The next day you may bump into her at the neighborhood library and you'll hardly recognize her for her sensible attire. She'll probably have five or six books under her arm—on five or six different subjects. In fact, she may even work there.

You'll probably find her a dazzling and fascinating creature—for a time, at any rate. Most men do. But when it comes to being serious about love you may find that your sparkling Eve leaves quite a bit to be desired. It's not that she has anything against being serious, it's just that she might find it difficult trying to be serious with you.

At one moment, she'll be capable of praising you for your steadfast and patient ways. The next moment she'll tell you in a cutting way that you're an impossible stick-in-the-mud.

Don't even begin to fathom the depths of her mercurial soul—it's full of false bottoms. She'll resent close investigation anyway, and will make you rue the day you ever took it into your head to try to learn more about her than she feels is necessary. Better keep the relationship fancy free and full of fun until she gives you the go-ahead sign. Take as much of her as she is willing to give; don't ask for more. If she does take a serious interest in you, then she'll come across with the goods.

There will come a time when Gemini will realize that she can't spend her entire life at the ball. The security and warmth you offer are just what she needs for a happy, fulfilled life.

The Gemini mother will be easygoing with her children. She'll probably spoil them and dote on their every whim. Because she has a youthful outlook, she will be a fun playmate for her kids.

CANCER MAN
CANCER WOMAN
The Cancer woman needs to be protected from the cold cruel world. She'll love you for your gentle and kind manner. You are the kind of man who can make her feel safe and secure.

You won't have to pull any he-man or heroic stunts to win her heart; she's not interested in things like that. She's more likely to be impressed by your sure, steady ways—the way you have of putting your arm around her and making her feel that she's the only girl in the world. When she's feeling glum and tears begin to well up in her eyes, you'll know how to calm her fears, no matter how silly some of them may seem.

The Moon Child, like you, is inclined to have her ups and downs. Perhaps you can both learn to smooth out the roughed-up spots in each other's life. She'll most likely worship the ground you walk on or place you on a very high pedestal. Don't disappoint her if you can help it. She'll never disappoint you. The Cancer woman will take great pleasure in devoting the rest of her natural life to you. She'll darn your socks, mend your overalls, scrub floors, wash windows, shop, cook, and do anything short of murder in order to please you and to let you know she loves you. Sounds like that legendary old-fashioned girl, doesn't it? Contrary to popular belief, there are still many of them around and the majority of them are Cancers.

Treat your Cancer mate fairly and she'll treat you like a king. There is one thing you should be warned about, though. Never be unkind to your mother-in-law. It will be the only golden rule your Cancer wife will expect you to live up to. Mother is something special for her. You should have no trouble in understanding this, for your mother has a special place in your heart, too. It's always that way with the Cancer-born. They have great respect and love for family ties. It might be a good idea for you both to get to know each other's relatives before tying the marriage knot, because after the wedding bells have rung, you'll be seeing a lot of them.

Of all the signs in the Zodiac, Cancer is the most maternal. In caring for and bringing up children, she knows just how to combine tenderness and discipline. A child couldn't ask for a better mother. Cancer women are sympathetic, affectionate, and patient with children. Both of you will make excellent parents, especially when the children are young. When they grow older you'll most likely be reluctant to let them go out into the world.

CANCER MAN
LEO WOMAN

The Leo woman can make most men roar like lions. If any woman in the Zodiac has that indefinable something that can make men lose their heads and find their hearts, it's Leo.

She's got more than a fair share of charm and glamour and she knows how to make the most of her assets, especially when she's in the company of the opposite sex. Jealous men lose either their cool or their sanity when trying to woo a woman born under the sign of the Lion. She likes to kick up her heels and doesn't care who knows it. She often makes heads turn and tongues wag. You don't have to believe any of what you hear—it's most likely just jealous gossip or wishful thinking. Needless to say, other women in her vicinity turn green with envy and will try anything to put her out of commission.

Although this vamp makes the blood rush to your head and makes you momentarily forget all the things you thought were important and necessary in your life, you may feel differently when you come back down to earth and the stars are out of your eyes. You may feel that although this vivacious creature can make you feel wonderful, she just isn't the type you planned to bring home to Mother. Not that your mother might disapprove of your choice—but you might after the shoes and rice are a thing of the past. Although the Leo woman may do her best to be a good wife for you, chances are she'll fall short of your idea of what a good wife should be.

If you're planning on not going as far as the altar with that Leo woman who has you flipping your lid, you'd better be financially equipped for some very expensive dating. Be prepared to shower her with expensive gifts and to take her dining and dancing to the smartest spots in town. Promise her the moon if you're in a position to go that far. Luxury and glamour are two things that are bound to lower a Leo's resistance. She has expensive tastes, and you'd better cater to them if you expect to get to first base with the Lioness.

If you've got an important business deal to clinch and you have doubts as to whether you can swing it or not, bring your Leo along to the business luncheon. Chances are that with her on your arm, you'll be able to win any business battle with both hands tied. She won't have to say or do anything—just be there at your side. The grouchiest oil magnate can be transformed into a gushing, obedient schoolboy if there's a charming Lioness in the room.

Leo mothers are blind to the faults of their children. They make very loving and affectionate mothers and tend to give their youngsters everything under the sun.

CANCER MAN
VIRGO WOMAN

The Virgo woman is particular about choosing her men friends. She's not interested in going out with anybody. She has her own idea of what a boyfriend or prospective husband should be. Perhaps that image has something of you in it.

Generally, she's quiet and correct. She doesn't believe that nonsense has any place in a love affair. She's serious about love and she'll expect you to be. She's looking for a man who has both feet on the ground—someone who can take care of himself as well as her. She knows the value of money and how to get the most out of a dollar. She's far from being a spendthrift. Throwing money around turns her stomach, even when it isn't her money.

She'll most likely be very shy about romancing. Even the simple act of holding hands may make her turn crimson—at least, on the first couple of dates. You'll have to make all the advances, and you'll have to be careful not to make any wrong moves. She's capable of showing anyone who oversteps the boundaries of common decency the door. It may even take quite a long time before she'll accept that goodnight kiss at the front gate. Don't give up. You are perhaps the kind of man who can bring out the warm woman in her.

There is love and tenderness underneath Virgo's seemingly frigid facade. It will take a patient and understanding man to bring it out into the open. She may have the idea that sex is reserved for marriage. Like you, she has a few old-fashioned concepts. And, like you, it's all or nothing. So if you are the right man, gentle and affectionate, you will melt her reserve.

When a Virgo has accepted you as a lover or mate, she won't stint in giving her love in return. You'll be surprised at the transformation your earnest attention can bring about in this quiet kind of woman. When in love, Virgos only listen to their hearts, not to what the neighbors say.

Virgo women are honest about love once they've come to grips with it. They don't appreciate hypocrisy—particularly in this area of life. They will always be true to their hearts—even if it means tossing you over for a new love. But if you convince her that you are earnest about your interest in her, she'll reciprocate your love and affection and never leave you. Do her wrong once, however, and you can be sure she'll call the whole thing off.

Virgo mothers are tender and loving. They know what's good for their children and will always take great pains in bringing them up correctly.

CANCER MAN
LIBRA WOMAN

It's a woman's prerogative to change her mind. This wise saying characterizes the Libra woman. Her changes of mind, in spite of her undeniable charm, might drive even a man of your changeable moods up the wall. She's capable of smothering you with love and kisses one day and on the next avoid you like the plague. If you think you're a man of great patience, then perhaps you can tolerate her sometime-ness without suffering too much. However, if you own up to the fact that you're a mere mortal who can only take so much, then you'd better fasten your attention on a girl who's somewhat more constant.

But don't get the wrong idea—a love affair with a Libra is not all bad. In fact, it can have an awful lot of pluses to it. Libra women are soft, very feminine, and warm. She doesn't have to vamp all over the place in order to gain a man's attention. Her delicate presence is enough to warm any man's heart. One smile and you're a piece of putty in the palm of her hand.

She can be fluffy and affectionate. On the other hand, her indecision about which dress to wear, what to cook for dinner, or whether or not to redecorate could make you tear your hair out. What will perhaps be more exasperating is her flat denial of the accusation that she cannot make even the simplest decision. The trouble is that she wants to be fair or just in all matters. She'll spend hours weighing both sides of an argument or situation. Don't make her rush into a decision; that would only irritate her.

The Libra woman likes to be surrounded by beautiful things. Money is no object when beauty is concerned. There will always be antiques and objects of art in her apartment. She'll know how to arrange them tastefully, too, to show them off. Women under this sign are fond of beautiful clothes and furnishings. They will run up bills without batting an eye—if given the chance.

Once she's cottoned to you, the Libra woman will do everything in her power to make you happy. She'll wait on you hand and foot when you're sick, bring you breakfast in bed on Sundays, and even read you the funny papers if you're too sleepy to open your eyes. She'll be very thoughtful and devoted. If anyone dares suggest you're not the grandest man in the world, your Libra wife will give that person a good sounding-out.

Libras work wonders with children. Gentle persuasion and affection are all she uses in bringing them up. Her subtlety sets a good example for them to follow.

CANCER MAN
SCORPIO WOMAN

When the Scorpio woman chooses to be sweet, she's apt to give the impression that butter wouldn't melt in her mouth . . . but, of course, it would. When her temper flies, so will everything else that isn't bolted down. She can be as hot as a tamale or as cool as a cucumber when she wants. Whatever mood she's in, you can be sure it's for real. She doesn't believe in poses or hypocrisy.

The Scorpio woman is often seductive and sultry. Her femme

fatale charm can pierce through the hardest of hearts like a laser ray. She doesn't have to look like Mata Hari (many of them resemble the tomboy next door) but once you've looked into those tantalizing eyes, you're a goner.

The Scorpio woman can be a whirlwind of passion. Life with her will not be all smiles and smooth sailing. If you think you can handle a woman who can spit bullets, try your luck. Your stable and steady nature will most likely have a calming effect on her. You're the kind of man she can trust and rely on. But never cross her—even on the smallest thing. If you do, you'd better tell Fido to make room for you in the doghouse—you'll be his guest for the next couple of days.

Generally, the Scorpio woman will keep family battles within the walls of your home. When company visits, she's apt to give the impression that married life with you is one big joyride. It's just her way of expressing her loyalty to you—at least in front of others. She believes that family matters are and should stay private. She certainly will see to it that others have a high opinion of you both.

Although she's an individualist, after she has married she'll put her own interests aside for those of the man she loves. With a woman like this behind you, you can't help but go far. She'll never try to take over your role as boss of the family. She'll give you all the support you need in order to fulfill that role. She won't complain if the going gets rough. She knows how to take the bitter with the sweet. She is a courageous woman. She's as anxious as you are to find that place in the sun for you both. She's as determined a person as you are.

Although Scorpio loves her children, she may not be too affectionate toward them. She'll make a devoted mother, though. She'll be anxious to see them develop their talents. She'll teach the children to be courageous and steadfast.

CANCER MAN
SAGITTARIUS WOMAN

The Sagittarius woman is hard to keep track of: first she's here, then she's there. She's a woman with a severe case of itchy feet. She's got to keep on the move.

People generally like her because of her hail-fellow-well-met manner and her breezy charm. She is constantly good-natured and almost never cross. With the female Archer you're likely to strike up a palsy-walsy relationship. You might not be interested in letting it go any farther. She probably won't sulk if you leave it on a friendly basis. Treat her like a kid sister and she'll love it.

She'll probably be attracted to you because of your restful, self-assured manner. She'll need a friend like you to help her over the rough spots in her life. She'll most likely turn to you for advice frequently.

There is nothing malicious about a woman born under this sign. She is full of bounce and good cheer. Her sunshiny disposition can be relied upon even on the rainiest of days. No matter what she says or does, you'll always know that she means well. Sagittarius are sometimes short on tact. Some of them say anything that comes into their heads, no matter what the occasion. Sometimes the words that tumble out of their mouths seem downright cutting and cruel; they mean well but often everything they say comes out wrong. She's quite capable of losing her friends—and perhaps even yours—through a careless slip of the lip. Always remember that she is full of good intentions. Stick with her if you like her and try to help her mend her ways.

She's may not be the quiet, home-loving woman you'd be interested in marrying, but she'll certainly be lots of fun to pal around with. Quite often, Sagittarius women are outdoor types. They're crazy about things like fishing, camping, and mountain climbing. They love the wide open spaces. They are fond of all kinds of animals. Make no mistake about it: this busy little lady is no slouch. She's full of pep and vigor.

She's great company most of the time; she's more fun than a three-ring circus when she's in the right company. You'll like her for her candid and direct manner. On the whole, Sagittarius are very kind and sympathetic women.

If you do wind up marrying this girl-next-door type, you'd better see to it that you take care of all financial matters. Sagittarius often let money run through their fingers like sand.

A Sagittarius mother may smother her children with love on the one hand, then give them all of the freedom they think they need. It can be very confusing.

CANCER MAN
CAPRICORN WOMAN

The Capricorn woman may not be the most romantic woman of the Zodiac, but she's far from frigid when she meets the right man. She believes in true love. She doesn't appreciate getting involved in flings. To her, they're just a waste of time. She's looking for a man who means business—in life as well as in love. Although she can be very affectionate with her boyfriend or mate, she tends to let her head govern her heart. That is not to say that she is a cool, calculating cucumber. On the contrary, she just feels she can be more honest about love if she consults her brains first. She wants to size up the situation first before throwing her heart in the ring. She wants to make sure it won't get stepped on.

The Capricorn woman is faithful, dependable, and systematic in just about everything that she undertakes. She is quite concerned with security and sees to it that every penny she spends is spent wisely. She is very economical about using her time, too. She does not believe in whittling away her energy on a scheme that is bound not to pay off.

Ambitious themselves, they are quite often attracted to ambitious men—men who are interested in getting somewhere in life. If a man of this sort wins her heart, she'll stick by him and do all she can to help him get to the top.

The Capricorn woman is almost always diplomatic. She makes an excellent hostess. She can be very influential when your business acquaintances come to dinner.

The Capricorn woman is likely to be very concerned, if not downright proud, about her family tree. Relatives are important to her, particularly if they're socially prominent. Never say a cross word about her family members. That can really go against her grain and she'll punish you by not talking for days.

She's generally thorough in whatever she does: cooking, housekeeping, entertaining. Capricorn women are well-mannered and gracious, no matter what their backgrounds. They seem to have it in their natures to always behave properly.

If you should marry a woman born under this sign, you need never worry about her going on a wild shopping spree. They understand the value of money better than most women. If you turn over your paycheck to her at the end of the week, you can be sure that a good hunk of it will go into the bank and that all the bills will be paid on time.

With children, the Capricorn mother is both loving and correct. She'll see to it that they're polite and respectful and that they honor the codes they are taught when young.

CANCER MAN
AQUARIUS WOMAN

The woman born under the sign of the Water Bearer can be odd and eccentric at times. Some say that this is the source of her mysterious charm. You may think she's just a plain screwball, and you may be right.

Aquarius women often have their heads full of dreams and stars in their eyes. By nature, they are often unconventional; they have their own ideas about how the world should be run. Sometimes their ideas may seem pretty weird—chances are they're just a little bit too progressive. There is a saying that runs: The way the Aquarius thinks, so will the world in fifty years.

If you find yourself falling in love with a woman born under this sign, you'd better fasten your safety belt. It may take some time before you know what she's like and even then, you may have nothing to go on but a string of vague hunches.

She can be like a rainbow: full of dazzling colors. She's like no other girl you've ever known. There is something about her that is definitely charming, yet elusive. You'll never be able to put your finger on it. She seems to radiate adventure and optimism without even trying. She'll most likely be the most tolerant and open-minded woman you've ever encountered.

If you find that she's too much mystery and charm for you to handle—and being a Cancer, chances are you might—just talk it out with her and say that you think it would be better if you called it quits. She'll most likely give you a peck on the cheek and say "Okay, but let's still be friends." Aquarius women are like that. Perhaps you'll both find it easier to get along in a friendship than in a romance.

It is not difficult for her to remain buddy-buddy with an ex-lover. For many Aquarius, the line between friendship and romance is a fuzzy one.

She's not a jealous person and while you're romancing her, she won't expect you to be, either. You'll find her a free spirit most of the time. Just when you think you know her inside out, you'll discover that you don't really know her at all. She's a very sympathetic and warm person. She is often helpful to those in need of assistance and advice.

She'll seldom be suspicious even when she has every right to be. If the man she loves makes a little slip, she's likely to forgive it and forget it.

Aquarius makes a fine mother. Her positive and bighearted qualities are easily transmitted to her children. They will be taught tolerance at an early age.

CANCER MAN
PISCES WOMAN

The Pisces woman places great value on love and romance. She's gentle, kind, and romantic. Like you, she has very high ideals, and will only give her heart to a man who she feels can live up to her expectations.

Many a man dreams of an alluring Pisces woman. You're perhaps no exception. Even though she appears soft and cuddly, she has a sultry, seductive charm that can win the heart of almost any man.

She will not try to wear the pants in the relationship. She'll let you be the brains of the family. She's content to play a behind-the-scenes role in order to help you achieve your goals.

She can be very ladylike and proper. Your business associates and friends will be dazzled by her warmth and femininity. Although she's a charmer, there is a lot more to her than just a pretty exterior. There is a brain ticking away behind that gentle, womanly facade. You may never become aware of it—that is, until you're married to her. It's no cause for alarm, however; she'll most likely never use it against you, only to help you and possibly set you on a more successful path.

If she feels you're botching up your married life through careless behavior or if she feels you could be earning more money than you do, she'll tell you about it. But any wife would.

No one had better dare say one uncomplimentary word about you in her presence. It could set the stage for an emotional scene. Pisces women are maddeningly temperamental and can go to theatrical extremes when expressing their feelings. Their reaction to adversity or frustration can run the gamut from tears to tantrums and back again.

She can do wonders with a house. She is very fond of dramatic and beautiful things. There will always be plenty of fresh-cut flowers around the house. She will choose charming artwork and antiques, if they are affordable.

She'll have an extra special dinner prepared for you when you come home from an important business meeting. Don't dwell on the boring details of the meeting, though. But if you need that big idea, to seal a contract or make a conquest, your Pisces woman is sure to confide a secret that will guarantee your success.

Treat her with tenderness and generosity and your relationship will be an enjoyable one. A bunch of beautiful flowers will never fail to make her eyes light up. See to it that you never forget her birthday or your anniversary. These things are very important to her.

If you are patient and kind, you can keep a Pisces woman happy for a lifetime. She, however, is not without her faults. You may find her lacking in practicality and good old-fashioned stoicism; you may even feel that she uses her tears as a method of getting her own way.

Pisces is a strong, self-sacrificing mother. She will teach her children the value of service to the community while not letting them lose their individuality.

CANCER
LUCKY NUMBERS 2003

Lucky numbers and astrology can be linked through the movements of the Moon. Each phase of the thirteen Moon cycles vibrates with a sequence of numbers for your Sign of the Zodiac over the course of the year. Using your lucky numbers is a fun system that connects you with tradition.

New Moon	First Quarter	Full Moon	Last Quarter
Jan. 2	Jan. 10	Jan. 18	Jan. 25
0 3 8 1	1 5 8 6	6 9 9 3	3 7 1 0
Feb. 1	Feb. 9	Feb. 16	Feb. 23
4 4 6 1	0 4 2 5	5 9 6 1	4 7 2 7
March 2	March 11	March 18	March 24
9 9 4 7	7 5 8 3	3 6 3 6	9 4 9 2
April 1	April 9	April 16	April 23
6 9 7 7	7 1 5 8	8 3 6 6	1 0 6 8
May 1	May 9	May 15	May 22
6 4 7 7	2 5 9 3	3 0 1 9	5 7 2 5
May 30	June 7	June 14	June 21
9 3 6 1	4 8 2 2	2 5 9 5	7 4 8 2
June 29	July 6	July 13	July 21
7 3 7 1	0 5 8 0	2 6 2 4	8 2 1 8
July 29	August 5	August 11	August 19
6 9 4 4	7 1 5 5	0 3 7 1	8 3 6 5
August 27	Sept. 3	Sept. 10	Sept. 18
4 8 8 2	2 5 9 5	7 2 5 5	3 6 2 2
Sept. 25	Oct. 2	Oct. 10	Oct. 18
8 9 3 6	1 6 8 8	8 3 6 4	4 7 2 8
Oct. 25	Oct. 31	Nov. 8	Nov. 16
3 6 0 4	9 2 6 6	6 9 7 1	1 5 8 6
Nov. 23	Nov. 30	Dec. 8	Dec. 16
6 0 3 7	5 9 3 3	3 1 4 8	8 2 6 5
Dec. 23	Dec. 30	Jan. 7 ('04)	Jan. 15 ('04)
0 3 8 0	1 0 5 8	2 3 1 1	5 9 6 0

CANCER
YEARLY FORECAST 2003

*Forecast for 2003 Concerning Business
and Financial Affairs, Job Prospects,
Travel, Health, Romance and Marriage
for Persons Born with the Sun
in the Zodiacal Sign of Cancer.
June 21–July 20*

For those born under the influence of the Sun in the zodiacal sign of Cancer, ruled by the changeable and intuitive Moon, this promises to be a rewarding and productive year. You may begin to take life more seriously, with a greater sense of what can be achieved to ensure your long-term happiness. There should be opportunities for a deeper commitment with loved ones, giving you greater emotional security. Cancer people who are in the business world can expect a period when working practices need to be overhauled significantly. Investing in new ideas can pay off, but you will have to use your instinctive understanding of economics to get the best results. Where personal finances are concerned, maintain a cautious outlook. There are bound to be a few fluctuations in your bank balance throughout the year. Job prospects should be quite exciting if you are looking for a change. You are ready to take on more responsibility, which should include a higher salary. The outlook for travel is mixed because you do not know exactly what you want. While you could really do with a change of scene, there is also a strong pull to host visitors from abroad rather than traveling yourself. Usually Cancer people are reasonably health-conscious, and that continues this year. A few digestive problems are to be expected. However, if you are careful about your diet and exercise, you ought to stay well. Romantic prospects may be plagued by confused and volatile emotions that are aroused as the months go by. This year you may learn more about relating than ever before, allowing a bond to be forged with the one closest to your heart.

Business affairs will keep you on your toes, with a particular focus on income and production methods. A rival company could steal a march on you, making it necessary to thoroughly revamp your aims. This is bound to have a beneficial effect since out-moded ways will be weeded out. Relations with workers may be a little uncomfortable at times, especially when changes are being made. In such a situation it is vital not to put all the blame on one side or the other. Be sure to acknowledge where you might have gone wrong or have been insensitive, then make a sincere apology. There is a possibility of moving if your enterprise alters dramatically in size or output. The key is organization. Use your ability to try to plan for all eventualities so that business goes as smoothly as possible. A brief downturn in profits might necessitate laying off some employees. Consider the financial and other con-sequences quite carefully, especially if it then becomes necessary to bring in temporary staff. April and May could find you brain-storming with colleagues to find new ways to market or utilize an unusual product or service. It would be wise to prepare for an unexpected period of success followed by a brief lapse back into the usual level of profit. With careful management the first half of the year should prove unusually lucrative. Then it becomes your choice whether to invest in expensive but effective advertis-ing from the end of August onward. Your own position should not be in doubt, but as the year progresses you could quite nat-urally assume greater prominence and responsibility. It would not be surprising if you have a new leadership role by the end of the year. All in all, with thoughtful planning and careful use of re-sources, 2003 holds the potential to be productive and successful.

Personal finances are quite complex. On the one hand, money should flow freely into your account. You will get more pleasure than usual from spending it. However, you may become a little nervous about long-term prospects for financial security. This area needs close attention. It might not be possible to come up with a definite budget and investment plan, particularly if you do not have the resources with which to do so. That does not mean you cannot research likely ideas and at least lay the groundwork for success. A raise may be in the pipeline at work, but you will have to push quite hard to get it; it will not just be awarded automat-ically. Do not hesitate to spend on yourself and your home this year. You will enjoy life more if you feel secure in attractive sur-roundings and with favorite possessions. Since Cancer people are usually sensible with money, you should end the year better off than when it started.

The outlook for jobs and employment suggests you need to shake up your ideas about job security. Changes are just around the corner, and rumors to that effect at work should not be disregarded. Cancer people who are looking for a new direction could not choose a better time to break away from familiar routine. Something involving investigation or research would suit your natural ability to search out facts and hidden information. Relationships with co-workers need close attention this year. Someone could develop a grudge against you for no good reason. However, if you begin the year with a positive outlook, by March you should have established sound enough relationships to get through the rest of the year without difficulty. You might briefly toy with the idea of working abroad, and even do so for a period during spring and summer. In the end, however, you will feel more comfortable close to loved ones and familiar scenes. If you embrace the main changes, this should be a year of advancement and success.

Travel prospects are stop and go. You may be persuaded by adventurous friends to sign up for a bold and exciting trip to distant lands. At the last moment, however, your naturally cautious side might want to back out. To do so would be to miss out on a potentially memorable as well as educational experience. Your main aim with travel this year should be to get new impressions that open your mind to a bigger picture of life. Foreign cultures have much to teach you about new ways of living. Business trips might become quite a frequent feature of your work routine, so that you keep a suitcase partly packed all the time. Cancer singles hoping to enjoy a holiday romance need to keep a level head. The period between mid-March and mid-May is a good time for taking a vacation. After that be prepared to get more excitement than relaxation while away from home. Whenever you travel, you are bound to come back with dramatic stories to tell and many happy memories.

Your health this year should be reasonably good as long as you are cautious and sensible. Digestive problems could cause some discomfort, especially if you try out an unusual new diet. It is fine to experiment with food, but if your diet is producing adverse effects it would be foolish to continue with it. There is also a possibility of putting on weight if you are too sedentary. Try to set up a regular exercise routine, even if this seems boring at first. As time passes and you grow older, tune in to your body and see if it needs different treatment. If you find that you are more tired than usual, it could be time to cut down on late nights. Long-term problems could yield to alternative treatment, although it would not be wise to shun your usual physician. However, a treatment that works is worth pursuing. During the spring be careful to dress properly even if the weather becomes uncharacteristically warm.

Play safe, especially if that means avoiding chills so that you stay in enviably good health.

Your outlook on love and romance might change quite profoundly this year. As a Cancer you are no stranger to deep emotion. You are about to learn just what makes a relationship work on very basic levels. It may help to read popular myths and legends of love. In this way you will be able to recognize universal themes which you play out with your mate or partner. Cancers who have been single for a while should be reasonably content with independence. However, when the right person comes along you may begin a more serious relationship than ever before. Long-term partnership will certainly benefit if both of you acknowledge that love includes moments of irritation, disappointment, and anger. If you become more realistic about the complex nature of romance, it will be easier to accept negative emotions as simply part of the package; they by no means indicate failure of any kind. The difference between love which grows over time and instant physical attraction may become clearer to you as the year progresses. The accent is on deepening your relationships to achieve a true sense of emotional commitment.

CANCER
DAILY FORECAST

January–December 2003

JANUARY

1. WEDNESDAY. Challenging. You may be feeling impulsive as the New Year inspires you to try something completely different. There is a tendency for changes to erupt suddenly, perhaps resolutions that you decide to implement immediately. Start working out to improve your physical fitness. A better diet of wholesome foods is likely to cross your mind after all the rich holiday treats. You could have a hunch about a new investment. This is a time to make changes for the sake of your family as well as your own welfare. However, avoid any form of outright gambling. A better budget can ease your financial concerns.

2. THURSDAY. Promising. As a Cancer you may feel quite stubborn and self-willed. Because of this you are apt to overreact and be affected by an imbalance. Or deep-rooted habits could make you seek partnership only as a form of personal security. Chances are that you will feel drawn to a romantic relationship. This is also a starred time to begin a new business partnership. Look for a parental figure or at least someone who you know will be protective of your interests. This will enable you to be stronger because you are responsive and more alive when paired with a person you look up to and respect.

3. FRIDAY. Surprising. If you are trying to accomplish something big as the workweek ends, team up with another person. In this way you will find that the work goes a lot easier and more quickly as you share the load. Together you can make a game of any task. The reaction to your lighthearted flirtation could be surprisingly positive. Your playful energy is apt to become romantically charged. Your creativity will also be stimulated. Give it an opportunity to be expressed even if not completely original. Playing and experimenting could lead to something exciting as you break away from the ordinary.

4. SATURDAY. Misleading. You start the weekend with high intelligence, sensitivity, and imagination. You will probably prefer seclusion. This is a better time than most for doing research and learning something new. However, you may be slowed down by technical glitches. These may take the form of computer problems, difficulties with your car, or other electronic distress. Be sure to back up your computer files. Make plans to join forces with a person who shares your interests. Chances are that you can borrow tools or transportation if necessary. Keep evening plans simple and straightforward. Avoid socializing with a person or a couple who want something from you.

5. SUNDAY. Fair. Your intuitions are strong, except when it comes to financial matters. It would be best to defer any important decision involving family assets. Try not to make a big-ticket purchase because it may cause you to suffer a loss as it turns out to be not such a good deal. Your energy level is not as high as usual, so arrange to get extra rest and relaxation. An afternoon nap would be ideal. Because you are quite organized and disciplined, you can put this to good use by cleaning out old files, secret hiding places, or even the attic. You can make especially good progress dealing with matters and objects from the past. Try to eradicate a habit that you know is unhealthy.

6. MONDAY. Disappointing. As a Cancer you are deeply sensitive, interested in questions about life and living. Quite possibly you have psychic ability that you can use in an unconventional way, even to guide other people spiritually. Because you are feeling highly original and individualistic, you should try to avoid being silly or childish. You could be disappointed when people do not take your thoughts and ideas seriously. Instead they may consider your behavior eccentric and attempt to avoid you. Pay close attention to any insights you have into family finances. It is possible you will have a money-making brainstorm that involves a new partnership.

7. TUESDAY. Variable. As a Cancer you are noted for your receptive, imaginative mind capable of delving into philosophical ideas. The unknown attracts you; in your work you may delve into history or the more immediate past. This is a day for learning and studying new subjects. You might find it helpful to team up with a co-worker or friend who already has some of the knowledge you are seeking or may have valuable contacts. More than likely you will be able to access information by making long-distance calls or e-mail queries to foreign colleagues or experts. This is also a good day for travel, especially with your mate or partner.

8. WEDNESDAY. Positive. Your energy level is high and you have sufficient enthusiasm to accomplish your day's goals. A new project or idea is bound to stimulate your mind. You will enjoy intellectual conversations with teammates and partners. Cancer students will have an easy time learning subjects such as language, history, and philosophy. Gather knowledge through reading, conversation, and debate. Stay away from the quiet of the library and note taking, as you have a tendency to be vague and impractical. Arrange to get some physical exercise; a team sport would be ideal. Play for pleasure but not to lose.

9. THURSDAY. Excellent. This is a starred day for career matters. You are apt to be involved with the public as part of your job. You may be invited to attend professional or social activities, giving you limited private life today. However, you are full of energy and can socialize while looking for ways to get ahead. Devote some time to contract negotiation or a presentation. You are intuitive about what the public wants. Discussions will go especially well in one-on-one situations with an existing or potential partner. This may also be effective in a romantic or family situation where you are hoping to get someone to say yes to your plea.

10. FRIDAY. Rewarding. Strive to make money while the sun is shining on your career. Income could come from a contract that closes as the week ends, probably in the form of a bonus or commission check. You could also receive a raise. Complications may arise because a business partner or teammate is jealous of your success, and they were part of the reason you succeeded. Be sure to acknowledge everyone's contribution and reward those who helped you as generously as possible. Otherwise they may not be so helpful to your career the next time around. Aim to make it a win-win situation where everyone benefits even though your name may be in the newspaper.

11. SATURDAY. Helpful. Although the weekend has arrived, it is a better day than most to make progress in your career. You may need to complete work you brought home, or you might find yourself back in the office. Pay special attention to your intuition. You are apt to have sudden insights that could be very beneficial. It is also a good time to delve into complex issues. With some serious thinking you will likely find answers to questions that have puzzled you in the past. It is likely that you are being rigid and dogmatic in regard to certain opinions, but these traits will help you get to the bottom of financial and partnership questions. Do not take no or maybe for an answer.

12. SUNDAY. Pleasant. This is a good day to spend with friends, especially if you can participate in some outdoor sports together. Consider skiing, skating, and other favorite winter activities. The only topic to avoid this weekend is finances. Do not even try to balance the checkbook or manage family funds. It would be wise to let your mate or partner handle money issues as they arise. Your intuition is not as strong as usual, and your free advice is apt to be misleading. Avoid loaning money or anything of value to friends. You are most likely in the mood to act impulsively. However, being a Cancer you should be able to hold on to your cash and still have a good time.

13. MONDAY. Enjoyable. Your easy social charm attracts admirers. You will find yourself surrounded by friends and potential partners. This is an ideal time to communicate your hopes and dreams with people you trust. Invite an old friend to go out for lunch, or accept an offer you receive to attend a club meeting or society gathering. You are emotionally intuitive in dealing with people, although being with so many can drain some of your energy. You may be trying too hard to entertain them. Just be yourself and you will both stimulate and be stimulated by the companionship of like-minded individuals.

14. TUESDAY. Manageable. Because you are sensitive, receptive, and intuitive toward other people, you may find many coming to you for help and advice. You are apt to have deep, profound insights into the human condition. Try to spend more time than usual in quiet solitude. This is a better time than most to restore

yourself by thinking and meditating. You have a creative imagination that is stimulated when reflecting. You will be most at
peace if you are near water. Consider a walk around a nearby
lake, river, or beach. Answers and ideas will surface in mysterious
ways as you suddenly simply know what to do next.

15. WEDNESDAY. Changeable. Spend some time alone and you
will probably come up with ideas for making more money or for
a way to save more. Either approach should make your bank account swell. Because you are feeling particularly thrifty, this is a
good time to review your budget and calculate your net worth.
Shared family assets will make you feel secure. Try to relax rather
than being a critical perfectionist. Once you have finished your
calculations your emotions should stabilize. Spend this evening
doing what makes you happy.

16. THURSDAY. Favorable. Cancers tend to be sensitive, receptive, and intuitive toward other people, but also easily hurt. You
hide your real feelings behind that tough Cancer shell. Often you
need to get away to think and meditate. Be sure to spend some
time today alone with your thoughts. If at work, look for a quiet
place to do your job on your own schedule and in your own way.
Try to find an empty office or unused meeting room where you
can close the door. If not, at least go for a drive to a nearby park
or take a walk in solitude to stimulate your creative imagination.
Pay attention to sudden inspirations, which will bring you good
luck.

17. FRIDAY. Satisfactory. Your personal plans might not match
those of your mate or partner. Do not bother asking for permission; it is best not to allow your ideas to be shot down by anyone.
Just go ahead and act on your intuition, which is your best guide.
You have lots of energy and enthusiasm, and are passionate about
a new idea. Your vibrations will attract like-minded people. Co-
workers and colleagues are willing to help you realize your vision.
Tonight is a time to get some physical exercise and also to watch
what you eat and drink. Do not overdo in any area.

18. SATURDAY. Successful. Today's Full Moon could have an
unusual influence on any very specific personal plans that have
been on your mind. This day favors achieving your goals and making significant strides to get ahead. Your energy level is high and
you are full of drive. Whatever you apply yourself to do is apt to

succeed financially. This is a good time to make money from a hobby or pet project. If you need assistance, turn to neighbors and colleagues. A business or romantic partner may not understand your intensity, but do not let that deter you from your very promising mission.

19. SUNDAY. Reassuring. If you have money issues on your mind, first focus on those that are personal rather than joint. It is not a time to give other people financial advice, since chances are it will not work out well for them. However, you can take advantage of your own intuition. Lady Luck is on your side, so you might want to make a small wager or buy a lottery ticket. With your generous and protective nature, your family will end up benefiting from the proceeds. This is also a good day to help out around the house. Give a hand with domestic duties usually done by someone else. If you have time, write to a family member who recently suffered a serious loss.

20. MONDAY. Cautious. You are able to earn money creatively by using your imagination. Focus on selling to the public or appearing in public. Family financial affairs are in a state of flux and tend to be unsettled. It could be that your spouse has incurred a big expense for something unexpected like a car repair or dental bill. Fortunately your personal ability to make extra money is favored at this time. Take extra precautions if on the road today. Be alert and use defensive techniques whether driving or walking. If you are taking many short trips around town you could be easily distracted.

21. TUESDAY. Happy. You tend to think emotionally and have a strong imagination. Your love can easily be expressed to your romantic partner. When you share your feelings, it is likely that you will receive flattering comments in return. This is sure to lead to a harmonious relationship with your loved one. You have an inquisitive mind and good common sense. You could be particularly successful writing about yourself or about family members. You have a good memory but often change your opinion. You make a good impression when working with or appearing in public.

22. WEDNESDAY. Unsettling. Because your mind is active you are willing to consider new ideas and techniques. When working with people who share your interests you are a natural leader.

However, you can be moody and you could have a tendency to interfere in the lives of others, supposedly for their own good. Try not to offer any free advice or assistance; wait until you are specifically asked. Otherwise people may not appreciate your efforts, which could be discouraging. Job pressure could sap your physical energy. Consider why you keep saying yes to more work and volunteering for extra assignments. This is the time to practice saying no and meaning it.

23. THURSDAY. Favorable. Get an early start on the day. The roadblocks and annoying delays that have been slowing you down lately are now removed. The money you have been waiting for should become available. This is a time for projects to start moving forward once again. You may find the lines of communication with family members and partners reconnected. It is a time to reach agreement on your new ideas. Your intuitive powers are restored and you will get clear signals regarding what direction to take. Your vitality and liveliness help to keep you physically energized. You may crave exercise and fresh air; do not deny yourself some time in the sun.

24. FRIDAY. Good. If you can work from home you will really enjoy it. Make phone calls or be online. You will be most successful working alone and in seclusion. You will get more done if you wear comfortable casual clothes and your favorite slippers. If you must go into the office, try to leave a little early or at least exactly on time. This is a better day than most to spend with children or family members. Go out of your way to keep them entertained. You will also benefit from getting some extra rest. After this busy workweek, treat the whole family to a pizza and a video tonight.

25. SATURDAY. Dynamic. You could be experiencing deep-rooted, intense passion. This is an ideal time to direct your emotions into an art form. You are able to write or communicate from the heart. There is a tendency for you to fall in love secretly. You may want to compose a love letter to express your longing, and you will most likely be pleasantly surprised by the positive reaction from your romantic partner. A new level of understanding can be reached through truth and honesty. Seek out and share the pleasures in life. This is also a great time to interact with children, even if they are not your own.

26. SUNDAY. Mixed. Combine your playful mood with some fresh air and exercise. Consider going out with the family or even just with a pet to play together. You have lots of energy to run around. A skating rink or a toboggan hill can be special fun. The laughter of children will remind you of what life is all about. If you have no kids around, playing fetch with your dog will also showcase the simple pleasures of being present in the moment. Be sure to avoid dealing with money issues today. Focus on simple childlike pleasures that are free for the enjoying. Someone at a distance is still waiting for your answer or action.

27. MONDAY. Helpful. Pay special attention to your intuition. You are apt to receive deep insight that will help answer a long-standing question. You could suddenly find a cure for a chronic or annoying health issue. If looking for a way to accomplish a great deal of work in a short time, turn for help to colleagues and co-workers who owe you a favor or just happen to be interested in assisting. Your courage and liveliness are contagious; ask and you will receive whatever you need. Your strong powers of concentration could be useful for planning new strategy because you clearly see the big picture.

28. TUESDAY. Unsettling. Be prepared for impulsiveness in your thoughts and actions. There is a tendency for changes to erupt suddenly and for you to respond with thoughtless moves. You may want to consider changing jobs to find something that suits you better. You may feel unstable and indecisive about taking on any more responsibility. Unhappiness at work can adversely affect your health, making you especially prone to stomach trouble. Since you are intuitive and imaginative in a work situation, look for something that utilizes your artistic eye. Take some time to be independently creative.

29. WEDNESDAY. Frustrating. If feeling disappointed about your love relationship, spend part of the day alone. You will have strong intuition, so be open to change. The future is full of promise. In fact, you will attract luck through your willingness to change. Say yes to whatever life brings your way. Things will start going smoother when you stop resisting and complaining. Your health will also improve when you allow negative energy and criticism to pass right through you instead of holding it within. Aim to become conscious of your feelings and to acknowledge them.

They will then melt away on their own without you having to actively do anything to discharge them.

30. THURSDAY. Deceptive. Your natural Cancer intelligence, sensitivity, and imagination create an opportunity for powerful expression. You have an artistic eye and fine taste. You may receive ideas from your highly tuned psychic abilities. Trust them and act on your own intuition. Do not second-guess or compromise yourself by asking someone else for an opinion; it could be deceptive and lead you down another road. You will get the best results if you honor your own style and ideas. Take your journey of self-discovery without trying to please anyone else. Only you can capture the essence of the vision you alone can see.

31. FRIDAY. Calm. Security is very important to you in marriage and in all relationships. Cancer people are apt to marry a parental figure who is protective and understanding. You are responsive in partnerships and devoted in marriage. Finances right now may be unsettled because of marriage or an inheritance issue. Fortunately you can calmly find answers by searching within yourself. Because you are deeply interested in questions about life and living, you can map out a future full of promise. Use your good psychic ability in a practical way to solve money issues. You can also guide people along spiritual lines by showing the way to proceed.

FEBRUARY

1. SATURDAY. Opportune. This is an ideal day to begin a new project as long as it does not involve high finance. Especially avoid any opportunity that requires the use of other people's money or shared family assets. Your energy level is high and you can accomplish a great deal if you use your intuition and excellent concentration. Consider delving into your past with psychotherapy, self-help books, or a personal development workshop; you are sure to gain new wisdom and possibly transformation. Be prepared to take another step toward your maximum potential. This will most likely be expressed as a new level of understanding and acceptance of yourself and of other people.

2. SUNDAY. Starred. This is a starred day for your creative impulses. You are apt to be feeling idealistic and crusading as powerful emotions sweep through you. Do not miss this opportunity to express your highly original personality and style. Find time for your favorite hobby. Do not hesitate to be eccentric, even dramatic in your approach. If you can completely let go of normal restrictions including thoughts about limiting your spending, unusually pleasing results can be achieved. Romantically you are also inspired. Someone new on the scene may be intrigued because of your unorthodox views about love and life. Pursue a dream with all your might.

3. MONDAY. Easygoing. Physically your body may not be as active as usual. However, your alert mind can more than make up for this. Take advantage of your receptive imagination, which is capable of comprehending complex philosophical ideas. Cancer students will find higher learning of all kinds easy to absorb. It is a better day than most to hit the books, especially to spend time in the library studying. Also do not shy away from essay or report writing. Publishing projects of all types are favored. Foreign-flavored subjects are of special interest, including language, history, and geography. Begin to plan an upcoming trip for business or pleasure.

4. TUESDAY. Demanding. At work you should have great powers of concentration because you are intent on seeing results. You drive yourself hard, and you expect other people to perform at your level. As a result, you may tend to be intolerant and argumentative with co-workers. You will not get their cooperation in that way. Your best approach is to find one other person who has a work ethic that is similar to yours, someone who respects deadlines and knows how to deliver a project on time and on budget. Strange as it may seem, look for another busy person; they are the ones who know how to get things done.

5. WEDNESDAY. Promising. With your strong willpower and boundless optimism, you can get a great deal done today. Your positive outlook inspires confidence. It is a good time to display your leadership potential. Do not be concerned if a partner or teammate has difficulty working in a subordinate role. Together you can both make money providing your lead is followed without a lot of arguing. You are intuitive about what the public wants. It is a good day to be involved with the public in career, professional, or social activities. Look for a financial opportunity that appears as a result of a public announcement from a government official.

6. THURSDAY. Productive. You should have a good day on the job if you set out to be efficient. Keep your impulsiveness under control. You have sufficient vitality and energy to initiate new work methods. Pay attention to inspiration and insights that promise to help you streamline your tasks. You could design a faster way to produce goods, or you might find a more cost-effective supply of raw materials. As a result your company should soon be making or saving more money and you may receive a financial bonus or promotion, even a raise or commission check. Tonight is a good time to celebrate your good fortune with the people who have helped advance your career.

7. FRIDAY. Helpful. On this busy day at the office you can accomplish a great deal by working on your own. Do not be concerned if a partner or teammate decides to take the day off. Proceed with confidence, even if the people around you do not support your radical new ideas. You may be feeling somewhat reserved or reclusive, but this is a better time than most to work in isolation. You may find it hard to share your feelings and visions. Strive to develop ideas further before exposing them to the critical views of other people. If you need helpful advice, consult a female member of your family or staff.

8. SATURDAY. Stimulating. The weekend is an ideal time to get together with friends. As a Cancer you have a flair for entertaining in your home. Consider hosting a brunch or a spontaneous potluck party where everyone brings a favorite dish to share. Your easy social charm attracts many admirers because you are emotionally intuitive when dealing with friends and strangers alike. You will enjoy stimulating conversation, particularly with a romantic partner. You are affectionate, romantic, and popular, so do not wait for someone to make the first move toward getting to know you better.

9. SUNDAY. Changeable. If you lack confidence in yourself or in your dreams, talk them over with a romantic or business partner who believes in you and supports your hopes in life. Basically you need intellectual compatibility in marriage and in all partnerships. Someone who is lively and talkative will help draw you out of your Cancer shell. Verbal give-and-take characterizes your most important relationships. People who know you intimately will be able to ask the right questions and give you the encouragement you need to continue on your chosen path. This is not a time to second-guess yourself.

10. MONDAY. Disquieting. At some time in life goals shift and friendships are likely to change. Do not be surprised if this is one of those days when you need to take a firm stand on your ethics or beliefs. You may even have to distance yourself from unreliable friends and from a scandal not of your own making. It may be disquieting to suddenly come to this realization, yet it will work out for the best in the long run. You can now attract new people into your life who think and act like you. Take this opportunity to join a club, society, or volunteer group. Together you can make a positive difference in the world.

11. TUESDAY. Fortunate. You have the ability to persevere and succeed through your own efforts. This is a better time than most to get better organized. Find a quiet place to work out a new strategy. You may not be in the mood to be physically active, but just sitting still and meditating will pay off. Your intuition is strong. You have great powers of concentration and are intent about seeing results as soon as possible. Just take care not to overwork; your energy could be sapped by stress from the pressure of your job. Watch for ways to improve your family's financial position. Protect your health by getting adequate sleep as well as exercise.

12. WEDNESDAY. Fair. Because you are philosophical and have deep insights, this is a better time than most to strive for self-improvement. Be gentle with yourself rather than being critical or becoming a perfectionist. You may benefit from an inheritance or from money though a marriage partner. There is the possibility of achieving fame, so take pride in your current responsibilities; they will be your legacy. You may have an unusual outlook on life, possibly an interest in the mystical. It would be wise to explore such a passion further in hopes of gaining personal insights that take you to a new level.

13. THURSDAY. Sensitive. Try to be more imaginative in the way you express yourself. You are intuitive about other people and have the ability to understand human motivation. This is a good time to ask anyone except your mate or partner for something personal. Home and family mean a great deal to you, and you remember childhood sights and sounds with nostalgia. You want to be appreciated and admired, and would like to be famous. Although you are receptive, romantic, and curious, you can be moody. You have a tendency to expend your energy in too many directions. Use your penetrating mind to find a new way to communicate your insights. You also have a talent for research and analysis.

14. FRIDAY. Quiet. The end of the workweek is a good time to concentrate on personal plans, desires, and interests. You can make exceptional progress with your own affairs. Your personality is attractive to those in positions of authority. It should be easy to obtain cooperation since people are inclined to cater to your wishes. Since eyes will be on you, it would be a good idea to pay extra attention to your personal appearance. Consider a new hair color or cut, or a different style of clothes. Spend some time thinking about new ways of using your abilities and talents to make more money. Do not be limited by what has worked for other people.

15. SATURDAY. Opportune. Aim to make money and increase your personal assets. However, do not try to help other people by offering advice. Somehow your good luck works only for you. This is a better time than most to go shopping. You are apt to find some excellent bargains at a flea market, auction, or garage sale. You could find a treasure to add to your collection. You are tenacious with a keen sense for what will potentially be profitable. You are also security-minded with an ability to plan for the future. Because you are thrifty and careful, you can earn money by using your imagination and operating through the public.

16. SUNDAY. Tricky. By lending a hand to someone who asks, you could receive a gift or payment in the future. Be willing to assist a neighbor with an outdoor project such as shoveling snow or helping with renovations. You might also help family members with household chores. Make yourself physically useful and active. Just be aware that you have a high emotional level. It will not take much to quickly get your temper stirred up. Try to avoid the issue of money, especially when it comes to other people's funds. If you are expecting to be paid for your efforts, be sure to negotiate upfront or there could be a serious misunderstanding.

17. MONDAY. Unsettling. You are inclined to be obstinate, possibly due to a feeling of superiority. Or you could just be feeling totally original and independent. In any case, you should not be handling money while in such a mood because you are apt to make bad decisions. As a result your financial affairs could fluctuate and be unsettled for quite a while. As a Cancer you are usually thrifty and careful, but today you may be careless. This is not a good time to go shopping; more than likely you will be foolishly extravagant. It would be wise to leave money matters to your mate or partner so that you do not spend money you do not have.

18. TUESDAY. Frustrating. You tend to think emotionally and have a strong imagination but you can be moody. You have a tendency to interfere in the lives of other people. Co-workers could thwart your progress at work, particularly if your task depends on them delivering certain results. Although you may want to work alone, you will have to pitch in and do part of their job, too. Rather than get frustrated, just roll up your sleeves and get working. The day will go much smoother if you work together as a team. Actively look for a partner with whom you can communicate all of your ideas. This is a good day for taking short trips around town to run errands.

19. WEDNESDAY. Excellent. As a Cancer you are protective toward your family and able to be a devoted parent. Because you are something of a visionary, you are always seeking to give your life more meaning. You may notice strong intuitive powers, particularly related to finances that you share with your mate or partner. Pay close attention to insights regarding joint investments, retirement plans, and mutual funds. With your idealistic desire to help people who are in need, you may consider adopting a special-needs child or sponsoring underprivileged children in a foreign country. Real estate or family possessions can be turned into usable cash once you make a commitment.

20. THURSDAY. Difficult. Expect a feeling of being pulled one way and then the other. Your physical energy is also in flux, which could make you bad-tempered or susceptible to injury as your mind wanders. Pay special attention to the road while driving or you could make an error in judgment. This is a time to avoid making any serious financial decision. It would be wise to postpone buying big-ticket items; more than likely you will find a better deal if you keep alert for a sale. Ask around and you might get excellent advice from colleagues or co-workers who have exactly what you are looking for. Do not be too proud to accept help.

21. FRIDAY. Deceptive. You may experience an impulsive streak that seems to have negative implications, but it is also powerfully creative. Be sure to pay close attention to your intuition, which can lead you in a new artistic direction. It is important to have fun and be somewhat childlike with your explorations. It will probably be easier for you to get loose if you are working from home. At least try to leave the office early if you cannot take the whole day off. Do not be surprised by a surging interest in mysticism and all that is spiritual. The only subject to avoid is money, which must not be one of the basic motivators in your life or your family's.

22. SATURDAY. Complicated. You are apt to be in a playful mood. This is a time to get plenty of exercise, especially with a partner or a child. It would be wise to keep activities lighthearted. Play for enjoyment, not to win or prove a point. If you have important lessons to teach, they might be better received as a game or story. You have an idealistic desire to help people in need but can be overprotective and possessive of family members. You may suffer disappointment or be deluded if you think you know what is best for everyone. Allow other people to learn their own lessons while you are close by to offer support and understanding if needed.

23. SUNDAY. Disquieting. Although you are apt to be in a playful mood, you have some serious thinking to do. Exercise during the early morning, then settle into your duties. You may have deep new insights to ponder as you strive for self-improvement. Take pride in handling your responsibilities to the best of your ability. You may have to bribe yourself with little treats and breaks throughout the day in order to keep your mind on track. Do not be surprised if you arrive at an unusual outlook on life and mystical subjects. Your ideas related to family and relationships could be unconventional, yet this makes you unique and attractive.

24. MONDAY. Varied. Expect a certain impulsiveness in all of your actions. There is a tendency for changes to erupt suddenly.

These are likely to work to your advantage when it comes to handling other people's money. Your intuition is strong regarding financial matters. You have a good head for figures and can do quick, accurate calculations. You are intuitive and imaginative in work but can be unstable and indecisive about home responsibility. Whenever possible, delegate tasks. Otherwise you could burn out from stress by taking on too much work yourself. Try to expand your circle of friends and helpers.

25. TUESDAY. Challenging. You should wake up full of vim and vigor, ready to tackle a new challenge with courage. Use this mood to motivate co-workers and colleagues. Because you feel a responsibility to other people, you can naturally assume a leadership role. Your enthusiasm will be contagious, helping to lift the spirits of everyone around you. You may receive sudden financial benefit from an unexpected source, perhaps an inheritance related to marriage or a bonus through your spouse. Pay extra attention to your health and you may come up with a cure for a chronic or bothersome injury. Consider looking into alternative medicine such as acupuncture or homeopathy.

26. WEDNESDAY. Good. This is a better day than most to work as part of a team or partnership. Security is very important for Cancer people in marriage and all relationships. Chances are that you will marry someone older or at least more worldly-wise than you. Family members and friends will be protective. You are responsive in partnerships. If traveling for business or pleasure, try to go with a compatible companion. That way you will enjoy sharing and exploring new places. For Cancer students this is a good time to join a study group, especially to practice conversing in a foreign language. You are sufficiently versatile and flexible to accept whatever comes along and make the best of it.

27. THURSDAY. Exciting. Use your penetrating mind to look for some way to communicate your newest insights. You have the ability to see into human motivation, especially related to money that comes to you through a distant family member or your marriage partner. You have a talent for research and analysis. This is a time to deal with insurance or legal issues. Your intelligence is higher than normal, and combining it with your sensitivity and imagination gives you an edge on any and all competitors. Quite possibly you have psychic ability that you can use in a practical way.

28. FRIDAY. Slow. Since it is the end of both the workweek and the month, chances are that you prefer seclusion. Find a quiet office or meeting room, then close the door and get down to work. This is a time to catch up on financial matters such as your expense report, tax preparation, or accounting statements. You should be disciplined and well organized. Your concentration is unusually good and you can get to the bottom of complex situations or calculations. Use your intuition to guide you into the right area. Just avoid giving money-related advice to anyone at this time.

MARCH

1. SATURDAY. Auspicious. Expect to jump out of bed full of energy, ready to get things done. If there is a large amount of work, get others to assist by joining in the project. Neighbors and family will become members of your team. Use your intuition to guide you to seek assistance from those people with the required skills. You can contribute high intelligence, sensitivity, and imagination to the cause. Be willing to delve into complex issues; you can see clearly what needs to be done. This is an excellent time for introspection and self-analysis. You have psychic ability that you can use in a practical way to improve your own chances of success.

2. SUNDAY. Buoyant. You are likely to act like the original, highly individualistic personality that you are. You have an inventive, unconventional mind and are often attracted to odd ideas. You may dress in an unusual manner, create your own aura, and invent new gadgets. People are attracted to your far-out point of view and may consider you weird and eccentric. You will not readily conform or be restricted by peer pressure. Although this could make you abrupt, rebellious, or unpredictable, you can harness your ingenuity to create something so new that it is immediately recognized by the public.

3. MONDAY. Disquieting. Start the workweek with a new project. This is a better time than most for learning. You have a receptive, imaginative mind that is capable of contemplating philosophical ideas. The unknown attracts you; in your work you may delve into the past. However, keep in mind that you have to be open to accepting incoming information. You may feel stubborn and self-willed, wanting to do things in the same old way that you are comfortable with. Deep-rooted habits are hard to break unless you are conscious of them. Awareness is the first step to making a positive change in your life.

4. TUESDAY. Surprising. As a Cancer you have a talent for scientific thinking. You can be stubborn and eccentric, but also a genius. Your career can get a huge boost from an inspiration that comes to you today. Pay special attention to any ideas that pop into your head about a different way of handling routine matters. Be open to change and suddenly you may find an easier way of getting work accomplished. A team of people is gathering around you to be part of your project. Thanks to them you do not have to come up with all the answers or do all the work yourself. Your primary contribution is in supplying the vision; other people can work out the details.

5. WEDNESDAY. Rewarding. Your career is about to take a major leap forward as you are rewarded for your recent efforts with a promotion, raise, or new contract. There is a possibility that you will change your occupation to one that comes with additional perks such as a new car or a private office. All of this will be because of your creativity. Cancer people have psychic abilities, connecting to a higher plane of consciousness. This brings you in touch with hidden memory, dreams, and vision that can lead to a better future. Try to be more involved with the public in career, professional, or social activities. You are intuitive about what the public wants; people are willing to pay top dollar for it.

6. THURSDAY. Helpful. With your great powers of concentration you are intent on seeing results. The work you do can inspire other people to try harder. Since you are normally reserved and somewhat solitary or reclusive, you will probably find yourself working in isolation. Cautiousness may lead you to place limitations on yourself. It may be hard for you to ask for help, yet you will most likely find that colleagues are willing to lend you a hand. Take up their offer so that you do not strain or overwork. Arrange to get some physical exercise to relieve ongoing stress. Go outside for some fresh air and deep breathing to clear the cobwebs from your mind.

7. FRIDAY. Fair. The end of the workweek brings positive change. Expect to receive a sudden insight related to mutual finances. You will have noteworthy success dealing with corporate funds or other people's savings. Your energy level is high and you will enjoy getting together with friends this evening despite the day's stress. Consider inviting teammates out for an impromptu gathering tonight. Because you are in the mood for lots of conversation, you will learn a great deal from older persons or from someone born into a foreign culture. It is also a good time for travel and for conducting long-distance business. Try to brush up your conversational skills in a foreign language.

8. SATURDAY. Useful. If you want to learn about a new subject, call up a friend. Chances are you know experts in many fields of interest. Their techniques of acquiring knowledge may be different than yours, but do not discount their ways as being any less useful. This is a good day to get out and socialize. Accept an invitation to any gathering. Even a club meeting or sports event will put you in contact with interesting people. If there is nothing on your social calendar, consider hosting a spontaneous potluck dinner where everyone brings a dish to share. Any excuse for a party will do. You will be surprised how much you learn just by chatting casually.

9. SUNDAY. Uncertain. Your easy social charm attracts many admirers. Right now, however, your life goals are about to shift and friendships are likely to change as a result. You may have recently learned something about an old friend that makes you uncertain about your relationship. Best not to jump to conclusions, since your intuition is not as clear as usual. Normally you are emotionally intuitive in dealing with people, but today it would be wise to have a direct conversation to get all sides of the story. Guard against basing your information on gossip or hearsay. Remember to give other people the benefit of the doubt.

10. MONDAY. Bumpy. You might receive a lot of conflicting information. Be prepared for a long-distance call that suddenly forces you to change your plans. You could be required to travel on short notice, or perhaps a planned trip has to be postponed. In any case, be alert to what this enables you to achieve. If you become disturbed or overwhelmed, spend some time alone. If you are in doubt about what to do, contemplate your existing options and simply choose all over again. New offers should not create a problem. If you listen to your intuition, you are unlikely to make a wrong choice or a false move.

11. TUESDAY. Sensitive. Normally you enjoy seeing new places and exploring new ideas, but today you may prefer to be alone with your thoughts. As a Cancer you stand by your word and tend to be idealistic. Today, however, you may be critical or too much of a perfectionist. As a result you could become fanatical about your own ideas. This may cause co-workers and friends to resist your suggestions. If you are able to get away to think and meditate, you will find another way to make your point. Because you are sensitive, receptive, and intuitive toward other people, you can find the best approach to influence them.

12. WEDNESDAY. Good. Concentrate on your own plans and projects. You have artistic talents that need to be expressed. Make time to explore your creativity. The tricky part is having to negotiate with your mate or partner, who may have plans that include you. Explain that inspiration like this does not happen every day, then make a deal that gives you an hour or two to yourself. You may have to offer in exchange something they want or will need later in the day. You can increase your energy by working on what you feel most passionate about. Break free of self-imposed barriers and boldly venture into the unknown.

13. THURSDAY. Difficult. If you are finding it challenging to learn a new subject, find a quiet place to work. Otherwise you will be continually interrupted by telephone calls. Cancer students will have an easy time doing research and studying in the quiet of a library. Writing of all kinds is favored, particularly if meant for publication. Cancer novelists, poets, and screenwriters should have success contacting an agent or publisher. You are imaginative in the way you express yourself and intuitive about other people. However, you need to protect your privacy and personal time since there is a tendency to let other people's priorities take precedence over your own.

14. FRIDAY. Calm. The end of the workweek finds you in a peaceful mood. You probably have been able to accomplish more of your personal goals than usual. Today you can obtain cooperation regarding your own desires. Spend extra time on your appearance. Consider getting a haircut or going shopping for new clothes. You will enjoy treating yourself to a well-deserved reward. Tonight take it easy at home. A pizza and watching a video with loved ones will be a relaxing way to unwind. Home and family mean a great deal to you, and you could find yourself remembering childhood pleasures with nostalgia.

15. SATURDAY. Mixed. You can expect to have good luck with money, perhaps even winning or finding some. This is a better time than most to make a small wager on your favorite sports team or to buy a lottery ticket. However, avoid giving other people financial advice. It is also not a day to make a large investment or to buy expensive items. Your intuition is not as strong as usual, so you could easily make a wrong choice. You are able to earn money creatively by using your imagination and selling to the public or appearing in public. Focus on activities that are related to the healing arts, medicine, and health issues in general.

16. SUNDAY. Unsettling. If you work alone today you should be able to find new ways to make or save money. Try to come up with creative ideas that have earning potential. You might be able to sell assets in an auction or over the Internet, maybe even speaking or offering your expertise to the public. Do not worry if your financial affairs are in a state of flux at this moment. Actually, this will make you even more resourceful and ingenious. Information from family members or from someone distantly related to you could be causing you concern. It could be difficult to connect due to different time zones and travel schedules. Just keep trying to get your message through.

17. MONDAY. Demanding. Make communications with partners the focus of your day. It is a good time to meet with your business partner or to have a discussion with that special person in your personal life. This could be intense because you feel passionate about a particular subject. It is possible for you to inspire other people, but only if you do not become too blunt. Be sure to stay flexible and listen to their ideas, too. There is a risk that you will be increasingly rigid in your opinions. Do not become a strict disciplinarian due to a fear of change. Deal with facts and be open to what life brings your way. Check your mail for an interesting offer that has a tight deadline.

18. TUESDAY. Complicated. As a Cancer you tend to think emotionally and have a strong imagination. This is good because life is in a state of flux and requires that you come up with creative solutions. New information is available. It will be a busier day than usual for correspondence of all kinds, which may cause a change of plans. Be prepared for interruptions to your solitude. The phone may ring off the hook. Use your quick mind to sift through choices and deal with issues on the spot so that they do not pile up on your desk. Give yourself extra time if traveling. There are apt to be delays caused by traffic jams along the way.

19. WEDNESDAY. Sparkling. Relax and enjoy your passionate nature. Your love life will be marked by a sudden beneficial change that brings you new hope. Do not be concerned about a touchy situation with your romantic partner. You can reach a better understanding by sharing your true feelings. Be protective toward your family members, especially youngsters. There is a possibility that you will spend a lot of money on your home today, perhaps buying a new house near water. Or you might be planning a renovation with more running water, such as another bathroom. You will also enjoy shopping for items to beautify your home and add to your nighttime comfort.

20. THURSDAY. Opportune. You are diplomatic and ambitious, thorough in dealing with problems. Being conservative and patient will pay off handsomely in the end. This is a fine day to work alone, preferably from the comfort of your own home. You have financial insight when it comes to real estate or family possessions. This is a better day than most to buy or sell a home. You will enjoy spending more time than usual with your loved ones. Cancer parents may want to play educational games with children, especially if doing so helps to increase their knowledge of geography, language, and history.

21. FRIDAY. Happy. Because you are in a fun-loving mood, you could have a loose hold on your purse strings. You might find yourself picking up the tab for lunch with colleagues or customers. Most likely you feel energetic, so it is a good idea to get some exercise by playing a friendly game. Anything you can share with a partner will be particularly enjoyable. Generally you are serious and faithful in love. These traits can also be a constructive influence in a business partnership. You are apt to be rigid and dogmatic in your career as you become more focused and verbal about getting ahead.

22. SATURDAY. Variable. Although it is the weekend, your mind is apt to be on work. It is a time to focus your creativity on career-enhancing projects. You have a strong sense of self and a strong drive to succeed. If you play around with some new ideas, you will find a way to achieve your goals. You have leadership ability and the power to influence other people. However, there is a risk of being somewhat arrogant and dictatorial. Work alone if you can manage it. If not, at least keep a light and playful attitude toward your job. By making a game out of it, everyone will want to get in on the fun and be on your team.

23. SUNDAY. Fair. Pay close attention to what your body is trying to tell you and you could receive some insights that will keep you healthy. Take this opportunity to get extra rest by sleeping late or having an afternoon nap. Unhappiness at work can adversely affect your health, especially stomach trouble if you allow stress to get to you. It may be necessary to change jobs frequently until you find something that truly suits you. Although intuitive and imaginative in work, you can be indecisive about responsibility. Be willing to ask for help, and learn to delegate tasks.

24. MONDAY. Productive. Instead of working alone, try asking for assistance from co-workers. This is an excellent day for teamwork. Group energy creates many ideas. Your intuition is likely to be confirmed and supported by other people, giving you the confidence you need to proceed without further delay. Now you can give in to your impulsiveness. Be prepared for changes to erupt suddenly. Let go of your expectations. If you do not know or anticipate an outcome, you can be pleasantly surprised by results as they happen. Keep all of your options open. Avoid making any long-distance promises this evening.

25. TUESDAY. Eventful. You are likely to be full of courage and enthusiasm. This is a great day to be physically active and to seek a challenge. With your energy you can keep up with people much younger than you. Your strong powers of concentration enable you to eliminate obstacles as you encounter them. You have good judgment but may not like taking care of details. It is time to team up with a partner who can handle administration matters. Together you can be successful by offering a complete professional service. Consider becoming formal business partners and sharing the profits of your efforts.

26. WEDNESDAY. Tranquil. Focus on how important security is to you in marriage and in all of your relationships. Single Cancers might want to think of tying the knot or becoming engaged. This is a good time for commitment and contracts of all kinds. Chances are that you will marry a parental figure, someone who is protective of you. You are likely to become increasingly popular with the general public. It will be reassuring to be loved for who you are rather than the image of what you may become in the future. Be responsive in all partnerships. Let your loved one know how much you appreciate all that you are building together.

27. THURSDAY. Satisfactory. As a deeply sensitive person interested in questions about life, you quite possibly have psychic ability. You can use this in a practical way if you pay attention to your intuition. Thoughts regarding your career are especially important. You will be able to communicate your visionary ideas clearly to those in authority. It would be wise to be modest when it comes to spending money. It is not a good idea to handle other people's funds or investments at this time. Even your family finances may be unsettled because of marriage or inheritance. Avoid any big expenditures at this time; you probably will not be happy with whatever you purchase on credit.

28. FRIDAY. Confusing. You are apt to be unusually emotional and excitable. You may come up with an exciting idea just waiting to be expressed. If you find this unsettling, spend time in a quiet place. You will probably prefer seclusion. Time alone will allow you to do original work. It is likely that you are feeling unusual aspects of your Cancer personality that could translate into very textured creative work. The direct relationship of your feelings to work may be confusing. You may just be building an image bank for later use. Honoring your inspirations and passions when they occur is a very important part of the learning process.

29. SATURDAY. Surprising. If you allow yourself to try something new, you are apt to be surprisingly pleased with the results. This is an ideal time to use your artistic vision. Go out with your camera and experiment with shadows and sun, or head out to the countryside with a sketchbook. Be eccentric and unusual in your approach. Allow yourself total freedom from conformity and any type of restriction. You will learn a lot from breaking all the rules. You can enjoy travel as your natural friendliness and tranquil nature puts you in contact with people from another culture. They are sure to appreciate your highly individualistic personality.

30. SUNDAY. Productive. Whatever you put your mind to do you will be able to achieve. Higher learning of all forms is especially favored. Cancer students can make excellent progress preparing for exams or writing and doing research for term papers. All forms of studying will be enhanced by working with a teammate. Dealing with philosophy, geography, and language will be easiest. After teasing your brain, be sure to get some physical exercise. If you take several short breaks for fresh air you will be able to absorb more information. Travel of all kinds should go smoothly, but take along a book in case of delays or a boring seatmate.

31. MONDAY. Stimulating. Your receptive, imaginative mind is capable of delving into philosophical ideas. The unknown attracts you; in your work you may be put in charge of records because of your special abilities. At some time in your career you are likely to benefit from relatives of the person you marry or live with. You will have happy experiences while traveling or merely commuting. However, you have a tendency to be vague, dreamy, and impractical. Be sure to get a promise in writing, especially an agreement with co-workers or the boss. A quick memo or e-mail confirming the details will save you from future misunderstandings or even a lawsuit.

APRIL

1. TUESDAY. Favorable. When it comes to your career, you can orchestrate significant financial gains through today's effort. You might receive a promotion with a healthy pay raise, or close a sale that results in a commission check. This is also a better time than most to begin a new job. Cancer people who are currently temporarily out of work should follow instinctive insight regarding a possible opening. This is a time when your stubborn, persistent personality should reward you. With your strong sense of self and drive to succeed, chances are good that you will achieve something special. Reward yourself this evening with a special dinner.

2. WEDNESDAY. Successful. This is an outstanding day to advance your career. You can now take a big step up the corporate ladder, or perhaps reach a peak in your own enterprise. You might land a major account or find a buyer for a business or an idea of your own. Your chances of success are extraordinary. However, problems may arise if your ambition or career takes precedence over your important personal relationships. Take the time to review all that has been happening with your spouse or business partner. You have strong leadership abilities and the power to influence other people. This is a time to share your achievements and rewards with those who have stood by you all along the way.

3. THURSDAY. Exciting. Be prepared for positive surprises. You could receive a phone call from someone in a foreign country bearing good news regarding higher learning, publishing, or travel. Your application may have been accepted to a new school, or you might have won a trip and soon be flying off on an unplanned vacation. For Cancer authors, a manuscript might finally be published. You are bound to be excited by all of this potential. Get on the phone and call friends to share your good news. This is an excellent time to celebrate your success with an impromptu party. You deserve all the praise you are receiving.

4. FRIDAY. Cautious. There is a very good chance that you will come into some money having just won a lottery prize or sold a valuable asset. Do not be surprised when a friend calls you for a loan or investment advice. It would be wise to keep business and pleasure separate. Otherwise you could get confused and lose both the friendship and your money. If you are careless now you are apt to become embroiled in a legal entanglement. Feel free to share your hard-won expertise. In fact, you might want to teach what you know about financial dealings and making money. Do not put off preparing your tax return.

5. SATURDAY. Pleasant. You should be surrounded by many acquaintances. Your easy social charm attracts many admirers because you adapt yourself well to a variety of people. Use your flair for entertaining at home to host a potluck dinner for neighbors and family members. Your friendships are based on intellectual rapport, and the conversation should be very stimulating. Because you are socially active you may want to get involved with a group, club, or society devoted to a good cause. You will be clever at thinking of ways to help achieve such a goal. A fund-raising event may keep you dancing long into the night.

6. SUNDAY. Inspiring. Use your independent mind to widen your intellectual horizons. You are known for your unorthodox views as well as a strong interest in unusual subjects of study. If you spend some quiet time alone, there is a good chance that you will make a dramatic breakthrough. An opportunity for travel may come up suddenly, and you may soon find yourself participating in exciting events in a foreign country. Be adventurous and open to new experiences. If you feel somewhat rebellious, this is a good time to try something different that you can share with one or two friends.

7. MONDAY. Demanding. Job pressures might sap your physical energy. You are in a perfectionist mode and may be too critical of your own efforts. Although you have great powers of concentration and are intent on seeing results, you tend to overwork. During the day be sure to take several breaks and to get out for a little fresh air. You will be able to accomplish more by heeding the signals your body gives you. This is also a good day to work alone in secret. Put your phone calls on hold for a few hours and stay behind a closed door. Without interruptions you can make excellent progress.

8. TUESDAY. Active. As a Cancer you are imaginative in the way you express yourself and intuitive about other people. Communicating with groups is favored. This is a good time to call a meeting or to make a formal presentation. Accept any and all invitations to travel, especially if a friend suggests you take off together for a spring vacation. A weekend workshop might also appeal; you could learn a great deal about yourself. Consider registering for a self-improvement course to improve your appearance or public speaking. Home and family mean a great deal to you. Remembering your childhood may fill you with nostalgia; perhaps it is time to plan a trip back to your hometown.

9. WEDNESDAY. Mixed. On the job you want to be appreciated and admired, perhaps even become famous. Chances are good that you will receive some kind of honor in life. Generally this is a better day than most to promote your personal plans and interests. People tend to cater to your desires if you do not ask for too much. There is a risk that you could come across as arrogant and dictatorial. If you look for ways to make a win-win situation for everyone, it will be easy to obtain cooperation. You might find new ways of using your abilities and talents to make extra money.

10. THURSDAY. Sensitive. Try not to be sensitive and moody. Disagreements with a romantic or business partner will have a tendency to dissipate your energy. It could be that you want to work overtime but your mate is looking forward to spending the entire evening with you. Or your business partner may be resisting your recommendations. Avoid anything that has to do with money; people are right to be skeptical about your financial ideas. You are susceptible to errors in judgment, so this is not a good time to make investment decisions. Heed your mate or partner's advice. Your career is on track and your passion will inspire colleagues to join forces with you.

11. FRIDAY. Disappointing. As the end of the workweek arrives, you may be unhappy with one or more colleagues who have let you down. Someone may not have completed accounting statements on time, or someone may have overspent the budget. You could even be disappointed with a friend or associate concerning a money matter. Although you are generous and have a protective nature, you may feel they have taken advantage of you. It is time to get creative and use your imagination to raise more funds. You have a good sense for what is potentially lucrative. Use your ability to plan for the future rather than just letting events dictate your actions.

12. SATURDAY. Favorable. Be ambitious about acquiring material comfort. This is a better time than most to make long-range financial plans. You are thrifty and shrewd when it comes to investments. Investing in cautious blue-chip stocks is more your style than get-rich-quick schemes. Instead of wanting money to come in quickly, aim for gains that are slow and steady. You are willing to put in considerable effort, and your perseverance and hard work is starting to pay off. The value of your home may have increased significantly. You might spot a new opportunity advertised in the weekend paper that would boost your earnings.

13. SUNDAY. Eventful. Communications with friends could reveal surprising information about a distant acquaintance in another country or city. You may have lost touch, but you will still find the news disturbing. Consider calling or writing a letter to reconnect. You are thinking emotionally and have a strong imagination. Because you naturally dislike routine, your day will be marked by many short trips. You have a good memory but tend to change your opinion often. This could cause confusion around the house. You can be moody and have a tendency to interfere in the lives of other people. Try to give support rather than advice.

14. MONDAY. Manageable. As a highly independent individual you will not give up your sense of self in marriage or partnership. A relationship begun impulsively at this time could be significant. You will probably be aggressive because you know what you like when you see it. You tend to be ardent and passionate in love. Do not be discouraged if your initial conversations are not very meaningful. You could find it hard to share your feelings, but you have the ability to persevere and will succeed through your own effort. On the job you will be most successful working alone or in seclusion.

15. TUESDAY. Harmonious. Continue to be protective toward your family and devoted to your loved ones. This is a day to enjoy domestic happiness. Family finances are settled or at least improving. Now you should begin to look for ways of improving your future economic security. Investigate pension and retirement plans. Your intuition may guide you into a lucrative new investment. It is also a good time to review insurance policies. Consider any addition or renovations you have made to increase the value of your home, plus any major purchases. You have good financial sense when it comes to real estate and family possessions.

16. WEDNESDAY. Variable. Today's Full Moon could play havoc at home and the office. You might have to appease upset family members or irate customers. This could keep you out later than normal. As a result your spouse or children might feel they are last on your priority list. Probably you can make it up to them by taking everyone out for dinner, or at least bringing home a pizza and ice cream. You will not feel like cooking after dealing with all the problems of the day. If you need help around the house, you will find loved ones willing to assist. Your energy should start to return as soon as you reach home.

17. THURSDAY. Enjoyable. Because you are in a fun-loving mood, games and sports will appeal, along with children and their laughter. You may want to take the day off or at least leave work early. You may find yourself being overprotective and possessive of your mate or children. You are romantic and have a creative imagination. Today you are apt to be impulsive in your actions, which is not good when it comes to finances. Do not trust your intuition about love or money; disappointment or incompatibility could result. Try to keep your childlike innocence and sense of humor.

18. FRIDAY. Contradictory. If you find yourself falling in love with a friend, it is likely that the attraction relates to all that you share. You will gain from the experience as you each mirror back a part of the other person. It might be time to incorporate a new aspect into yourself rather than projecting it on your mate or partner. Your energy level is high when it comes to relationships, but you may not be too interested in everyday tasks such as work. No one will appreciate you daydreaming on the job. If you are looking forward to a social event this evening, leave work a little earlier than usual.

19. SATURDAY. Beneficial. By helping other people or volunteering assistance you could benefit through an unexpected gift or reward. You may be given something that you have been wishing for, probably related to your health or physical fitness. A colleague who has skills in massage or knowledge of alternative medicine may perceive that stress or nervous tension is adversely affecting your health. You may be especially prone to stomach trouble. Let your intuition guide you to a person who can help heal a chronic problem. Avoid gossiping with a neighbor; what you say in confidence may soon be known by everyone.

20. SUNDAY. Frustrating. You are probably feeling impulsive. There is a tendency for changes to erupt suddenly and for you to respond with thoughtless moves. This may relate to an underlying shyness or lack of self-confidence. Or you could just want to be alone to work on a personal project. If family members keep asking for your help, promise to assist later. It is actually a better day than most for routine, run-of-the-mill jobs around the house. Take care of your practical responsibilities first, then set aside some quiet time for yourself. Do not neglect tending to pets and plants.

21. MONDAY. Rewarding. Because you are passionate about life and have a strong drive toward new partnerships, you may suddenly be attracted to the occult. Medicine and the healing arts could also appeal. This is a good time to schedule a medical check-up, especially with a naturopathic or alternative healer. You can be a brilliant researcher since your thirst for knowledge and information runs deep. This is a better time than most for writing reports, articles, and essays that are meant for publication. If faced with a job that is too big, arrange to team up with a like-minded person. Friends are apt to be more helpful than co-workers.

22. TUESDAY. Useful. Apply your good common sense and shrewdness to partnership and friendship matters. You may have the opportunity to team up with a friend on an interesting project. If the two of you share the same hopes, wishes, and aspirations, you could get involved in a humanitarian or altruistic venture. Together you can strive to make the world a better place. You are becoming popular with the public. Although you are responsive in love, you are changeable about your relationships and may not want to make a commitment right now.

23. WEDNESDAY. Sensitive. You are full of courage and ready to tackle a large work-related issue. Your liveliness is based on a strong hunch that this project will work. You have excellent powers of concentration and can assess problems and find solutions. However, there may be a financial issue that you are unable to settle today. Perhaps you are too close to the problem, especially if it has to do with family funds or using other people's money. There is a risk that someone will perceive your total confidence as an effort to be domineering. It would be wise to consult experts or at least listen to various opinions with an open mind.

24. THURSDAY. Mixed. Because you will probably be sympathetic and warmhearted, colleagues and co-workers will turn to you for advice. Your insights are reliable. You might be gifted as a person who provides answers, thanks to your strong powers to know what is in people's mind. You may prefer seclusion so that your visions have a chance to formulate. You need time alone or you could get high-strung and anxious as psychic energy flows through your body. Evening plans may have to be canceled on short notice.

25. FRIDAY. Variable. Since it is the end of the workweek you may be feeling somewhat reserved or reclusive. It is possible that you are limiting yourself because of fear. Nothing will go against you that you cannot handle. Trust your powers and relax. You might find it hard to share your feelings with other people. You may be carrying a secret that upsets you. Now is the time to look into your own past and find a way to overcome personal limitations. You can tear down barriers and discard worn-out habits that are no longer appropriate for who you have become.

26. SATURDAY. Good. You are socially popular, able to attract and keep friends. In turn, you will benefit from their faith and support. If you receive an invitation to a house party or other social event, accept if there is no conflict. You will enjoy getting out and participating in stimulating conversations. You have high goals in life and an optimism that wins people to your cause. Use your imagination to delve into ideas and consider alternatives. If you are traveling, start early to avoid delays caused by transportation problems or confusion regarding your reservations. Travel as light as possible.

27. SUNDAY. Helpful. Your receptive, imaginative mind is capable of exploring new ideas. Catch up on world events by reading every section of the Sunday newspaper. You might even head to the local library or log onto the Internet to do some research. The unknown attracts you, and you may find yourself immersed in history. Although your mind is hungry for information and higher learning, your body needs extra rest because you have been overworking lately. Take a Sunday afternoon nap. If you are away from home and traveling, expect delays. Take along a good book or some handwork to reduce the stress.

28. MONDAY. Fortunate. Use your Cancer charm and diplomacy to further your special interests. Strive to mix and mingle with important people. You may be attracted to artistic or cultural work because in some way you want to be involved in creating beauty. You should be popular with the public since you are intuitive about what they want. There is also a good chance that a partnership could enhance your career. You may benefit in particular through female family members. Heed your intuition when it comes to making money. You will be rewarded for your artistic eye and love of nature.

29. TUESDAY. Expansive. Your career should proceed full-steam ahead as both your intuition and co-workers help you succeed. You are also having good luck with money. If your company is expanding, you are apt to be on the receiving end of a raise or bonus. However, do not let all your good fortune go to your head. Be wary of spendthrift tendencies. If going out to celebrate, set a budget. Because you are in such good spirits, it is likely you will have harmonious relationships. Love can be easily expressed. Be sure to acknowledge the help you receive on a daily basis from your mate or partner.

30. WEDNESDAY. Favorable. On the career front you will be rewarded for being diplomatic, patient, and thorough in dealing with problems. As a Cancer you are ambitious but quiet and conservative. You will be most successful working alone and in seclusion. Shut yourself away in an empty office or unused meeting room so that you can think without interruption. If you need help or advice, turn to old friends or acquaintances. It is surprising how much you can learn just by making a quick phone call. Communications with a foreign country or actual travel is favored.

MAY

1. THURSDAY. Mixed. Being socially charming you attract many admirers. Most likely you will be surrounded today by friends and associates at a club or social meeting, perhaps a luncheon. Although this is a good time to get involved in a new project, avoid taking responsibility for a fund-raising event. Your normally strong intuition is obscured. You are idealistic in your desire to help other people, but if you give money to such a cause you may be disappointed or deluded. You could be a pawn in the hands of an unreliable person and become involved in a scandal not of your own making.

2. FRIDAY. Happy. Your intelligence and sensitivity are better than normal, making you very creative. You may become involved with artistic or cultural work, busy creating beauty. Look for ways to incorporate these aspects into your job, whether designing a new advertising campaign or coming up with an innovative sales pitch. More than likely you are a visionary and want to give more meaning to your life. Pay attention to your intuition. You may be gifted with strong powers, especially in divining secret information about friends or associates.

3. SATURDAY. Exciting. The weekend has arrived and you have lots of energy and passion for life. Your most important relationship could improve thanks to your strong desire to express your love. You are sensitive, receptive, and intuitive toward other people. You will also benefit from spending time alone. Get some outdoor exercise on your own, bicycling, walking, or jogging. This will be a form of active meditation that allows your imagination to soar. You may enjoy a favorite creative hobby. Take out art materials and experiment with new ways of looking at everyday objects.

4. SUNDAY. Deceptive. A certain vagueness or emotional unbalance could make it difficult for you to arrive at any decisions. As a result you are susceptible to deceit. When in doubt, spend time alone listening to your intuition. There is a chance that a partnership could enhance your career success. This is a better day than most to reposition joint finances. You may be able to get ahead faster by pooling resources and talents. Get extra rest because your physical energy has been sapped by job pressure. Stay home this evening despite an intriguing invitation.

5. MONDAY. Variable. If you are feeling thrifty, do not be coaxed into spending. Work alone on a personal pet project. You can put your perfectionism to work doing financial calculations regarding expenses and income projections. Your critical eye will find a way to save more money. Use your independent mind to widen your intellectual horizons. You will enjoy reading and studying, particularly topics like language, geography, and foreign culture. Cancer students should hit the books in a quiet place like the library. Pursue an interest in unusual subjects and you are apt to develop unorthodox views that make you stand out.

6. TUESDAY. Helpful. You are socially popular, able to attract and benefit from the faith and support of friends. Your high goals and optimism win people to your cause. Call a trusted friend if you need helpful advice. A lunch or dinner date would be a good opportunity for you to pick up the tab in thanks for recent support. Continue to be creative and idealistic, imaginative in the way you express yourself. You are intuitive about other people and know how to please them. You want to be appreciated and admired, and this is a day when you do not have to go fishing for compliments.

7. WEDNESDAY. Dynamic. Look your best, because today you are likely to be expressing your opinion in a public forum. You could find yourself speaking in front of a group of associates or an auditorium full of students. Your verbal skills are strong and your self-expression is apt to be passionate. The only risk is that your ideas may sound rigid or dogmatic. Your personal opinions could clash with an official position, but chances are good that your colleagues agree with you and will follow your lead. Your love life is marked by a sudden change that benefits both you and your mate or steady date.

8. THURSDAY. Bumpy. Show that you can be generous and protective toward your romantic partner. Your financial affairs may fluctuate or tend to be unsettled due to your family obligations. Do not hesitate to spoil loved ones with a gift, or take them out for a special dinner tonight. As a Cancer you are normally tenacious, never giving up easily. Your keen sense for what is lucrative will lead to new opportunities. Cancer people are the most security-minded sign of the Zodiac, with an outstanding ability to plan for the future. However, today you may be uncharacteristically greedy or extravagant, spending money emotionally and unwisely.

9. FRIDAY. Mixed. Watch your wallet, especially if you go out with a group of associates or friends. There is a good chance that you will be left to pay the tab for lunch or dinner. If you are on a tight budget, be sure to ask for separate checks. Select a modest restaurant with good food at reasonable prices, or consider inviting people to your house for a pot-luck meal. If everyone contributes a favorite dish and brings along a bottle of wine or soda, expenses can be kept very low and you can enjoy their company without a lot of fuss. In addition, this gives you a chance to show off your home as well as your latest creative work.

10. SATURDAY. Slow. You are able to earn money creatively by using your imagination. Deal directly with the public, not through a middleman. You might be able to sell possessions or assets through an ad in your local newspaper. This is a better day than most to hold a garage sale or attend a flea market. You are apt to either make a tidy profit or find a real steal of a deal. Take it easy and look after yourself later in the day. Your health may be under stain due to overwork or because you tend to neglect eating a wholesome diet. If there is work that needs to be accomplished today, look for support or assistance from family members or even a neighbor.

11. SUNDAY. Fair. You will be thinking emotionally and have a strong imagination. For Cancer parents, this is a better time than most to communicate with children. You can have fun teaching them while playing together. You should be feeling silly and playful, which is ideal for games. You might also enjoy doing arts and crafts together. Regress and live for the moment just like you are a kid again. It would be wise to let go of achieving results. Aim to inspire people with your actions and ideas. You may also enjoy getting together with friends. Outdoor exercise would be a good stress reliever, especially golf, tennis, or even a game of catch.

12. MONDAY. Disappointing. You are apt to feel reserved and somewhat reclusive. You may place limitations on your options because of fear or excess caution. Your thinking may be hazy as you have difficulty concentrating. You will be most successful working alone in seclusion. Try to find an out-of-the-way office or meeting room so that you are not interrupted by a constant stream of phone calls and associates. It would be wise to avoid dealing with other people's money because you may unconsciously deceive them. What has profit potential for you may disappoint a more aggressive investor.

13. TUESDAY. Sensitive. This is an excellent day to focus on domestic issues. Continue to be protective toward your family, particularly with youngsters. During your lifetime you can expect to move fewer times than other people. Cancer people like to live near water and to have a solid, secure home base from which to operate. If you are considering relocating due to your job or love life, this is a positive day for arranging a mortgage or for buying furniture for your new house. You have good financial intuition regarding real estate or family possessions. You will most likely be very accurate when it comes to timing a sale or any purchase involving a bank loan.

14. WEDNESDAY. Important. You have excellent artistic gifts and a strong sense of design and color. It would be wise to capture your latest ideas on paper and to act on your impulses. These may not be directly related to your career but something you need to do to beautify your home or office. Long term, if you feel cozy and comfortable in your surroundings you will be more productive. You should also be feeling romantic and unusually passionate. This is a very constructive influence for all partnership matters. You are serious and faithful in love; once you choose your mate you will attempt to hold on for life.

15. THURSDAY. Emotional. Unlike yesterday, you are apt to be impulsive about love today, following your heart rather than your head. This unusual behavior could cause you to take foolish chances or to make an unwise choice. If you are having a secret love affair, it is likely to become public knowledge unless you take extra precautions. Avoid sharing private information with friends or what you reveal could become gossip. It is also not a good day for handling money or making any financial decisions. Since you are in the mood for fun, direct your romantic and creative imagination toward your family. Include a pet in your evening plans.

16. FRIDAY. Tense. The Full Moon could play havoc with your friendships. A trusted friend may have made a slip of the tongue, making you the subject of gossip. Or someone you know well may let you down by forgetting an appointment or neglecting to follow through with a special favor. Say that you are disappointed, but true friends forgive each other's mistakes. At work you may have to diffuse a tense situation that arises when you are faced with a sudden change of plan or information. A colleague may not deliver work on time, or electrical equipment could break down. Do not procrastinate or you could get caught short.

17. SATURDAY. Helpful. There is a risk of impulsiveness and a tendency for changes to erupt suddenly. Avoid thoughtless moves. You will most likely find family members and neighbors usually helpful. This is an ideal time to straighten out joint financial issues. Perhaps you can ask the people living next door to share the cost of a new fence or of tree removal. Balance your checkbook and review family investments, particularly your pension plan and locked-in savings. Also check that your insurance policy still covers the current value of your assets, particularly if you have recently made home improvements or renovations.

18. SUNDAY. Exciting. This morning your quiet reverie may be interrupted by a family member who needs your help for a special project. Team up with a romantic partner or a friend and you will learn something new and exciting. Opportunity could even involve unexpected spontaneous travel, perhaps to the countryside or to visit friends who live in an unusual location. This is an ideal time to stimulate your creativity and intelligence. Being in the mood to meet new people, you can accept all invitations that involve meeting visitors from another part of the country or from overseas. Diversify to avoid stagnation.

19. MONDAY. Manageable. Do not hesitate to talk about partnership with friends or associates. Teamwork is the theme of the day. You will be able to accomplish a great deal by cooperating with like-minded people. However, when it comes to choosing your mate, keep in mind that security is very important in both marriage and all relationships. The best choice is a parental figure of some kind, or at least someone who is protective of you. It is vital to trust the people you are with. If the subject of money comes up, it would be wise to keep friendship and finances separate. Otherwise there is a risk that you could lose both simultaneously.

20. TUESDAY. Favorable. You will be relieved as the things that have been holding you back are suddenly removed. Obstacles and delays are over, and this is a favorable time for you to make progress. Team up with a partner or friend who has connections. Together you can make significant gains, particularly in a philanthropic project. Chances are also good that you can make a profit from business ventures with friends. This is a starred time for fund-raising for a good cause. You will enjoy a social function and activities where you can talk about reform and humanitarian ideals.

21. WEDNESDAY. Deceptive. As a Cancer you are deeply sensitive and quite possibly have psychic ability. You can use these traits in a practical way to improve your own life and your family's. Pay attention to your intuition. However, when it comes to money issues, it would be best to avoid giving advice to friends and associates. There is a risk that you could lose even on a sure thing. Your finances may be unsettled because of marriage or inheritance. Sleep before making any decisions. Use your strong powers of concentration to do more research. More than likely you will prefer seclusion this evening but you have to give in to your mate or date's wishes.

22. THURSDAY. Reassuring. You have great powers of concentration and are intent on seeing results. However, take care because you often overwork when in such a mood. Take more of an interest in medicine and your health. You could personally be gifted in the healing arts. Pay close attention to what your body is trying to tell you. You could benefit from a change in diet or a natural treatment to cure a problem that has persisted for quite a while. Consider massage therapy or some other body treatment to relieve stress. Job pressures may sap your energy unless you learn relaxation techniques.

23. FRIDAY. Changeable. Your receptive, imaginative mind is capable of delving into serious ideas. The unknown attracts you; in your work you may come up with a new product or concept. You are highly individualistic and may even be considered eccentric or unusual. You will not conform or be restricted. Arrange to work alone today further developing your ideas. If friends or associates interrupt you, use them to test your pet theories and original notions. A friendly audience will not lead you astray. You have a tendency to be vague and impractical, but this is a good time to let your dreams have free rein. Be open to all possibilities despite the probabilities.

24. SATURDAY. Low-keyed. You may be feeling a little under the weather, with your moods and emotions swinging to extremes. You might be jealous of a co-worker's success. There is a risk that you could be overly skeptical and susceptible to errors in judgment. To avoid being rash or erratic, find ways to soothe your nervous strain. Spend some time alone mediating or contemplating. It may be helpful to get some physical exercise to relieve stress and get any anger out of your system. Talking with a close friend or reading a favorite inspirational book can also be soothing.

25. SUNDAY. Buoyant. You have great physical energy and self-confidence. Allow your ambitions to run wild and see what develops. Since you are feeling courageous you may want to tackle a major project. Your passion and enthusiasm will carry you far. The work you do can inspire other people. Working in private for part of the day will allow your receptive, imaginative mind to experiment with new ideas that could lead to a job promotion. Your home life should be harmonious as you adapt to the needs and demands of your loved ones. Around the house you work well together with family members and should not have to hire any outside help.

26. MONDAY. Varied. This is an excellent day for making money. You might finally get that raise you have been waiting for or close a big contract. If the extra money is burning a hole in your pocket, go shopping. Treat yourself; you deserve something special for your recent efforts. This is also a good day for handling money on behalf of other people, perhaps making investment recommendations for clients or negotiating a bank loan for a family member. Just avoid pooling money or getting involved in a speculative investment with friends. These will probably not pay off or even hold their original value.

27. TUESDAY. Successful. With your charming speech this would be an ideal time to give a presentation related to work or on behalf of a group. Try to find the best balance between mental activities and your love of art and beauty. Chances are that you will be involved with the public in career, professional, or social activities. As a result you may not have much of a private life. Although you are intuitive about what the public wants, you may be dealing with an intricate situation that involves friends and associates. You will find less resistance if you use your crab-like tendency to circle around delicate issues rather than tackle them head-on.

28. WEDNESDAY. Changeable. You have strong intuition. Be open to the future; you will attract luck through change. New information may suddenly come to light which causes you to begin to explore other options. Do not worry if financial aspects are vague. For now do not let money issues stand in your way. Instead, consider what you would like to do regardless of potential financial rewards. There are many measures of success. Focus on your secret hopes and wishes. Friends will understand and support your creative needs. Brainstorm together to find ways of making your dreams become reality.

29. THURSDAY. Mixed. Your physical energy level is not as high as usual, but this is more than compensated by your high intelligence, sensitivity, and imagination. Use brainpower instead of muscles. You have an artistic eye and can indulge in a creative project that also satisfies your love of luxury. Work with rich colors and intricate textures. You should be surrounded by a large number of acquaintances. Your friendships tend to be based on an intellectual rapport. If you feel social, consider getting involved with a new group, club, or society that does good work.

30. FRIDAY. Uncertain. Because you are receptive and intuitive toward other people, you could be overwhelmed by sensory information. This could cause nervous tension and make you temperamental. You can be easily hurt while trying to hide your real emotions. You may be feeling insecure. This is a better time than most to get away to restore yourself, think and meditate. Your creative imagination can help you discard worn-out old habits and approaches that are now proving unsuccessful. Try to finish neglected work and minor matters that you have kept on the back burner, clearing the way for exciting new projects.

31. SATURDAY. Auspicious. This is an ideal time to begin a new project, especially one you can work on in private or secret. Put your stubborn, self-willed behavior to good use by directing your energies within. Deep-rooted habits can be effective because of your determination. More than likely you will receive a financial reward or prize for your newest idea or creation. You could be a visionary, gifted as a medium or possessing strong extrasensory powers. Using your idealistic desire to help people who are in need will give more meaning to your own life.

JUNE

1. SUNDAY. Good. This is an ideal day to spend time alone. You are in the mood for quiet reflection and introspection, and you have the necessary energy and courage to look deeply within yourself. There is a chance for your intuition to guide you to appropriate help. Use your good powers of concentration to delve into personal matters which have eluded you in the past. Consider a retreat or workshop to learn more about your own needs. You may find out why you are a perfectionist. Try to be more tolerant and forgiving of what you see as personal faults. You have the right to please yourself. Remember who should be number one.

2. MONDAY. Exciting. Expect positive changes. You may suddenly have an opportunity to travel, perhaps on an all-expense-paid business trip to a city you have always wanted to see. Try to book a few extra days to explore the area as a tourist. Or you may soon be starting your vacation. This is an ideal time to travel because transportation connections should merge smoothly. You can learn a lot if you meet and speak with foreigners, even on the telephone if not in person. Unusual offers or business deals could come in the form of import or export ventures. Higher learning is also featured. It is time to learn another language.

3. TUESDAY. Cautious. Avoid dealing with money, either your own or your family finances. You might have a disagreement with your mate or partner regarding the budget or a major purchase. Postpone any investment decisions or accounting until another day when you may have more luck. However, this is an excellent day to spend with friends and associates. Arrange a lunch date or get together at a club or social gathering tonight. You have a lot to say about future hopes and dreams. It will be good to line up supporters who believe in your plans and projects and are willing to back you with action as well as words.

4. WEDNESDAY. Important. Meditate on your current financial situation and you should receive some insight about ways to make money. You may opt to begin a creative project that you work on in secret. Or you may come up with a way to pool your funds with other people to achieve an important goal. In any case, you are destined to find a way to improve your personal net worth or family assets. You are imaginative in expressing yourself and intuitive about other people. It is natural to want to be appreciated and admired, even famous. Chances are you will gain profound insights on how to achieve this relatively soon.

5. THURSDAY. Unsettling. Your financial affairs could fluctuate, tending to be unsettled. Cancer people are usually thrifty and security conscious, but today you may be uncharacteristically wasteful and careless. If your mate or partner has blown the monthly budget with an extravagant purchase, do not go out and do the same. If you have been tenaciously building savings for the family's future, you may have to start over. This incident may make you angry or at least discontent. However, becoming too critical could strain your romantic relationship. This is a time to show your generous and protective nature by being willing to forgive and make allowances.

6. FRIDAY. Chancy. If you are in the mood to spend money, make sure it is your own. Do not disburse finances for your spouse or any other family member. You are apt to regret making investments or giving advice to loved ones or friends. This is not a time to loan money or make any recommendations. Use this day to run errands and catch up on the week's correspondence. You may receive a disquieting message or phone call but do not worry. This is just a temporary glitch that will most actually provide you with a much needed change and a little extra time. Welcome a new challenge to prove your worth.

7. SATURDAY. Volatile. If feeling unsure of yourself or lacking in confidence, you will enjoy spending some time alone meditating on issues from the past. If family members interrupt your reverie, wait until this evening rather than getting mad. You might learn that family members are planning a summer visit at your house. Put out the welcome mat. You may also get a phone call with surprising information that is unsettling. Time will be the best healer. As a Cancer you tend to think emotionally and have a strong imagination. Be aware of your reactions as they occur. You can learn by simply recognizing when you are being illogical.

8. SUNDAY. Mixed. This is a day to spend around the house. You may have personal projects in mind, but actually it is an ideal time to be with friends and family members. Consider hosting a Sunday brunch or an afternoon barbecue. You will enjoy conversing about philosophic topics. Together you can come up with ways to make local changes that could have a global impact. Recycle, reuse, and reform the world. You have a good memory, are willing to change your opinion, and make a good impression when talking in front of an audience. With your inquisitive mind and good common sense you can be successful writing about yourself or your family.

9. MONDAY. Problematic. You are likely to be feeling protective toward family members, particularly children. If you have a chance to work from home, take it. Devote some time to household finances. You may need to arrange a loan or to refinance your mortgage. You should have good luck when it comes to finding the funds you need. You may be able to borrow money from your parents or in-laws, especially for a new home or a change of residence due to a job relocation. The only possible problem is a chance of aloof behavior that makes you seem uninterested when you are with family members and other loved ones.

10. TUESDAY. Lucky. Your intuition will lead you in the right direction, so pay close attention. Your energy level is high, and so is your enthusiasm for a new project. You are a powerful, brilliant researcher. You will have excellent concentration and are intent on seeing results as soon as possible. Your work can inspire other people. There is a good chance that you will get help from loved ones or co-workers. You are ambitious and diplomatic, which makes it easy to deal with current issues. If you have a chance to work in quiet privacy, your artistic and creative urges will thrive.

11. WEDNESDAY. Uneasy. You are not only in the mood for fun and games but eager to learn something new. On the job this could translate into trying to acquire new skills or tackling a project you have never done before. You may not get the results you want on your first attempt, but do not let this stop you. Failure is an important part of the learning curve if you pay attention. Just do not invest a lot of money in materials or supplies. Speculation, especially with other people's money or company funds, can get you into a tight bind. Your energy level may not be as high as usual, yet intellectually you are very sharp. Stick with what comes easily to you.

12. THURSDAY. Disquieting. Because you are impulsive about love you tend to follow your heart rather than your head. For Cancer people involved in a secret romance or infatuation, it is possible that the affair will become public knowledge. This might actually be for the best, so that you can live and love openly. Seek out the pleasures of life. You may not be as quick as usual mentally or physically; get extra rest and relaxation. This is a good time to explore your creative talents. You may be able to capitalize on your artistic abilities by turning a hobby into a commercial proposition. This might even become a major source of income.

13. FRIDAY. Beneficial. It may be Friday the thirteenth, but this could be your lucky day. Financially the gods are smiling upon you. You might want to make a little bet with co-workers, perhaps in regard to a sporting match you will be watching or participating in together tonight. Trust your intuition, which is especially stronger than usual in regard to family finances. You may be inclined to speak very little because you are protecting a secret or there is a project you wish to work on alone. Just be aware that your colleagues and family members are more than willing to help. If you need assistance due to sudden changes at the end of the day, do not hesitate to ask.

14. SATURDAY. Sensitive. Today's Full Moon makes you more impulsive than usual. Be prepared for changes to erupt suddenly and for thoughtless moves as a result. You have lots of energy and may find yourself acting too quickly or erratically. Take extra care if driving; preferably get a loved one to be your chauffeur. Your mind is preoccupied with thoughts and cares. Ideally you would tune into your intuition, but it is likely that family members will continually interrupt you. Best to be physically and mentally present with them and with your surroundings. Important ideas and insights will filter through in a flash.

15. SUNDAY. Changeable. Put aside personal opinions and listen to what your mate or partner has to say, although this might at first seem to interfere with your plans or projects for the day. You may have been planning to rest but your loved one wants to take a trip. You will enjoy yourself once you get out of the house. You could be pleasantly surprised by a special event. Live on the wild side and find out what life has in store for you. If you look at the faces in a crowd you might spot a former neighbor or schoolmate. This is a good day for receiving news. Check your e-mail and any unopened correspondence. Keep the phone line free this evening.

16. MONDAY. Quiet. Give more attention to your personal affairs, especially romance. Consider the needs and desires of your romantic partner. You can show in many small and intimate ways that you are thinking of the time you spend together. Consider making a series of phone calls, mailing a love letter, or sending flowers. Prove your appreciation for the constant love and attention you receive. As a Cancer, security and comfort are very important. This is a good time to tend to any legal or contractual issues. You may even want to make your romantic or business partnership official.

17. TUESDAY. Fair. Your intuition will be strong. The best way to clearly receive insights is to spend plenty of time in a quiet place. You will probably prefer seclusion throughout the day. If at work, try to find an empty office or a vacant meeting room where you can hide out. Try harder to uncover secrets or hidden information. You will be able to compute complex financial matters. This is a good time to prepare accounting statements or revenue projections. As a Cancer you are unusually sympathetic and warmhearted. You may even understand what motivates other people almost as soon as they realize their intentions.

18. WEDNESDAY. Varied. Because you are deeply sensitive and interested in questions about life, you may be developing an interest in mystical or metaphysical subjects. Quite possibly you have psychic ability that you can use in a practical way. Focus on how to help other people; you may be able to guide them in spiritual matters. Also consider how to improve your health. Listen to what your body and unconscious mind are telling you. Finances may be unsettled because of marriage or an inheritance tie-up. This is not a good day to handle family funds or other people's money. Get expert advice before investing or opening an account.

19. THURSDAY. Challenging. Most likely you are full of energy and ready to apply yourself to a new challenge. Chances are that the first thing required is to gain knowledge. This probably means hitting the books even if you are not a student. It could also be an excellent time to write a book, an article, or proposal. The problem is that you are feeling lively and the last thing you want to do is sit quietly in one spot. Be sure to start your day with some exercise to burn up some of that excess juice. Then you will find that your strong powers of concentration can be applied. Also, listen for the little voice of your intuitions guiding you gently to the best source.

20. FRIDAY. Deceptive. What you most want to know is probably being kept from you. Secret meetings could be occurring, or there may be talks going on behind the scenes. If you pay close attention to the signs you can pick up clues. Use your insight and follow your hunches. You will find that information comes to you from unusual sources, perhaps a friend or colleague from the past. This is the time to go underground to find out what is happening. Working alone will stimulate your creativity. Try to capture your ideas on paper, before they evaporate. You can count on a friend but probably not on a neighbor.

21. SATURDAY. Variable. With your gift of speech, this is a better time than most to initiate conversations and make presentations. If you do not feel like being in the public eye, consider writing down your ideas. It is an ideal time to work on something intended for publication. Also strive to complete a personal project. You have the right balance between mental activities and your love of art and beauty. Although a project may not be directly related to your career, you will probably find that it leads to an interesting new opportunity. Ignore the regular weekend routine and take advantage of your creativity. Break with tradition and see what develops.

22. SUNDAY. Pleasant. Although it is a day off from work for most Cancers, your mind is probably back in the office. If you brought work home, tackle it early in the day. By being dressed in your comfortable casual clothes you will relax and accomplish a great deal. You should not be interrupted by telephone calls or questions from colleagues. In the quiet of your own house you will find it easy to come up with new money-making ideas. Pay particular attention to research and ongoing investigations. Luck is with you. Take your inspirations seriously and you should be very pleased with what you are able to accomplish.

23. MONDAY. Important. To get the best out of this day, focus on your career. Work alone. You are an instinctive researcher and will be especially contemplative and insightful today. You can work things out for yourself. Utilize your insights into the actions of co-workers. They may not understand your methods or behavior, yet you can clearly see their motivation. You should enjoy a harmonious relationship when it comes to romance. You will find it easy to express your feelings. You will have good luck when it comes to both money and love. This is an important day to declare your feelings as well as your intentions.

24. TUESDAY. Lucky. Honor your serious sense of purpose and you can become a self-made success. It is likely that important people will want to spend time with you. Put on your best suit and be a polished professional in all that you do. Those in authority will notice your energy and confidence and will be impressed. Not only that, but you can dazzle them with your unique views. As a Cancer you undoubtedly have unorthodox or radical ideas. Today everyone is ready to listen while appreciating your creativity, so do not hold back or sit on the fence. This is an opportunity for you to make a name for yourself with people who matter.

25. WEDNESDAY. Successful. You are full of vim and vigor, chomping at the bit to get ahead. This is an ideal day for higher education and all aspects of learning. Get some physical exercise early in the morning or you may have difficulty sitting still long enough to read or write. Personal projects related to publishing are favored. Try to avoid dealing with money or financial issues since you do not have the patience to exercise good judgment when it comes to dollars and cents. You may be in the mood to work in secret or alone, but expect some interruptions from co-workers. You have the support of friends and their admiration as well.

26. THURSDAY. Helpful. If your hopes and dreams need support, turn to trusted friends. They will have unusual but worthwhile advice for you. You may also receive positive information from some unexpected sources. Be especially alert to signs and indications from someone at a distance. This could be in the form of a long-distance phone call or e-mails from colleagues and associates. All forms of travel are favored. You can learn something new and valuable from foreigners. Be open to the unconventional ways in which your questions are being answered as virtual strangers lend you a hand.

27. FRIDAY. Varied. At the end of this busy workweek your energy level is lower than normal. However, this can work to your advantage, forcing your mind to come up with creative ideas. If you are at the office, try to find a quiet place to work, or at least get out for a meditative walk during the lunch break. The time you spend in reflection and contemplation will be valuable. You can make progress finishing tasks that have been neglected. Tidy up your desk and empty the in-basket, getting organized and making room for something new to capture your attention.

28. SATURDAY. Enjoyable. This is an ideal weekend to indulge in artistic projects. You are apt to be in a meditative mood, connecting with the creativity within you. Play with rich colors and textures. There is a good opportunity to make money from a favorite hobby. Contemplate ways to sell your ideas or products to the public. Since you feel tranquil and loving, it should not disturb you if family members or friends do not actively share your vision. What is important today is to please yourself and allow your own style to develop. Stay close to home this evening.

29. SUNDAY. Fair. Concentrate on yourself. Begin by contemplating what makes you happy. Start the day by meditating. Let ideas float up from your unconscious mind. Because you are in the mood to learn something new, you may suddenly find that you are interested in higher education. If you are thinking of taking a summer class or workshop, now is the time to register. Or you might want to begin learning another language in preparation for a vacation you are planning. You have the intelligence and concentration to pick up new skills quickly and to retain information.

30. MONDAY. Stimulating. Pay extra attention to your appearance. Be sure your shoes are polished. Put on your best outfit. You could suddenly find yourself in the limelight. Those in authority will note if your image suits the job. You could be asked to speak in public, make a presentation, or serve as the chair of a meeting. You are imaginative in the way you express yourself and intuitive about other people's needs. You are bound to be appreciated and admired by your peers and may even become famous one of these days.

JULY

1. TUESDAY. Opportune. This is a starred day to work on personal pet projects. Focus on pursuing your own special ambitions and interests. The best way to get ahead is to be methodical and patient. You have good powers of endurance, to the point of almost being obstinate. You are apt to win all debates and discussions. Do not hesitate to ask people for what you want; more than likely they will cater to your desires. You should also have an opportunity to increase your assets or income by using your original ideas. Pursue your passions with commitment and the money will follow without any extra effort. Break with the old and chase what is new.

2. WEDNESDAY. Successful. Use your intense style of communication to make money by giving presentations and sales pitches. Because you speak with conviction and enthusiasm, your words will be compelling and motivating. The one subject to avoid is household or shared finances. Although you are feeling generous and protective, your comments may come across as criticism. As a Cancer you are generally very determined when it comes to protecting and building a nest egg. Your mate or partner is apt to be more extravagant when it comes to enjoying what money can buy, forcing you to reach a compromise.

3. THURSDAY. Pleasant. You are able to earn money creatively by using your imagination. This is a better day than most to work alone in seclusion. You should receive insights as a result of this period of contemplation. You could also get ideas from unexpected or secret sources. Your financial affairs are settled, so you may enjoy doing some shopping for yourself or for loved ones. You are likely to find a good deal since you are thrifty and careful when it comes to money. You have a keen sense for what could increase quickly in value. Review your investment portfolio or savings plan now that your income is increasing.

4. FRIDAY. Changeable. Your energy may not be as robust as normal, yet your brain is sharp. You probably will not miss a beat when there is a sudden change in plans. New information could come to light at the last minute on this Friday afternoon. You may have to modify a speech or other presentation on short notice; not to worry since your communication skills are strong. You also have personal charisma, leading people to support your ideas and be more cooperative than usual. A group you recently joined is looking for a leader who can think fast. You are the one to rise to the challenge and save the day. Those in authority will be impressed with all of your actions.

5. SATURDAY. Fair. Sleep late, if possible. You are apt to be rigid and dogmatic in your opinions, basically indicating it is your way or no way. If you are the resident expert, you may get away with this behavior. However, there is a risk that your family will not toe the line. You have to be diplomatic and conciliatory when it comes to group decision-making. Try to see other people's points of view and you will have a lot less to argue about. Consider why it is so important that you be right. Spend some time working alone on personal projects so that you can do as you please and not have to report to anyone.

6. SUNDAY. Unpredictable. Your plans for the day may have to be put on hold because your help is needed around the house. Your mate or partner may request assistance with domestic chores, or the kids may need to be driven to their sports events. In any case you are bound to be involved with other people. Expect sudden changes in all plans. Stay flexible and be relaxed in your attitude. Pay close attention to your intuition and you are apt to receive insights related to loved ones. It might be fun to go on a spontaneous family outing. Let yourself be a kid again to get the most enjoyment out of this day.

7. MONDAY. Variable. If you can work from home, you will accomplish a great deal. You may have to attend to domestic duties, perhaps waiting for a plumber, repairman, or delivery van. Try to get a colleague to cover for you at the office, or you might be able to make some work-related phone calls from home while you are waiting. You can probably surprise yourself by making some money from the comfort of your residence. You can save by negotiating personally with contractors and decorators. Throughout the day, wherever you are, focus on your residence and family. You will feel more secure when your to-do list has been checked off.

8. TUESDAY. Problematic. As a Cancer you have a strong sense of duty, which makes you very conservative in picking a love partner. Your feelings of affection are sometimes sacrificed for personal ambition. Right now there are a number of projects you need to accomplish for yourself, projects that are important to your feelings of self-worth. At the same time, you need the support of your romantic partner. When the workday is done, clear your mind so that you can be fully present and attentive to that special person in your life. Seek out pleasures in life to share them with your loved ones.

9. WEDNESDAY. Happy. Because you are in a fun-loving mood, avoid dealing with anything serious such as money and high finance. You will likely follow your heart rather than your head, so you will not do the homework or research that is necessary. Do not rely on a hunch or your instincts, because they are not dependable right now. It is a time to focus on yourself and your ambitions. Your communication skills are strong and you will find it easy to gain the cooperation of other people. They will appreciate your lighthearted touch even when dealing with complex questions.

10. THURSDAY. Low-keyed. You might not feel as energetic as usual because something is distracting you emotionally. Or you could be feeling a little under the weather due to poor eating habits. This could make you less tolerant to sudden changes in plans. The boss may issue a new directive, or a client may want to modify an order. This will probably cause you more work, which you are not in the mood to tackle. However, it would be best not to become argumentative. Instead, look for ways to get additional assistance. Ask for more resources, for more time, or for a co-worker to lend a hand. The end results will be worth the extra effort.

11. FRIDAY. Auspicious. If you feel a strong impulsive urge, go with it. Trust your intuition. Lady Luck is on your side. Your health is good and you should be full of vim and vigor. Focus on what you would most like to accomplish. By being fully occupied with your vision and intent, you attract whatever you need to be successful. Chances are that people will come to you bearing gifts. These could be free advice, money, or contacts. The old adage about asking and you shall receive is true for you. Colleagues and co-workers are on your side. Just remember to say thank you for all that is given to you, without expecting more and more.

12. SATURDAY. Fair. Since you are feeling physically fit and energetic, start the morning with a favorite form of exercise. Try to get a partner to join you. Be open to share the day with your mate or steady date. Stay open and flexible regarding the main activity of the day. Chances are that there will be an unexpected change in plans as something occurs that points you in a new direction. A loved one may need your help around the house or might want to go on a trip across town or into the countryside. Since you are in the mood for new adventure and travel, sit back and enjoy being together for the ride.

13. SUNDAY. Tense. Today's Full Moon could play havoc with one or more of your personal relationships. As a Cancer person, security is very important to you. You may be romantically involved with a parental figure of some kind, someone who is protective of you and makes you feel loved and cherished. Today, however, this person may be pushing some buttons that make you want your independence. As a result, you could feel ready for a change in your love relationship. This is probably just a phase that will pass with the changing Moon. In the meantime, you can make money with a new business partnership. Join forces with someone who complements your talents.

14. MONDAY. Complicated. You can afford to go into matters deeply. This is an ideal time to do research and to analyze complex issues related to your relationships or to big business. The only subject that it will be difficult to deal with is money. Your finances may be unsettled because of marriage or inheritance. To avoid suffering a loss, it would be wise to get expert opinion. Gather information from accountants and investment analysts. You can find ways of improving the future economic security for yourself and your family if you look into retirement plans, wills, and insurance coverage that is guaranteed.

15. TUESDAY. Sensitive. Today you will most likely prefer seclusion. It is a time to contemplate all of your current choices. Count your blessings and all that you have to be thankful for. Although your intuition is usually strong, there is a risk related to monetary matters. You may be too attached to your possessions to clearly see your priorities. Or you may be operating from the incorrect perception that there is not enough to go around. Examine your fears. You will do better basing your life on the principle of abundance rather than of deprivation. Be generous; share with other people.

16. WEDNESDAY. Unsettling. Your best bet is to stay open-minded and flexible. Things are definitely going to change. It could be that travel plans need to be altered due to a traffic jam or missed connections. This may not be the smoothest day to start a vacation or business trip. Progress is apt to be slower than usual. However, you could find yourself in surprisingly interesting situations. Look for opportunities to meet new people and to experience other cultures. If all else fails, a good book will help you pass the time. Be daring and try being someone completely different. Here is your chance to be eccentric.

17. THURSDAY. Variable. You should bound out of bed this morning, full of energy and enthusiasm. Pay extra attention to your appearance since you might find yourself in the public eye. This is an excellent time to work on personal projects. You have the courage to learn something new and should use your strong powers of concentration to delve into the unknown. You may be attracted to a different philosophical idea, foreign culture, or age-old language. For Cancer summer school students, studying will go easily. Your mind is receptive and imaginative. It is also a good day to be traveling for fun or business providing you have made reservations in advance.

18. FRIDAY. Helpful. The end of the workweek includes a happy experience while commuting or traveling some distance. If you have not yet taken your summer vacation, it is time to at least make definite plans. Call a travel agent to explore some ideas and possible itineraries. It is also a good time to catch up with the people you have played telephone tag with all week. Make long-distance phone calls early in the day, then wait to receive helpful information from around the country. Cancer writers will find special inspiration and support, and may even receive good news from an agent or publisher.

19. SATURDAY. Confusing. Perhaps you had plans for this weekend to work on pet projects or hobbies. However, chances are that your career is forcing you to put in some extra time. Actually it is a good day to make money; you may be paid double time for your efforts. Follow your intuition to sniff out profitable deals and sales opportunities. Just avoid handling other people's money or pooling your funds in an investment scheme. To avoid confusion and conflict of interest, keep all money-related transactions clear and simple. Be sure to get any contract or commitment in writing.

20. SUNDAY. Eventful. You could be involved with the public in career, professional, or social activities. Even though it is the weekend, it would be wise to expand your circle of useful acquaintances. Chances are that you will meet and network with people you will eventually do business with. Keep in mind that most sales are made with people who are not viewed as strangers. Focus on new contacts and connections. Cancer people who are temporarily out of work could learn more about career changes and options by talking with a counselor. People will be helpful with suggestions and someone may even be able to arrange an important introduction to an influential decision-maker.

21. MONDAY. Successful. Expect a productive day. Even if you do not get your own way, you will be able to make significant progress. There are apt to be sudden changes to your plans. The boss may issue new directives, or a customer may need a rush response. In any case, drop what you are doing and shift priorities. You should find colleagues and associates willing to assist. This is a good day to get together with friends, so call to arrange a lunch date. You may also be invited to a club meeting or other social gathering. If you accept the offer, you are likely to learn something new and useful.

22. TUESDAY. Buoyant. Pay attention to signals received from friends and associates. You will be doing a lot of talking as you make presentations. Your words are bound to be passionate and inspirational, enabling you to move and motivate other people. Your easy social charm attracts many admirers. You may find yourself in a leadership role because your enthusiasm is infectious. As a result it might be difficult to listen to what is really being said. Normally you are emotionally intuitive in dealing with people. However, today you are apt to tune into unreliable friends. Do not mix money and friendship or you could lose both.

23. WEDNESDAY. Positive. This is a time to mix and mingle with like-minded people. You might be attracted to participate in a humanitarian cause. Consider lending your talents to a fund-raising event, but resist the urge to simply write a check and then walk away. You can do the most good by volunteering your time and energy to help make a difference in the situation. You might donate your art to an auction. Or you can help find corporate sponsors who are also intent on making the world a safer place. Your focus may be on saving an environmentally sensitive area or stopping the destruction of a natural treasure.

24. THURSDAY. Disquieting. Your physical energy may not be as robust as usual, which might make you wish to withdraw from planned activities. Or you may need to get away to study and reflect on a complex subject that needs instant attention. To avoid any interruption of your thoughts, find a quiet place to work. Look for a room where you can close the door or at least unplug the telephone. You may also find it helpful to take a walk in a park where you can connect with nature. As a Cancer you are sensitive, receptive, and intuitive. You have a creative imagination, especially when it comes to solving financial issues.

25. FRIDAY. Fair. Spend most of today in quiet reverie. Start the day with a long walk alone or with a pet. Your intuition about money matters is very strong. You might come up with new ways to earn extra dollars, or a way to make substantial savings. You can even handle other people's finances successfully. Review insurance policies, bank loans, and any existing mortgages. If possible, work in an empty office or unused meeting room. You may have to do some complex math and accounting, but interruptions from your colleagues could cause you to lose count. With your good luck it should add up to your advantage.

26. SATURDAY. Fortunate. When it comes to communicating about the subject of money you have a lot to say. Because you are feeling optimistic you can be positive about raising funds. This is a better day than most to make a sales pitch. You are imaginative in the way you express yourself and intuitive about other people, who more than likely will not be able to resist your offer. As a result you will end up earning more money. It may not be for your personal use, however, since you are definitely philanthropically inclined. With humanitarian projects and altruistic ventures on your mind, you can have a lasting impact on your world.

27. SUNDAY. Varied. This morning you should bound out of bed. Even though it is the weekend, you probably will not sleep late. Start the day with some vigorous physical exercise, perhaps an early morning jog, a few laps in the pool, or even a walk as the sun comes up. Think about your personal appearance. Nothing makes you look and feel better than being fit and active. However, do not let yourself become too critical about your body. It is most important to eat and exercise in moderation. Now that the weather is warm, be sure to drink more water also. Aim for improvement, not perfection.

28. MONDAY. Enjoyable. Dedicate this day to your own personal enjoyment. Start by treating yourself to some little luxuries, perhaps a scented bath or a leisurely swim topped off by a good breakfast. Most likely you are feeling open and friendly toward other people. As a result they will find your personality more attractive and irresistible than usual. It should be easy to obtain cooperation because people will want to cater to your desires. You may find new ways of using your special abilities and talents to make money. With your artistic eye you can create something beautiful from natural materials or even from scraps you had thought about discarding.

29. TUESDAY. Slow. You might not be as energetic as usual. In fact, your get-up-and-go might feel as though it got up and went. Your drive to succeed is less directed than normal because you are in a recharging cycle. Allow yourself to get more rest, perhaps even a nap before dinner. This will enable you to start thinking about new opportunities. Your mind can come up with plenty of money-making ideas; take note of them and keep them in a safe place while they germinate just a little longer. When the time is right these ideas will be ready to sprout. Right now you can afford to let your thoughts be obscure, knowing that they will pay off eventually.

30. WEDNESDAY. Good. If you are looking for change or a new challenge, try sharing your good fortune with other people. You should be feeling generous and protective. Consider treating your loved ones to gifts or other surprises. Presents are best when there is no real reason for giving them. This is also an excellent day to communicate your feelings. Make a sales pitch to a new customer or negotiate a raise with your boss. There is a good possibility that people are in the mood to buy whatever you are selling. Colleagues and co-workers will be happy to assist in your endeavors providing you recognize their contributions publicly.

31. THURSDAY. Changeable. There will be lots of new information that causes you to change your plans. However, you have the ability to cope effectively. Your intelligence is sharper than usual, plus you have sensitivity and imagination. All you need to do is gather facts and then use your common sense to make a decision. It is also important that you relay your intentions to those who will be affected. Your strongest tool is your ability to communicate. This is a good time for writing letters, making phone calls and undertaking short trips around town. Clients and neighbors will be especially pleased to hear from you in person.

AUGUST

1. FRIDAY. Frustrating. It is quite possible that co-workers or colleagues will let you down as the workweek draws to a close. Be prepared for people to call in sick or to take the day off. If you have a busy work load, you might need to call a temporary agency for help. Otherwise, just do the best you can under the circumstances. You may have to handle all of your own communications, which could mean that you answer the phone and take messages for other people while doing your own work. Rather than becoming frustrated, concentrate only on what is most important. This is a better time than most to catch up on correspondence.

2. SATURDAY. Opportune. This is an excellent day to make money from the comfort of your home. If you brought work from the office, it is a time for writing proposals and making business plans. You might have something to sell at a craft sale or flea market. If you earn some extra cash, shopping for something to beautify your home will be satisfying. The challenging part of the day concerns being selfish with your time and energy. Domestic duties such as lawn and garden work are apt to take you away from hobbies and family fun. Try to enlist the help of loved ones and spend part of the day outside together.

3. SUNDAY. Satisfactory. Pay close attention to your intuition. You could get flashes related to a new or improved place to live. You may notice an open house when walking around your neighborhood; it could give you ideas for your own decorating or renovations. If you like living where you now are, you might have found your next house. Even if it is a fixer-upper, you have the vision to see all of the potential. You can rely on your financial common sense when it comes to real estate or family possessions. Take some time for rest and relaxation; your body will appreciate some extra pampering. Share a healthy Sunday dinner with family members.

4. MONDAY. Misleading. Your ideas or fantasies about money could be leading you astray. It would not be wise to borrow funds from other people. Also avoid purchasing any expensive item. You are apt to be feeling impulsive and are sure to regret being extravagant. Be conscious of what attracts you, but ask yourself if you really need to own it. Maybe you can borrow the item or rent it until the thrill wears off. Do more research before making any major spending decision. You may change your mind once you read pertinent consumer reports or news releases.

5. TUESDAY. Reassuring. If you have had difficulty explaining yourself recently, you will be glad to regain the conviction in your voice today. You are clearer about your personal needs and desires, and it will be reassuring to know your own mind. This is a time to speak up and share your ideas. Your energy level is high and so is your enthusiasm. Seek new ways of using your abilities and talents to make money. People are apt to be so impressed with your creativity and self-confidence that they may agree to fund your project or to purchase a quantity of what you make.

6. WEDNESDAY. Bumpy. You are likely to be impulsive about love, following your heart rather than your head. This could cost you money because you want to take your loved one out for a fancy meal at an expensive restaurant or purchase an expensive gift even if you are short of cash. Although this could be disturbing to your budget-conscious Cancer temperament, at least you will know that you are serious about this romance. Your actions speak louder than words. Most likely your efforts will be rewarded but not immediately. Seek out the pleasures in life, living each moment and not waiting for the future.

7. THURSDAY. Deceptive. You could be feeling unusually impulsive. There is a risk of changes erupting suddenly, and for you to make thoughtless moves as a result. Take a few deep breaths or count to ten before reacting. Co-workers may debate or question your actions; ask yourself why they are making you argumentative. Watch for financial issues to interfere with your love life. You and your mate may disagree on the family budget. Your verbal skills are strong, so be assertive rather than aggressive when making your points. Use your intuition to look for money-making or saving opportunities. Open your mind to options that have never occurred to you before.

8. FRIDAY. Favorable. The end of the workweek offers you another way to increase your bank account. You may be offered a promotion with a raise, or a job you recently applied for may come through. Either way you will soon be going home with more cash or assets. This is also a good time to fully utilize your talents. You may be able to close one more contract before the end of the day. There is a potential partnership where you can learn something new. You may suddenly get a hot tip or a lead from an unlikely source. Consider going away for the weekend with that special person in your life.

9. SATURDAY. Harmonious. This is an excellent day to share with your loved one. You will probably want to be together all day since you have been apart too much lately. The conversation should be flowing, allowing you to do a lot of catching up. Communications of all kinds are featured. This is a good time to run errands together and take short trips around town. Let go of any specific goals and dreams of accomplishment. With all your pent-up energy, this is an excellent day for sports and recreation. Try to spend time near water, perhaps a nearby river or lake. A picnic lunch or afternoon barbecue would be pleasant and probably memorable.

10. SUNDAY. Promising. This weekend is an excellent time for working as part of a team. You may be a member of a sports club or coaching a kids' league or even helping with a fund-raising drive to build a ball park. In any case, your communication skills will both motivate and teach people. You can see though the opposition and come up with a winning strategy. Pay attention to your first reactions; in the heat of the moment, go with your instincts. This is also a good time to get in touch with family members and former neighbors. Write that birthday card or letter you have been putting off for almost too long. Send flowers or a balloon bouquet if the mail would be too slow.

11. MONDAY. Tricky. If you have a preference for seclusion, do not ignore it. Chances are your subconscious is trying to get an important message through. Take time for meditation or reflection on a specific question that has been on your mind lately. Write your thoughts in a journal or tape-record them. By doing some psychic detective work, you can reach hidden meaning. This is a starred time for self-analysis. If you are feeling confused, consider talking to a counselor or taking a workshop to learn more about your own motivation. More than likely you will have a flash of insight and could find an answer to a problem that has dismayed you for a long time.

12. TUESDAY. Cautious. The Full Moon may affect you directly in the wallet. Be careful if you go shopping because it could cost you much more than you expect. You are apt to be feeling extravagant and purchase something totally beyond your budget items. Or you might think that you are getting a good deal only to discover that you are not happy with the quality when you get home. When it comes to work-related expenditures, ask for a second opinion from colleagues, who will be the voice of moderation today. In fact, it would be a good idea to let someone else monitor your spending all day as a type of savings plan.

13. WEDNESDAY. Useful. Today you are apt to be highly original and individualistic. You will not willingly conform or be restricted by anyone else's demands or opinions. In fact, you are so sure of yourself that you are apt to come across as completely decisive. As a Cancer you have the courage to stand by your convictions, not caring if people consider you eccentric or unusual. In fact, more than likely you would take that as a compliment. It is an excellent day for long-distance travel and to begin learning a new language. Your strong powers of concentration will make any type of studying and research easier than usual.

14. THURSDAY. Inspiring. You have a receptive, imaginative mind capable of delving into philosophical ideas. Higher learning of all types is bound to attract you. Look into taking a weekend workshop or learning a new skill as part of a vacation package. A sports clinic could greatly improve your abilities. The unknown attracts you, prompting you to delve into history or the past as part of your job. The boss or colleagues may try to dissuade you from digging in the archives, because perhaps they have something to hide. Of course, that is even more reason to follow your hunch and carry on with your search even if you must do so on the sly.

15. FRIDAY. Calm. Chances are that you can wrap up a deal by the end of the day. At the very least you can straighten up your desk and leave with a clear conscience of a job well done. You will have happy experiences connected with travel. If you have not yet been away on a summer vacation, this is the time to depart or to plan a getaway. Consider a spontaneous adventure this weekend, packing your car right after work and taking off. Or call a travel agent for a last-minute bargain seat to somewhere fun. You will find that two days away can feel like an entire week, bringing you back home refreshed and rested.

16. SATURDAY. Fair. Although it is the weekend, your mind may be back on the job. You may get flashes of intuition related to your career, perhaps even inspiration that will help you climb the corporate ladder. If you get passionate about an idea, follow it up. It may help to phone a few colleagues and bounce your ideas off them, asking for feedback. It is also a better time than most to brainstorm about ways to utilize company financing or a bank line of credit. You will probably need a sponsor or financial adviser to help pull this idea together. Chances are people will be helpful once you are able to explain your intentions. Just be sure to keep grounded in reality.

17. SUNDAY. Good. Even though this is supposed to be a day of rest, you can make a lot of progress by focusing on your career. Suddenly your hopes and dreams seem like they could come true. You are full of creative ideas. Discussions with friends and supporters will prove fruitful since they might have just the contacts you need to raise money or to sell your idea. It is time to polish your professional appearance. Buy yourself a new suit. Do not forget the finishing details like shiny shoes, stylish accessories, and an updated haircut. It is likely that you will be closely involved with the public in career, professional, or social activities.

18. MONDAY. Enjoyable. You should feel warmhearted toward your friends and more sociable and charming than usual. As a result you will attract new admirers who share your views and support your vision of life. It would be wise to accept any invitation to lunch or to a club meeting. You are emotionally intuitive in dealing with people. By networking and mingling, you could be introduced to potentially lucrative contacts. Physically you should be feeling strong and healthy. Exercise of all forms will be invigorating, especially with a group all working to achieve the same goal. Eat well without overindulging.

19. TUESDAY. Helpful. Expect friends and associates to support your dreams. If you need advice, call on a trusted relative or friend. It would be a good idea to invite this person out for lunch or arrange to meet for a drink after work. Your presentation skills are strong, making this a better time than most for sales pitches and contract negotiations. During the process of explaining yourself, everything will become clear. Catch up on correspondence. Your mail might be heavier and contain more useful information than usual. Cancers who earn a living with words will find that writing flows easily. The difficulty today is settling down to work.

20. WEDNESDAY. Disappointing. At some time in life goals shift and friendships are likely to change. A club or society you have belonged to for a long time may no longer suit your needs because you have outgrown it or mutual values have shifted. You may be asked to make a financial contribution to an organization, or a friend may ask you for a loan. Resist the urge to give away money. You can be generous in many other ways, offering your time, expertise, or experience. You can help by various means that do not involve cash. Spend some quiet time alone reflecting on how to share in the most meaningful manner.

21. THURSDAY. Comforting. It is a time for digging into your past and taking care of old business. This might mean clearing up neglected work lurking at the bottom of your in box. You will feel a lot better when such items are off your mind. As a Cancer you have a strong sense of duty and want to do the right thing. This could make you conservative. In picking a love partner, feelings of affection may sometimes be sacrificed for your personal ambition. There is a risk that you will be attracted to a person just for the security or prestige you would be given. It may be comforting but will only truly be satisfying when combined with real love and devotion.

22. FRIDAY. Lucky. The end of the workweek is a time to have some laughs. With your cultured mind and good sense of humor, you might be the one cracking the jokes. Life keeps surprising you with funny moments. From the ridiculous to the absurd, you are apt to have a permanent smile on your face. In fact, you could find yourself laughing all the way to the bank. Lady Luck may drop cash or prizes in your lap. This is a better time than most to buy a lottery ticket or a raffle chance. Somebody is going to win, and it might as well be you. A small sports gamble could pay off big. Be careful not to let a surprise at home catch you off guard.

23. SATURDAY. Unsettling. This morning you should wake up with lots of energy and enthusiasm for a personal pet project. However, your attitude might lead you to bite off more than you can reasonably chew. It would be a good idea to pace yourself so that you do not get disappointed or frustrated with the progress you are making. Chances are that you will try too hard to get it right the first time. As a Cancer you are a perfectionist, which makes you very critical. If you attempt to cut corners in an effort to be thrifty, you will only find that less is not always more. You may end up with results that could upset your expectations. Recognize the concept that learning includes an occasional failure.

24. SUNDAY. Unpredictable. Strive to be imaginative in the way you express yourself. You are intuitive about other people, being receptive, romantic, and curious. This is an ideal day to spend with your loved ones. If you share long, intimate conversations, you will probably be surprised by what you learn when you ask and then listen. The results might be unpredictable, but your intimacy and appreciation will increase. Home and family mean a great deal to you. As you look back on your own childhood with nostalgia, share some stories about the good old days with children or reminisce with your siblings. Sunday dinner with your extended family is sure to be enjoyable.

25. MONDAY. Quiet. Things are likely to be slow at the start of this workweek. This is a good opportunity for you to concentrate on personal tasks. If you have to run some errands, do some shopping while you are traveling around town. Take more time with your personal appearance. Get your shoes polished and your hair trimmed. You are apt to be in the public eye, so look your best. You might be called upon for your opinion in a meeting of higher-ups. Or you could find yourself making a sales presentation on short notice. If you look like a winner, you will feel even more confident.

26. TUESDAY. Sensitive. You are able to earn money creatively by using your imagination and sensitivity. More than likely you will be interacting directly with the public, perhaps selling to them or making a personal appearance. Your financial affairs are in a state of flux and tend to be unsettled. As a Cancer you are sometimes thrifty and budget-conscious, at other times wasteful and careless. Today you are probably in spending mode, intending to purchase something special you have been saving for. Just make sure you use your own funds and not money or credit you share with someone else. There could be a dispute if you need to first get family or corporate approval.

27. WEDNESDAY. Mixed. Do not hesitate to be generous and protective, especially toward your loved ones and neighbors. You may hear of a sudden setback in the life of someone you know well, even someone from a distance. You will want to help. You are in the mood for a change or a new challenge, and this crisis will give you a special focus. There are times when your stubborn, self-willed nature is a strength that other people can lean upon. You should be able to take care of complex communication issues.

If you need to reach many people in a short period of time, use high-tech solutions such as e-mail, fax, or even satellite transmission.

28. THURSDAY. Frustrating. Prepare for glitches with electrical appliances. Your computer may crash at the worst possible moment, so be sure to make back-up copies before trouble strikes. If your car has been thumping lately, take the hint and drop it off for maintenance before it strands you. You may also experience delays with communications, so it would be wise to use a courier for any urgent document. In order to avoid frustration, do not procrastinate. There is a risk of all types of disruptions. Think ahead and plan alternative ways of accomplishing what needs to be done.

29. FRIDAY. Favorable. Your health should take a definite turn for the better. You will feel that old passion for life surging through your veins once again. Your mind is sharper and you are wittier than usual, plus you have heightened sensitivity and imagination. Do all that you can to turn your vitality into action. This is an excellent time for taking a short trip. Run errands while commuting to customers or suppliers. You will enjoy meeting with people and it will give you an opportunity to talk about personal subjects. All forms of communication are favored. Good news is apt to reach you by phone or mail.

30. SATURDAY. Fulfilling. Because this will be a busy day around the house, you probably will not have much time for any of your own personal projects. Cancer parents might be busy driving children to special events or trying to keep them entertained at home. It is likely that you will be asked to assist with gardening or some type of outdoor activities. Just make yourself useful. Focus on domestic duties. Stay flexible and be prepared for a sudden change of plan. You may receive a phone call or invitation from neighbors. An evening barbecue might be just what everyone needs to relax after an intense day of yardwork and errands.

31. SUNDAY. Enjoyable. This is an ideal day to have fun with games and amusements that the whole family will enjoy, especially those that involve learning or education. Consider visiting a museum, science center, or zoo. You will probably learn as much as the kids do. Since you are feeling physically fit and active, this is an ideal time for sports and physical exercise. If you are playing a match, more than likely you will be the winner. You want to make a little wager on the result. Do not compete with your spouse to see who will be cooking dinner tonight. Romance is in the air, so follow your impulses when it comes to love.

SEPTEMBER

1. MONDAY. Happy. Because you are feeling impulsive about love, you might find yourself following your heart rather than your head. This is especially likely when it comes to telling that special someone how you really feel. Writing a love note or letter should come easily as romantic ideas of all kinds flow from your mind. This is also a good day for catching up on phone calls and running errands. Love may arise as a result of travel or through long-distance correspondence. You are cheerful and creative, making it easy to express your feelings in both speech and writing. You will win attention for your ideas in a way that people find charming and compelling.

2. TUESDAY. Mixed. Stay alert so that you are versatile in handling people and projects. You can efficiently cope with details. People will be drawn to your wit and humor. This is a better time than most for you to make presentations and proposals. You have unusual eloquence when it comes to expressing yourself. Although you may be trying to help other people, the results are apt to be disappointing. You could wind up nervously worrying about minor matters or be indecisive when it comes to making relatively basic choices. As a result there is a risk of quarrels with relatives and friends. It might be simpler and smarter to let them make the decisions today.

3. WEDNESDAY. Slow. Your energy level is not as high as usual. If you need help on the job, ask co-workers to lend a hand, they probably owe you a few favors. Even though you may not wish to be physically active, you can make progress by other means. You are intuitive and imaginative in work. One or two shortcuts will help speed things up with little extra effort on your part. Follow a hunch when it comes to money. You are shrewd in handling personal finances. You will be stable and decisive about work-related responsibility. You may experience deep-rooted and intense passion this evening, when you could fall secretly in love. Just be wary of getting involved with someone who is on the rebound.

4. THURSDAY. Variable. Communication with colleagues may become confusing. There are bound to be misunderstandings, so try to state your intentions in at least two different ways. Also ask them to repeat or paraphrase your statements to be sure they have been clearly understood. It would be wise to get any important details in writing. Send out a memo or an e-mail as a backup in case you need proof later of what was agreed to today. This is a better day than most for partnership matters. You are apt to learn something new or surprising from someone you work closely with on a daily basis. Collaboration with experts or foreigners could provide useful information.

5. FRIDAY. Productive. The end of the workweek should be productive because you still have lots of vim and vigor. You can accomplish the most by teaming up with another person. Communications among and between your teammates will be motivating. If you act in a leadership role you can reach your goal before the weekend arrives. Your personal life may be more delicate and emotional than usual. Security is very important to you in all of your relationships. However, today your love relationship is changing. You may be strongly attracted to another person. Explore this a little further to see if it is just a passing infatuation.

6. SATURDAY. Good. Partnership and communications are the joint themes of the day. If there is something you have wanted to talk about with your romantic partner, there could not be a better time. You will be able to express your feelings and emotions clearly. There is no time like the present to be open and honest. Share a long, lazy breakfast, then linger over coffee as you talk. Spend the day together and you will have plenty to discuss. You may also be in the mood for taking short trips around town, but you definitely need a navigator or driver. Share the adventure and you will double the pleasure, making this a day to remember.

7. SUNDAY. Expansive. You are something of a visionary as you seek to give your life more meaning. You may be gifted as a medium or possess strong ESP powers. You are apt to prefer seclusion today, so find a quiet place where your intuition can come through loud and clear. Pay attention to any insights you receive. Finances you share with a partner could be a source of trouble or confusion. As a Cancer you are idealistic in your desire to help people in need. However, you may suffer disappointment when they do not heed your advice. Try to be sympathetic and warm-hearted toward their actions even if you do not agree with them.

8. MONDAY. Favorable. Utilize your great powers of concentration and you should soon be seeing results. You may become increasingly interested in medicine and health-related issues, perhaps discovering that you are gifted in the healing arts. In some way your work can also be inspiring. People most likely want to hear what you have to say. Use your charm of speech to get important messages across. Seek a balance between mental activities and your love of art and beauty. If possible, dedicate some time to a creative project that uses words. Write down thoughts and insights as they occur to you; keep a pad of paper and a pen by your bedside.

9. TUESDAY. Mixed. For some reason you may find yourself at a loss of words. You may be traveling in a foreign country where you do not know the language, or studying a new subject and not understand the terminology. It is apt to be upsetting when you cannot express yourself easily. Look for more simplistic or universal ways of making your points. If all else fails, consider pictures, actions, and hand gestures. This gives you an opportunity to be eccentric and unusual. You do not have to conform or be restricted by the rules. Try hard to keep your sense of humor. Everyone loves an open smile, the class clown, and a good laugh.

10. WEDNESDAY. Difficult. Today's Full Moon makes this day more challenging. You are apt to overwork due to an excess of crazy customers or other people's strange behavior. As a result you might find that your physical energy is being sapped by job pressures. Try to take frequent short breaks to restore your vitality. During lunch you might enjoy escaping into a book or magazine. As a Cancer you are basically persistent and have good organizing abilities. However, co-workers may not want to follow your orders, especially if you come across as stubborn and set in your ways. Try to be patient and to accept a little lunacy.

11. THURSDAY. Disquieting. You are apt to be rigid and dogmatic in your opinions. As a result, it might seem as though everyone is resisting or ignoring your points of view. You need to be more flexible and open to contrary thoughts. Look for common ground and try to arrange a compromise. You might learn something new as different philosophical ideas attract your attention. Your receptive, imaginative mind is capable of delving into a wide variety of topics. The unknown attracts you; in your work you may make a remarkable discovery. At some time in your career you are likely to benefit from relatives of the person with whom you live.

12. FRIDAY. Variable. You are likely to become involved with the public in career, professional, or social activities. As a result you may not have much time for your private life. There is the possibility that you will soon change your occupation. Your career may get a boost from a female colleague or from a female member of your family. You are intuitive about what the public wants and in fact could be something of a visionary. Trust that your talents and work will soon be recognized. Just be patient and put on a show of confidence even if you are a bit shy and feel slightly nervous. Keep negative emotions under tight self-control. For now just be industrious and your powers of endurance will help you succeed.

13. SATURDAY. Favorable. Although this is not a regular day of work, your career is highlighted. You may be called in for some lucrative overtime if co-workers run into a difficult problem and need your expertise to solve it. If you brought work home for the weekend, this is the day to tackle it because you have strong powers of concentration. You should come up with good results because ringing telephones and colleagues' questions will not interrupt you. Take care not to overwork. Be sure to stretch frequently and go out for a walk or get some other form of exercise.

14. SUNDAY. Lively. This is an excellent day to get together with friends. Do not be surprised if someone drops by unannounced or you receive a phone call from an old acquaintance who now lives out of town. Consider a vacation back to your childhood home to stir up memories and get a chance to reunite, even have a reunion and share the current gossip. Now is the time to catch up on correspondence, especially to distant relatives. You have lots of energy for travel. A drive into the countryside or to a nearby lake or park would be enjoyable, particularly if you invite some friends to go along for a picnic.

15. MONDAY. Fair. As a Cancer you have an unusual outlook on life and possibly an interest in all that is mystical. You may receive a sudden financial benefit from an unexpected source. Your romantic involvement is likely to be unconventional. Although you feel a responsibility to other people, take care not to try to rescue them. You could find yourself being taken advantage of by someone who is actually quite capable. Remember they have to do it for themselves, but you can be supportive. Your intuitions may not be very accurate right now. There is a risk of financial loss through a business deal that goes sour, so it would be wise to postpone any investment decisions.

16. TUESDAY. Changeable. Your easy social charm attracts admirers. You will especially enjoy the intellectual stimulation of like-minded people. This is a time to get involved in group events, such as a club meeting or a business association luncheon. Either will motivate you by the energy of the whole group. Try not to volunteer for a demanding position such as treasurer or fundraiser. This is not a favorable time for you to handle other people's money because there is a risk of being duped by an unreliable friend and getting involved in a scandal not of your own making. You will enjoy spending a quiet night at home after being surrounded by people throughout the day.

17. WEDNESDAY. Uncertain. You are sensitive, receptive, and intuitive with other people, yet you could have difficulty explaining your side of the story. Your feeling or intuition may not easily be put into words. Sometimes it is best just to hold onto your visions and let them germinate rather than exposing them to early criticism. If you tend to be easily hurt, retreat alone to a quiet place where you can hide your real feelings. Get away to restore yourself, think, and meditate. You have a creative imagination; even though things are unclear now, have faith that they will soon be clarified enough for you to take action.

18. THURSDAY. Sensitive. This is definitely a day for working alone or in secret, especially if you are feeling insecure. There could be a disappointment through your mother or another female family member. This is an ideal time to reflect back on your past in order to learn from your mistakes and avoid repeating the same errors. Now that you are no longer a child you can discard worn-out habits and approaches that prove unsuccessful. Simply decide to change, then do it your own way. You no longer need anyone's approval or permission. This is also a time to complete minor matters that have been kept on the back burner. Finishing up neglected work will clear the way for exciting new projects.

19. FRIDAY. Lucky. It would be worthwhile to start your day off quietly contemplating or meditating. Open your mind to a profound new insight or sudden flash of intuition that sets your direction for the rest of the day. You have lots of energy and enthusiasm. Apply this to a personal goal or project you want to achieve. This is a day for furthering your interests and desires. It is likely that other people will cater to you. You should have good luck finding new ways of using your abilities and talents to make money. It is important to communicate your ideas because those in positions of authority are listening.

20. SATURDAY. Successful. If it seems that unseen forces have been slowing you down, you will be relieved to know that your path ahead is now clear. Strive to move forward with all of your projects. Now your persistence will pay off; the delay just gave you time to get better organized. You are well positioned for your talents and work to be recognized and rewarded. More than likely you will be very industrious with good powers of endurance. Communications of all types are favored. You might want to dust off an old manuscript, write a proposal, or devise a project plan. Being a perfectionist could come in handy, but be careful not to be overly critical at this early stage.

21. SUNDAY. Favorable. With your active, creative mind you have a need to communicate your ideas. You should be successful in writing, teaching, or lecturing. If you need to prepare a speech or a classroom lesson, do so now. Also catch up on all forms of correspondence, from formal letters to birthday cards. For Cancer students, this is an ideal time to write essays and term papers. Your ability to express yourself can make you a leader in your chosen field of expertise. More than likely you will be especially fluent in a second language today. Run personal errands during the afternoon rather than putting them off.

22. MONDAY. Eventful. If you are going shopping, chances are that you will find bargains for your home. These could involve building and renovation materials, or perhaps furniture and decorating items. You are able to earn money creatively. Use your imagination as you look for new ways to work from home. You may have extra space that you could rent out. Consider hosting a foreign student so that your family can learn another language and appreciate another culture. Or you might want to think about opening a bed and breakfast for tourists. At the moment your family's financial affairs are apt to be unsettled, but it will not be long before additional income relieves the stress.

23. TUESDAY. Cautious. As a Cancer you are sometimes thrifty and careful, at other times wasteful and careless. Normally you have a keen sense for what could be profitable. Today, however, you are not as security-minded or apt to plan for the future. You may be greedy or extravagant. If you are feeling under the weather, treat yourself to a special food in an effort to perk yourself up. This is not a good time to go shopping because you are apt to spend money emotionally and unwisely. Doing so could create stress with your mate or partner regarding the household budget. Best to consult before making any major purchase, even if you stumble upon a sale.

24. WEDNESDAY. Excellent. Your creativity is heightened. If you are interested in mysticism, try to combine the two traits into a new work of art. You could have a flash of inspiration that starts you off on a new path. This is a better day than most to capture your ideas. You have powerful artistic potential but need firm direction. Consider enrolling in a workshop or art class to gain the skills you must have for realizing your vision. If you already have a mentor, ask for input and support. You have a magical gift of words and a charming way of speaking. All forms of written work, from fiction to business proposals, are favored.

25. THURSDAY. Frustrating. Your mood and emotions are apt to swing to extremes, especially when it comes to interacting with your colleagues and co-workers. You may feel jealous of the credit or rewards they have received. However, it would be wise to congratulate and learn from them. In the future you may even be able to team up together. On the personal front you may be upset or disappointed about your current love relationship. Getting angry or frustrated will only bring about unpleasant changes. Instead, try to pinpoint the cause of the difficulty. You might find it easier to write in a journal rather than talk to your mate or partner or to a marriage counselor.

26. FRIDAY. Pleasant. This is a better time than most to begin a new project, especially one that is connected to your home. Think about moving. Cancer people enjoy living near the water. Your home is usually a showplace and you like to surround yourself with beautiful items. You may soon be starting to renovate or redecorate. Enjoy conjuring up happy memories of childhood. You may want to call your mother or a favorite aunt for a chat. There will be harmony in all domestic relationships. Do not hesitate to have a heart-to-heart discussion with loved ones.

27. SATURDAY. Exciting. As your energy returns you will find yourself full of new ideas. You are independent in thought and open to change. This weekend you can enjoy travel and distant adventure. Fight for your convictions. Seek out new experience as you strive to live life to the fullest. Higher education may be on your mind. You will gain in honor or financially by improving your knowledge. This is a good time to search the Internet or to borrow books from the library in order to learn more. You will also enjoy being physically active around the house, helping with gardening and other outdoor activities.

28. SUNDAY. Demanding. You are apt to be impulsive about love, following your heart rather than your head. As you seek the pleasure in life there is a risk that your thinking will be illogical. You have a tendency to rush into a commitment before considering your actions from all points of view. However, you have lots of energy and enthusiasm, enabling you to juggle several balls at the same time. Be aware that one of your liaisons could soon become public knowledge. This weekend you are romantic and have a creative imagination. With your wit and sense of humor, you should be able to talk your way through any tricky situation.

29. MONDAY. Dynamic. You are even more alert than normal. As a result, you will be versatile and able to adapt to different people and projects. You are practical and efficient when it comes to coping with details. You may also be successful in getting co-workers to assist with various aspects of your job. People are drawn to your wit and frequent laughter. Make a game or race out of work and everyone will want to play along, especially if you offer a motivating prize. This is a better day than most for making a formal presentation or sales pitch. There is an eloquence and passion in your self-expression that will be difficult to resist.

30. TUESDAY. Varied. Pay attention to your intuition when it comes to your health. You may be overworking or letting stress build up inside you. Unhappiness at work may adversely affect your health, making you especially prone to stomach trouble. This is the time to exercise to burn off excess adrenaline. Consider joining a fitness club or enrolling in a sports clinic, or find a co-worker or neighbor to challenge to a regular game. It will help to have someone to motivate you on rainy days or when you could easily justify that you do not have any extra time. It might also be a good idea to schedule an annual checkup with your doctor.

OCTOBER

1. WEDNESDAY. Bumpy. You could be feeling quite impulsive. If things are not going well at work, there will be a tendency for disputes to erupt suddenly. Disagreements with co-workers or the boss might lead you to think about quitting on the spot. However, try not to make any thoughtless or irrational moves. Right now you are apt to be indecisive about taking on any new responsibility. It would be wise to search for a position that truly suits you while you are still employed. At home you will find that your family supports you no matter what you decide. Try to unwind and put the office behind you this evening.

2. THURSDAY. Beneficial. Work should go smoothly because you are tuned into the needs and motivations of your boss and your colleagues. You may also have greater insight into your own health and well-being. Be sure to avoid too much caffeine and junk food. Look for wholesome alternatives that provide your body with nutritious energy. Your vitality level will pick up with extra vitamins and minerals. If you have a lot of extra work to do, try to find a partner or teammate. Brainstorming regarding marketing or advertising ideas is favored, as are all forms of communication. Travel could be worthwhile.

3. FRIDAY. Slow. If you are trying to slow down as the work-week ends, focus on catching up with correspondence. Offers from a distance may be more useful than normal, perhaps containing money, a contract, or helpful information. Communications with a business partner or teammate will be productive. You might want to call a meeting to review a possible project or an unexpected opportunity. If you need assistance with a job, ask your partner for help. Be careful not to be self-indulgent or lazy, however, or your request could backfire. If you have been disappointed in love, this is a good night to have a heart-to-heart talk with your romantic partner. Be willing to compromise anything except your principles.

4. SATURDAY. Comforting. Security is very important in marriage and in all relationships. Cancer people can be especially happy marrying a parental figure. Your spouse will probably be protective of you. Continue to be responsive in partnerships and particularly in marriage. This is an excellent day to dedicate to your loved one. Start with breakfast in bed, or linger over an extra cup of coffee. You should be very perceptive when it comes to recognizing the desires of your family members. You will enjoy spending the day in the house together, cooking a special meal or puttering in the garden. A beautiful home makes you feel secure as well as comfortable.

5. SUNDAY. Sensitive. Although you are probably feeling sympathetic and warmhearted toward loved ones, you will probably prefer seclusion. As a Cancer you are deeply sensitive, interested in questions about life and the afterlife. You have psychic ability that you can use in a practical way. A personal problem that you share with your mate or partner could be a source of trouble or confusion. Pay attention to your intuition regarding this matter. You can guide other people in a spiritual way. Since you have an idealistic desire to help anyone in need, take time out to listen and respond to the hopes and fears of your own loved ones.

6. MONDAY. Worrisome. Because you are apt to be feeling original and highly individualistic, you may find yourself dressing in a flamboyant, extroverted manner. Expounding upon your unusual outlook on life can bring new people into your sphere. You will be attracted to the mystical and unconventional, which family members may find worrisome. However, do not let other people restrict your actions. Have the courage to be unique and eccentric. Seek out different experiences in order to live life to the fullest. Be wary of people who refuse to take a stand.

7. TUESDAY. Cautious. Your receptive, imaginative mind is capable of delving into sophisticated philosophical ideas. Today, however, you have a tendency to be vague, dreamy, and somewhat impractical. If you are having difficulty expressing your thoughts, do some research at the library or buy a book on the subject. The unknown attracts you; in your work you may pursue knowledge of the past. You might encounter some opposition from a colleague who would rather leave facts buried in the archives. At some time in your career you are likely to benefit from an introduction at a family gathering. You will have happy experiences on a trip, especially a long-distance voyage, but be prepared for delays.

8. WEDNESDAY. Calm. You will most likely be involved with the public in your career. Focus on professional or social activities related to business. You are intuitive about what the public wants but will not have much private life. However, you should enjoy and profit from this easy day of mingling and chatting with people you are just getting to know. Take some time to attend a trade show or training course to increase your knowledge and gather feedback from clients. Also watch people's reactions and note how they respond verbally. Your career may benefit from female members of your family who are involved in charity work or as hospital volunteers.

9. THURSDAY. Manageable. If you use your home as a place of study or work, you may need to make some changes in your residence. Or you may be transferred or have to depart on business-related travel. Your parents and early home life stimulated your curiosity to learn. Now you are mentally active and probably have contacts throughout the world. You are apt to be feeling romantic and artistic. You might attract a most interesting person because of your unusual ideas about love. Suddenly you could become very sentimental regarding traditional family life. Cancer singles may soon be ready to settle down, although not necessarily in a marriage relationship.

10. FRIDAY. Emotional. Today's Full Moon could make you more touchy than usual. Because Cancer people are very sensitive to lunar influences, it is possible that you will experience more shyness than normal. The Moon could also affect your self-confidence, making you hesitant or doubtful about your choices. You may be pulled back and forth between home and career due to a sick family member. Or there could be a reason you have to work late tonight that causes you to miss a family gathering. Get home as soon as you can since you are likely to be craving warmth and affection. Tonight you will be in an unusually romantic and passionate frame of mind.

11. SATURDAY. Helpful. Although this is officially a day off work for most people, you might find yourself called back to the office. Work you brought home with you should not be put off. Today is actually a better time than most to make career progress, even if it is just thinking about ideas while you are helping with chores around the house. In the process of daydreaming, there is a good chance that you will have an inspiration which leads to receiving sudden financial benefits from an unexpected source. Tonight you will enjoy getting together with friends. Your energy level is high, so you can participate in something physically active such as dancing or playing a team sport together.

12. SUNDAY. Positive. This is an excellent day to invite friends to your home for Sunday brunch or an afternoon barbecue. Also be open to accept a spontaneous invitation for a visit. You are in the mood for intellectual stimulation and good conversation. It is also a better time than most to catch up on personal correspondence. If you have long overdue letters to write or e-mails to answer, take this opportunity to get in touch. You are persistent and have strong organizational abilities, making this a starred time to clean out closets or a spare room. You never know when you will have company sleeping over unexpectedly.

13. MONDAY. Unsettling. Your easy social charm attracts many admirers but also makes you accessible to unreliable friends. Through them you might be dragged into a scandal not of your own making. Your goals are about to shift and friendships are likely to change. Fortunately you are emotionally intuitive in dealing with people, which will probably help you sort out good company from bad. You have a natural flair for entertaining at home. Invite new neighbors to come over so that you have a chance to get to know each other better. When they let their guard down, you will discover their real intentions.

14. TUESDAY. Frustrating. You may feel rigid in your attitude, which could lead you to be a strict disciplinarian with children. Because you want to stick to clearly defined rules, your communications could seem abrupt or overly blunt. Ask yourself what is making you afraid. More than likely you are resisting change, which can be very frustrating. Try saying yes to a new situation and you will probably breathe a huge sigh of relief. If you can get away to think and meditate, your intuition will serve as an excellent guide. Stop trying to control all situations and allow life to help you reach your maximum potential.

15. WEDNESDAY. Fair. If you are feeling stressed out from overwork, try to stay home today. If that is not possible, at least find a quiet spot where you can work alone behind a closed door. Otherwise it is likely that colleagues and associates will keep interrupting your thoughts. You have good common sense and exceptional shrewdness, especially related to home and family affairs. Cancer parents will find it easy to chat with children about secrets. With your creative imagination you can easily relate to their worries and self-doubts. Communication with your romantic partner regarding home life should be harmonious.

16. THURSDAY. Favorable. Because you are sensitive, receptive, and intuitive toward other people, you can see behind the scenes. Your intuition is strong. There may be some behind-the-scenes maneuvering by certain people, but they will not be able to fool you. Opportunities or propositions received from peculiar or unlikely sources can be well worth looking into. Someone may unexpectedly reappear out of your past. This is a good time for picking up the pieces of an old romance and making a brand-new beginning. Concentrate on developments in the background away from public view.

17. FRIDAY. Rewarding. The end of the workweek puts you in the mood to take a lighthearted approach. You could play the part of a witty conversationalist, tossing out lots of jokes and funny stories. You will enjoy being the center of attention. When the spotlight is shining, you come to life. People in authority will notice your way of handling an audience. You are versatile, flexible, and restless, definitely ready to try something new. You could also be inclined to suddenly change your mind. Avoid making any serious decisions that are irreversible, especially regarding issues related to your home and to your current work.

18. SATURDAY. Deceptive. The personal projects you want to tackle today might have to wait because domestic duties need your immediate attention. You could suddenly have a pipe that needs to be repaired or a leaky faucet. It may turn out to be the perfect weather for autumn garden cleanup. Or you may spend most of the day driving children to sporting events or helping with a school project. In any case, your time is not going to be your own, so just surrender to the moment. Consider that a weekend break of any kind can be good luck compared to having to be on the job. This evening you should enjoy domestic bliss and harmony in your closest relationships.

19. SUNDAY. Chancy. Anything involving a substantial sum of money will be a risky proposition. You might think that you have found a real treasure at an antique shop, only to be disappointed when it turns out to be an expensive forgery. What appears to be a bargain will probably not be worth its price. Avoid flea markets and auctions where the temptation to buy may overcome you. As a Cancer you are normally thrifty and careful, but today you are likely to be wasteful and careless. You could be feeling greedy and extravagant, basically eager to spend money emotionally and unwisely. Leave your wallet at home and spend time with family members in your own backyard.

20. MONDAY. Good. You are able to earn money creatively, possibly even from home. Focus on a product or service that you can offer to the public. Consider converting a passionate hobby or interest into a money-making enterprise. You might need to look for a partner to help get started. Turn to someone you already like working with, such as a colleague or committee member who you enjoy spending time with socially as well as in a working situation, someone who makes work seem like play. You are serious and faithful in love. Shower your romantic partner with some extra attention by going out for a special dinner at a restaurant where you can linger.

21. TUESDAY. Tiring. This is the kind of day when you could shop until you drop. There may be a sale or clearance that you just cannot afford to miss. It could be an estate sale or a store that is closing. This might be an opportunity to buy something special for your home such as an old Persian carpet or dining room suite. If you miss out you will regret it, because it is probably a one-of-a-kind item. Your energy is not as high as usual, so try to minimize the number of trips and errands you undertake. At work it would be wise to concentrate on clearing up paperwork rather than launching anything new.

22. WEDNESDAY. Stimulating. If you are looking for a change and a new challenge, try writing. You will find that ideas flow easily through your pen or computer keyboard. Communications of all kinds are favored. You can inspire people with your thoughts. As a Cancer you have good self-discipline and are patient, industrious, and have good powers of endurance. You want your talent and work to be recognized. You like socializing and being in the spotlight. You can attract romance and possibly a new lover as your words go straight to the heart of the person you are hoping to impress.

23. THURSDAY. Easygoing. Realize that you are thinking emotionally and have a strong imagination. Because you dislike routine your life is marked by many short excursions. You have a good memory, are willing to change your opinion based on new evidence, and make a good impression when working with the public. You have an inquisitive mind coupled with good common sense. You could be successful writing about yourself or your family. You are creative and fond of pleasure and good living. Follow up on your interest in art, theater, or sports by reserving tickets for a special show or event. Surround yourself with people, including children, who make you happy to be exactly where you are.

24. FRIDAY. Slow. This is a good day to take off from work, especially if it appears that not much will be happening. Instead you could do what is necessary from the comfort of your home. You will be more productive dressed in casual clothes and sitting in an easychair. Focus on financial calculations including budgets, accounting, and banking. Double-check figures that involve other people's money. Your intuition is strong, making this a good time to review family investments. Be sure that your insurance, will, and pension plan are all in order. Get out for some exercise tonight. Games with children will be especially enjoyable.

25. SATURDAY. Promising. You are apt to feel stubborn and somewhat self-willed. Deep-rooted habits can sometimes work to your advantage, as today when they relate to a new creative project that looks very promising. You have a dramatic way of expressing yourself and possess artistic talent. More than likely you can excel at communicating with the public today. You also like the idea of change and of getting to know new people. Cancer singles may begin a new romance. A lover must keep you intellectually interested or you quickly become bored. Now more than ever you need to seek adventure and new experiences.

26. SUNDAY. Happy. Your Cancer personality exudes friendliness and a tranquil nature. This is a day of rest and a time to indulge your love of luxury. Linger over your morning coffee and the Sunday newspaper. You might want to spend the afternoon with a good book for company. Your artistic eye takes pleasure in all forms of creative work. Consider visiting a few galleries around town to refill your well of inspiration. With your talent you should be able to succeed in the artistic or entertainment world. Take center stage, making yourself visible, and allow the magic to begin. Do not settle for anything less than your best.

27. MONDAY. Disquieting. You are impulsive about love, with an intuition that could be leading you on a wild-goose chase. You may find yourself attracted to someone who is not available. If you are on the rebound from a disappointing romance, you could be drawn to the exact opposite of your former mate. There is a tendency to follow your heart rather than your head. The results might not be what you imagine, but you are sure to have an interesting experience. Seeking the pleasures in life is a good thing. If your energy is lower than usual, pay extra attention to your diet and get some exercise by taking a brisk walk.

28. TUESDAY. Buoyant. Because you are active and have a courageous personality, this is a better time than most to be physically active. Give free rein to your creativity. Consider dance or martial arts as possibilities. You also have a very practical mind that can be of help or service to other people. A colleague may need a hand, or you could impulsively volunteer to assist with a new project. You have a literary ability, so writing is meaningful. You are also a forceful debater who can help promote a worthy cause. Just try to avoid getting involved in financial matters. You can contribute the most with strength of action and words.

29. WEDNESDAY. Favorable. Pay attention to any intuition you have regarding a possible new job. You may suddenly find yourself with an offer that comes out of the blue. Something you volunteered with or helped in the past has prepared you for a new opportunity. If this is more than you think you can handle on your own, look for a partner. If you are indecisive, consult your romantic partner. Right now you are ready for a challenge. You may change jobs frequently until you find one that truly suits you. You are intuitive and imaginative in work; find a way to use these traits to achieve long-term success.

30. THURSDAY. Tricky. Be enterprising in using your creativity. Your high energy level will direct you to take action with a partner. Be assertive about expressing your needs, one of which is to have fun while working. However, be aware of scheming tendencies. Your thinking may be hazy and you might have difficulty concentrating for any length of time. As a result you could accidentally deceive just the person you want to impress. Security is very important to you in marriage and in all of your relationships. Marrying a parental figure will probably give you some added confidence. In partnerships of any kind, be responsive without giving in entirely.

31. FRIDAY. Enjoyable. Take pleasure in today's social life and being in the spotlight. You are apt to attract romance and may even find a new partner. Enjoy all forms of creative work. The laughter of children will be the highlight of the day. Cancer parents may enjoy going to a family G-rated movie or watching a video at home. You have the talent to succeed in the artistic or entertainment world, especially because you love applause. You also need the support and admiration of your family. You feel secure having a solid home base to ground yourself. Being surrounded by loved ones gives you the confidence you need to succeed.

NOVEMBER

1. SATURDAY. Sensitive. You might prefer seclusion because you are getting strong psychic signals. With some quiet time you can find the direction in which these impulses are trying to move you. Sitting and contemplating near a body of water such as a pond, fountain, or river can be especially useful. Even submerging yourself in a hot bath might be beneficial. You have sound financial judgment; with patience and persistence your investments will grow in value. You also have an active mind with a broad outlook which enables you to see far into the future and then plan accordingly.

2. SUNDAY. Exciting. You are an original and highly individualistic person so you may want to experiment with personality changes. You could dress in a completely different style or try a new sport or game just for the fun of it. Friends and family members may consider your new behavior eccentric or at least unusual. However do not conform or be restricted, even if no one understands or wants to play along. Just because some people are uncomfortable is no reason to limit your potential. In fact, this is probably part of your creative self-expression. Enjoy being in the spotlight and getting attention and applause.

3. MONDAY. Misleading. Your strong powers of concentration could be very helpful when it comes to higher education. Focus on learning something new such as sign language. You might find yourself traveling, which could force you to deal with another culture. A long-distance call from someone native to a foreign country may require you to communicate in new ways. Your intuition is apt to be misleading you. Also be aware that you are susceptible to deception. Confusion and misunderstandings cannot be ruled out. Get important information in writing for future reference and support.

4. TUESDAY. Variable. Your receptive, imaginative mind is capable of contemplating philosophical ideas. The unknown attracts you. In your work you may delve into history or the more recent past. Think about going back to school to learn more. This is a better day than most to do research in preparation for a presentation or for a report. Cancer students will enjoy the ease with which an assignment can be completed. Communications of all forms should be informative and educational. Take extra care of your health. Too much sitting at your desk or in front of a computer will sap your energy. Take stretch breaks and short walks to refresh your mind and body.

5. WEDNESDAY. Reassuring. Do not hesitate to become involved with the public in career, professional, or social activities. Strive for harmony and good relationships with associates on the job. Working together as part of a team can ensure good progress, especially if other people are willing to handle the hard physical part of the work on your behalf. A work situation may lead to romance. Since you are interested in art, theater, and sports, consider inviting a colleague to join you this evening out on the town.

You are energetic and creative, fond of pleasure and good living. Your health is good, but guard against a tendency to overindulge in rich food and alcohol.

6. THURSDAY. Promising. Pay attention to your intuition on the job. There is a possibility of changing your occupation. Your career may benefit through a woman boss or a female member of your family. You have good insights about what the public wants. All of these shortcuts to success do not require any particular endurance or persistence. Let go of your stubborn ways of maintaining control and you will soon find yourself on the fast track. Right now you are attracting good luck. Be energetic and creative. Enjoy pleasure and good living. A love affair is likely to reignite your passionate nature and zest for life.

7. FRIDAY. Favorable. When it comes to your career, you attract luck through change. Remain open to all future possibilities. Today you are apt to have a sudden insight or idea, perhaps even a flash of genius. This could lead to a new invention or a humanitarian movement, more than likely an action that will be original and unorthodox. Because you are independent and resourceful, people might be attracted to your far-out points of view. You might even be psychic in some regards but not all. This is a better time than most to be rebellious or unpredictable at work. Sudden and dramatic events will have a surprisingly positive effect on your job.

8. SATURDAY. Lively. Your easy social charm attracts many admirers. Since you have a flair for entertaining at home, invite out-of-town friends for a visit. You are full of energy and need to find a way to stay active. Consider a group game or adventure, whether it is a few rubbers of bridge or a tennis foursome. There may be a community event such as a dance or festival that you can attend; check the newspaper for ideas, times, and places. You will enjoy intellectual stimulation and long conversations. Your mind is not content with a little knowledge; you want to know more. A new book might be an eye-opener.

9. SUNDAY. Tense. Effects of last night's Full Moon can make life more dramatic than usual. You are apt to be very playful and fun loving. A friend may not appreciate your lighthearted response to a difficult situation for which this person expected support and comfort. Normally you are emotionally very intuitive in dealing with people, but today you see humor in every situation. Rather than joking and making witty conversation, listen sympathetically and nod knowingly. Keep your unsympathetic response to yourself. Sometimes the most important part about being a friend is just being there even though you do not have the answers or any suggestions.

10. MONDAY. Chancy. Friends and acquaintances surround you throughout the day. You are apt to be attending a social function, club meeting, or business association together. At some point someone might invite you to join in a group investment that involves pooled resources or even a loan on your part. It would be wise to decline such an invitation because there is a risk of loss through a business deal with friends and associates at this time. In fact, an unreliable friend could lead you into a scandal not of your own making. At some time in your life your goals will shift and friendships are likely to change, but not quite yet.

11. TUESDAY. Uncertain. Although you have heightened creativity and powerful artistic potential, you need firm direction. Consider enrolling in an art or crafts class so that you set special time aside for projects. Look for a mentor or supporter who encourages you to keep experimenting. It is important that you learn by doing. Childlike self-expression and the freedom to focus on whatever intrigues you will help release fear. Get some quiet time alone to allow your ideas to bubble up without interruption. Your physical energy may be lower than usual, but your mind is active. Restful contemplation can lead to unusual sources of inspiration.

12. WEDNESDAY. Emotional. Because you tend to be a perfectionist, day-to-day problems can seem overwhelming. If you need quick answers, trust your hunches and gut reaction. You will attract luck by being open to change and positive about the future. Take a renewed interest in your health, diet, and personal hygiene. It is a time to get better informed about the latest on these subjects. As a Cancer you have a tendency to be nervous and may develop respiratory or stomach problems. Look into natural remedies such as homeopathy. Improve your diet with organic foods. Load up on extra vitamins and minerals. Exercise can be your best stress buster.

13. THURSDAY. Excellent. This is a better day than most to focus on personal projects. Be aware, however, that you are a perfectionist and may be too critical of your first attempts. Allow the process of learning to take place through trial and error. Practice is the way to improve. You are persistent, have excellent organizing abilities, and are capable of self-discipline. You are likely to be very industrious. Over time your talents and achievements will be recognized. Your energy level is high and you are determined to succeed. Seek out experiences that enable you to live life to the fullest. Higher education occurs outside the classroom as you gain real-life practice.

14. FRIDAY. Good. Be imaginative in the way you express yourself. Listen to your intuitive voice regarding other people. Home and family mean a great deal to you. Think back on your childhood with nostalgia. For Cancer parents, this might be a good time to tell youngsters about the good old days. Teach an old-fashioned game, rhyme, or story. You are full of vim and vigor and will have fun being physically active. Participating in a team sport is an excellent idea. Your powers of endurance are strong; you can probably run a marathon and still have energy left over. You have the ability to succeed in spite of negative circumstances. Do not hesitate to tackle a big project that someone else declined to take on.

15. SATURDAY. Manageable. Although it is the weekend, you should be able to earn money creatively. You are practical and efficient, especially in writing or any form of communications. You may be paid for authoring an article for a newspaper or magazine. Use your imagination to deal directly with the public. Consider selling items at a garage sale or through an on-line auction. You may accept an invitation to appear in public to speak on a subject you know well. If shopping today, watch your spending. Normally Cancer people are thrifty and careful, but today you are likely to be wasteful and careless.

16. SUNDAY. Active. If you are going to shop, concentrate on buying for other people rather than yourself. You may even want to start your Christmas shopping early and beat the rush. You should be able to find some deep-discount bargains or a clearance sale, more than likely saving money and finding some unusual specialty items. Also look for items to improve your own health and fitness: vitamins and minerals as well as exercise and sports equipment. Now is the time to get in shape for winter activities such as skating and skiing or just to look good in a bathing suit. Make plans for a winter vacation.

17. MONDAY. Unsettling. This is not a good time to make any financial decisions. You are in a careless mood and you will probably not do your homework or enough research before making a purchase. As a result you could find yourself making impulse buying decisions that upset you later. Your financial affairs are in a state of flux and tend to be worrisome. At work it would be wise to avoid handling other people's money. At home do not get into family assets or a joint checking account. As a Cancer you usually immediately recognize a potentially lucrative deal, but today you are not as alert as usual.

18. TUESDAY. Rewarding. You are apt to experience deep-rooted and intense passions. You have a tendency to fall in love secretly, especially with someone at work. This person could be a colleague or even a client. As a result you may suddenly be paying more attention to your body and physique. This is not just vanity but is actually good for you no matter what the motivation. Suddenly you could find yourself dedicated to a new fitness schedule. You are ready for a change and a new challenge. You are shrewd when it comes to handling finances. This is a good time to put together a complex business proposal or sales pitch. Your ability to communicate is excellent in person or in writing.

19. WEDNESDAY. Fair. You are thinking emotionally and have a strong imagination. As a result, communications with your colleagues are going to be challenging. You may be so lighthearted and flippant that no one takes you seriously, especially when it comes to discussing money. You dislike routine and being tied down, so fill your day with many short trips. Do not hesitate to run some errands while visiting customers and suppliers. You can make a good impression working with the public or appearing before a large audience. Get out there and mingle. You also have a talent for acting and could be put in the spotlight.

20. THURSDAY. Disconcerting. You might feel restless, hasty, or impulsive due to delays while commuting or traveling. Breakdowns in communication are bound to irritate you. Although you want to do something extravagant, you will be forced to bide your time. Get home as early as possible so that you can relax and be pampered. You are protective toward your family and also toward your pets. You can increase your assets through real estate or family possessions. If you are contemplating a change of residence, living near a soothing body of water could be your best move.

21. FRIDAY. Changeable. You are apt to be feeling somewhat erratic due to nervous strain from this busy workweek. If you have the chance, work from home today. You can get your work done in half the time if you are free from interruptions. Later in the afternoon you can help out around the house with a repair project or a few routine chores. You will enjoy being with loved ones, particularly children. Play games or teach a new skill. Prepare a special family dinner if you have the time. Otherwise, order a pizza and watching a video together. This is not a time to make any major decisions.

22. SATURDAY. Successful. As a Cancer you take pride in your work and have a talent for organization. At the same time, you need to feel appreciated. Your health is good and you have strong recuperative powers. Because you have been taking good care of yourself, you can fight off the standard winter cold or flu. If you have an occasional nagging health problem, look to alternative medicine for relief. A new doctor may be able to help you find the root cause of the problem rather than just treating the chronic symptoms. Enjoy some creative time, or call it play time if you are interacting with children.

23. SUNDAY. Tricky. You have a skeptical mind and, as a result, are susceptible to occasional errors in judgment. For example, you could be indiscreet due to being stubborn and self-willed regarding some particular matter. Someone may be pushing your buttons that causes you to act out of character. This could trigger a deep-rooted habit that you have been struggling to overcome. In any case it would be wise to ask for help from loved ones. Let someone you trust have the deciding vote on any important matter. Get some physical activity to discharge negativity from your system. This allows you to direct your energies into creative new endeavors that will be satisfying.

24. MONDAY. Tiring. Your physical energy may not be as high as usual, making you irritable. Avoid getting into an argument, particularly with a co-worker or your boss. You may be belligerent and ready to disagree about anything and everything. However, that will only drain you further. Use your intuition to find quick solutions or compromises. You are something of a visionary and may be gifted as a medium or possess strong extrasensory powers. Use this to see people's motivation and needs. If you can empathize with them, there may be no reason to disagree. Also support your body with nourishing food, and avoid caffeine.

25. TUESDAY. Bumpy. Your penetrating mind is susceptible to nervous tension. You have a talent for bringing about change through your writing. Be sure to capture new thoughts on paper because they are apt to come and go in a flash. These could be important ideas that can later be developed or published in book form. Your high intelligence, sensitivity, and imagination is today combined with impulsiveness. There will be a tendency for changes and ideas to erupt suddenly, then vanish just as quickly. It is important not to stagnate because your work can inspire other people to aim higher.

26. WEDNESDAY. Difficult. You may be feeling somewhat obsessive or combative. As a result you will be unhappy when forced to accept new terms or conditions. A colleague may be promoted and become your boss. Or you could find it difficult to accept that a younger co-worker knows more than you about a certain subject. Rather than become competitive, it would be wise to team up. You will both be stronger with your combined experience and different educational backgrounds. By being responsive in partnership matters, communication will be easier. This is a definite plus when you are united in your efforts to solve a complex problem.

27. THURSDAY. Favorable. Security is very important to you in marriage and in all of your relationships. Continue to strive for harmony and fulfillment in your partnerships. You are a natural peacemaker, which makes you popular with other people. Take a chance and make the first move toward a possible new liaison. This is a very favorable time for meeting new people. Cancer singles should definitely get out and mingle. You could experience love at first sight. It is a good time to make an engagement official. At some point in your life you are likely to gain prestige or financial benefit through a partner.

28. FRIDAY. Variable. You come across as sympathetic and warmhearted. Because of your idealistic desire to help people who are in need, a co-worker may come to you for advice or compassion. Your intuitions are very astute. Use your strong powers to identify problems and then seek the best solution. If you find that you are getting too emotionally charged, something as simple as putting your hands under running water or touching the earth will help get you grounded once again. Avoid evening plans that would take you far from your home base.

29. SATURDAY. Helpful. This weekend you should make yourself useful around the house. Help with domestic duties, or assist children with school projects. You probably have a preference for seclusion, so it would be wise to volunteer for things you can do alone rather than with a group. Meditation is vital to help you see the way ahead. You will be particularly talented in the areas of health, nutrition, and cleanliness. This is also a better time than most to take care of family banking and accounting. Just do not be too much of a perfectionist when it comes to these matters.

30. SUNDAY. Volatile. In the comfort of your own home you can be eccentric, original, and highly individualistic. You may decide to take up a unique new passion ranging from collecting bizarre artifacts to traveling to an exotic country. No matter what other people think of your choice, you will not conform or be restricted. You are apt to have happy experiences on a voyage. Because you tend to be vague, dreamy, and impractical, invite along a companion who is better organized and is able to handle details for you. Be sure bills are paid before the due date.

DECEMBER

1. MONDAY. Demanding. If you need to accomplish an important task, you can do it with courage and liveliness. Do not shy away from learning a new skill or studying another language. Your strong powers of concentration ensure success. For Cancer students, this is a good day for taking an exam. Your receptive, imaginative mind is capable of delving into the unknown. You may delve into history or the past and become active as a museum guide. You will have happy experiences while traveling even if there is a delay along the way. Take the night off to unwind from this mentally demanding day.

2. TUESDAY. Dynamic. Today you are more clever and original that usual. It is likely that you will come up with an interesting new idea or concept, possibly even an invention related to health or physical fitness. You may not have the specific background or education, yet you can find answers by doing research. At some time in your career you are likely to benefit from relatives, so keep them informed about your career. Seek intellectual compatibility in your personal as well as business partnerships. You will probably marry someone lively and talkative. Verbal give-and-take characterizes all of your relationships. This is a starred time to form a new business relationship.

3. WEDNESDAY. Expansive. As a Cancer you have a good imagination with artistic potential. This is an excellent day for creative self-expression, even at the office. Figure out what you can make as a handmade gift for someone very special in your life. Take pride in your work. With your talent for organization, you are also an efficient problem solver. Pay close attention to inspirations; you could come up with something very intriguing that benefits your career. Expect to be involved with the public in career, professional, or social activities. You are intuitive about what the public wants and have an idealistic desire to help anyone who is in need. Just keep in mind that charity begins at home.

4. THURSDAY. Favorable. With your great powers of concentration you are bound to see speedy results. An important project that you only recently became involved with can have a favorable impact on your career. Show that you are dedicated and passionate about the opportunity. You may be putting in long hours of overtime and as a result not have much private life. Take care that you do not overwork to the point where job pressure saps your physical energy. Your intuition may guide you to some shortcuts for accomplishing your goals. Your career may benefit also through a female member of the family who is perceptive and understanding.

5. FRIDAY. Good. Communicating with a business partner or teammate at work should be constructive. It is a time to build a team. Together you can discuss a project plan. Business partnerships in law, literature, or communications are particularly beneficial. As a Cancer you are sociable and adaptable to all kinds of people. Your easy casual charm attracts admirers because you are emotionally intuitive. With your flair for entertaining at home, consider inviting friends over. Start celebrating the holiday season before everyone is booked with Christmas parties and family gatherings.

6. SATURDAY. Sensitive. Make good use of your optimistic outlook. You are apt to be in a sensitive mood and want to share good tidings of the holiday season with people who are less fortunate. Consider getting involved in a community charity such as a toy collection or a food drive. You might be able to get your friends and family involved as well, or even get your company to contribute. Make a few phone calls to find out how you can help make a difference. Keep busy with a variety of intellectual interests. Your mind is not content with a little knowledge; you want to know more.

7. SUNDAY. Changeable. Because you are independent in thought and open to change, travel and adventure appeal. This is a good time to make reservations for a trip at Christmas or for a winter vacation. Be prepared for a sudden change of plans. Friends who were going to stop by for a visit might have to cancel, or people could drop by unannounced. You will enjoy talking about your hopes and dreams for the future. Discussions about humanitarian and altruistic projects should also capture your imagination and lead to taking action locally. You fight for your convictions because you want to live life as best you can.

8. MONDAY. Promising. Under the influence of today's Full Moon, pay attention to your intuition. You could be something of a visionary, giving your life deeper meaning by using psychic gifts such as strong extrasensory powers. You tend to be sensitive, receptive, and intuitive toward other people. Spend some time alone in a quiet place so that your insights become clear to you. Finances shared with a marriage or business partner could be a source of trouble or confusion. The Christmas budget may go a little overboard because you are the one who is being extravagant this year. Try to restrain an urge to splurge.

9. TUESDAY. Unsettling. This is a day to guard against interruptions by co-workers. Try to find an empty office or unused meeting room where you can close the door. In this way you will avoid the ringing telephone as well as the idle chatter of colleagues. You may feel a little under the weather or just stressed from the extra holiday workload. As a result there is a risk of being argumentative. You could become headstrong and even fanatical about a sudden idea. More than likely you will face resistance from people who are less creative or farseeing than you. If you are feeling insecure, get away to think and meditate on your own.

10 WEDNESDAY. Uneasy. If your gift-buying budget is limited, do not go shopping. Normally Cancer people are very thrifty, but today you are in a spendthrift mode. As a result you could be extravagant, then regret it almost immediately. You are a bit of a perfectionist; be careful that you do not come across as too critical with your mate or partner. Communications with your loved ones, workmates, or business allies could be tense because you insist that your way is the only way. Try setting a mutually agreeable goal, and then letting everyone find their own personal way of achieving it.

11. THURSDAY. Variable. Expect to have some conflict on the job because you want to take some time off at Christmas but so does almost everyone else. Or you may want to spend the holidays in your hometown with your relative but your mate or partner prefers to stay home. In any case, you should be able to talk it through and find an acceptable compromise. Love is easily expressed today and a reconciliation is more than likely. In fact, after resolving this one issue you should have a very harmonious time for the rest of the day. In addition, you will have good luck with money thanks to a family member.

12. FRIDAY. Lively. Focus on your high aspirations for advancing your personal plans, desires, and interests. You are full of vim and vigor. Potentially you can find new ways of using your abilities and talents to make money. Rely on those in authority who have decision-making power. You will have good luck obtaining cooperation from them because your personal drive and ambition will attract their interest. Ignore a jealous colleague who has the impression that you are too wrapped up in yourself and have a potential power complex. Just be sure that you are not in any way dictatorial. You may want to invite co-workers out for some holiday cheer after work.

13. SATURDAY. Confusing. You are able to earn money creatively by using your imagination. Try to deal directly with the public. You may have holiday gift items to sell at a market or craft sale, or you might be appearing in public as a performer or speaker. In any case, your creativity should provide some extra income. This will be quite helpful since your family financial affairs are apt to be unsettled due to all the extra seasonal expenses. As a Cancer you are thrifty and careful, but today you could exhibit opposite traits. Your keen sense for what is a good buy may desert you. Try to regain your ability to plan for the future security of your family.

14. SUNDAY. Fulfilling. This is an ideal day to do Christmas shopping. Be sure to take along a list because your intuition will not help you with suggestions. You are sure to find bargain sales that please your thrifty side, especially when you find the perfect gift in the right size and color for a substantial discount. It will be useful to take along a family member to assist you in going through the list quickly. Be sure to consider your own health and fitness. You need to get some fresh air and exercise other than walking through a shopping mall and a parking lot.

15. MONDAY. Helpful. At work you are noted for being persistent and self-disciplined. You have organizing abilities that you can put to good use on the job. This might be one of your last chances to send holiday cards to your clients and suppliers. It is also a good time to catch up on correspondence of all kinds. Your inbox may be loaded with greetings and gifts. Try to return phone calls on the same day you receive the message. You can tackle a long to-do list because you are industrious and have a strong sense of personal responsibility.

16. TUESDAY. Variable. Use your energy and initiative to advance career matters. You are apt to dominate other people because of your drive and determination to succeed. Now more than ever you need change and a new challenge that makes you sit up and take notice. You are ambitious and competitive when it comes to communicating, able to close a sale or make a very compelling marketing pitch. Work with a trusted teammate or business partner; avoid interacting with jealous co-workers or less motivated associates. Because you value your independence you must shy away from interference. Your self-reliance and executive ability will give you added status in your occupation.

17. WEDNESDAY. Complicated. As a Cancer you are protective toward your family, but right now your career has to take priority. You have been given an excellent opportunity to prove your special abilities during this very busy time of the year. A work-related crisis dealing with transportation or shipping problems can give you a chance to shine. In any case, you will not get to spend as much time at home as you would like. You may have to put in overtime tonight, but this is just a temporary situation. Keep your plans flexible so that you can go with the flow. You can do everything your way, but only until the boss tells you to change.

18. THURSDAY. Mixed. If you have any important shipments that must be delivered on time, find a dependable courier. Chances are that there will be delays if you mail at the post office. Even delivery trucks and airplanes could have problems meeting schedules due to bad weather. Plan alternate methods now before you hear from unhappy customers or disappointed children. There might be some stress in your primary relationship because of an ongoing argument. You may have to ask your loved one to take on extra responsibility around the house since you are probably overworking and overstressed. Ask for help before job pressures sap your physical and mental energy.

19. FRIDAY. Eventful. Home is where your heart is, so if possible work from the comfort of your house. You will find that you can get your tasks done in half the time, then be able to help with holiday preparations. However, if you must go to the office, spend time assisting colleagues. There could be electronic equipment breakdowns or communication delays. Fortunately you can handle such problems because you are an efficient problem solver who can get things moving again. Try to arrive home early so that you can put up the Christmas tree and decorate outside as well.

20. SATURDAY. Satisfying. You are in the mood for fun and festivities, making this an excellent time to take the family to a special holiday event. This could be a sport like sledding or skating, or it could be Christmas caroling or a concert. You are apt to be feeling impulsive when it comes to love and would enjoy sharing time with that special person in your life. In your romantic frame of mind you can use your creative imagination to come up with special plans for this evening. Seek out the pleasures in life, which might include spoiling children with a few extra surprises or treating yourself royally.

21. SUNDAY. Manageable. Although it is the weekend, you might have to be at work. Cancer people who are in the retail industry may have to help out with the last-minute shopping rush. Doing so will probably be well worth your while when your next paycheck arrives. You have leadership ability and strong initiative. There is a touch of inspiration and genius in your thinking. You are apt to be intense about a romantic involvement, perhaps with someone at work. You may inherit money from a loved one or a marriage partner, or you could gain from the career advancement of someone who loves you. In many ways, this promises to be a remarkable day.

22. MONDAY. Frustrating. Success is yours in marriage and in all forms of partnership, which should bring material, monetary, and social benefits. This is a time to be impulsive. That could mean getting engaged or eloping before the year ends. There is a tendency for changes to erupt suddenly in your life. This might be frustrating at first, since as a Cancer you are rather set in your ways and afraid of new beginnings. You may be concerned because you need to be dominant in your relationships. However, this is a better time than most to be impractical and reckless. Your partner will probably be prominent and of good, honorable character.

23. TUESDAY. Fair. Your energy may not be as high as usual. Unhappiness or stress at work may adversely affect your health, making you especially prone to stomach trouble. Try to take it easy. Focus on eating wholesome food rather than all the Christmas goodies. Although you are intuitive and imaginative at work, you can be unstable and indecisive about responsibility. If you need assistance with your workload, ask co-workers or a higher-up. They should be willing to give you a hand. You may be stubborn and self-willed when it comes to doing things in your own way, but try to delegate a few tasks to other people and then let them proceed on their own.

24. WEDNESDAY. Varied. This Christmas Eve you and your romantic partner are apt to be a little stressed from all the advance preparations. You are probably totally organized and ready but may have to lend a hand to family members with last-minute shopping or wrapping. With your good powers of endurance you will be ready well before midnight even if you had lots of last-minute errands and tasks to complete. Communication with loved ones should be harmonious, including good relationships with relatives who are visiting. Allow the Christmas spirit to enter your heart and home.

25. THURSDAY. Merry Christmas! You should feel tranquil and satisfied. A happy and friendly mood prevails for the entire day. Your love of luxury will be satisfied with the rich colors, tastes, and sounds of the holiday. Your artistic eye might capture these precious moments in photographs. Your energy level is high and you have ample enthusiasm, so let yourself become a kid again. Hopefully the children in your life will allow you to play with some of their new toys. Try to get some physical exercise later in the afternoon to work up an appetite for a traditional dinner feast.

26. FRIDAY. Uncertain. You probably will not be in the mood to join the crowds bargain hunting at the shopping malls. Today you will likely prefer quiet seclusion. Because you are sympathetic and warmhearted toward family members, you may lend a hand with chores around the house. It is also possible that your mind is back in the office. You may have had an idea over the holidays that you are anxious to work on, or you could be called in to deal with the volume of after-Christmas activity. Loved ones may not appreciate it if you have to tend to business, but do what you must. Just keep the evening free for socializing.

27. SATURDAY. Happy. This is an excellent day to spend with your loved ones. Everything you do together will double your pleasure, whether skiing, skating, or sitting on a beach. You will be happiest seeking intellectual company, someone who is lively and talkative. Your love life is most likely filled with lots of verbal give-and-take. Basically you want to know more about everything. Your learning mode may include reading a new book or signing up to take a course to improve your skills. Although your opinions are apt to be rigid and dogmatic, this leads to interesting and animated conversation. You are apt to win a debate if you stick to the facts and avoid becoming emotional.

28. SUNDAY. Slow. If you are feeling a little lazy, sleep late and then relax and read a good book for the rest of the day. You probably received a few books as gifts or brought one along for the holidays. You are in the mood for learning, with an open, receptive mind capable of delving into philosophical ideas. The unknown attracts you. History comes alive as you learn more about a certain time period. If you are traveling there is a good chance of delays. Be sure to phone ahead to confirm departure times. Leave early to avoid a traffic jam caused by bad weather. Rather than becoming restless or irritable, just settle back and be glad you brought along a book or magazine to help pass the time.

29. MONDAY. Disconcerting. If you are heading back to work you could have a lot to discuss with a colleague or business partner. Just thinking about this could make you anxious and nervous. You may not be happy with how things were handled over the holidays. You are apt to be high-strung from so much sugar and caffeine. Try to cut back on Christmas goodies now. Allowing your mood and emotions to swing to extremes could bring about unpleasant changes that prove to be counterproductive. Instead, focus on clearing up year-end business. Do some filing to get better organized for the year ahead.

30. TUESDAY. Manageable. This is a very important day for your career. Final year-end results hopefully will be positive. Use your good Cancer instincts to make decisions regarding your future. You and your mate or partner may disagree about what to do at this crucial point. It is a time to decide on definite New Year's resolutions. You are clever and original, able to go forward on your own if you must do so. You have an independent mind and a self-reliant nature. Think of going back to school for an advanced degree. Right now, however, is time for a well-earned vacation or at least to make plans for one.

31. WEDNESDAY. Fair. On this New Year's Eve, you might find yourself having to work. Cancer people who are in the hospitality business may be helping everyone else have a good time. At least this is a good opportunity for you to make extra money even though you might be disappointed not celebrating together with your romantic partner. You could be involved with the public in career, professional, or social activities and not have much private life. Making a resolution to improve the amount of time you spend with your loved ones will get you off to a positive start in the New Year.

CANCER
NOVEMBER–DECEMBER 2002

November 2002

1. FRIDAY. Disquieting. Trying to bully other people into doing what you want may work in the short term, but you will heap up a lot of trouble if you continuously do so. It is far better to be with people who are willingly going along with your ideas, though not at the expense of implementing their own. A social event is likely to be more expensive than you had planned for, which can be an embarrassment. Take a credit card with you to a gathering to make sure you are not caught short. This is a day when acting on your principles can be quite a challenge. However, it is important to follow your conscience, even if that means standing apart from the crowd or going out on a limb.

2. SATURDAY. Easygoing. This quiet day favors spending time at home or just hanging out with loved ones. Your memories will probably be vivid, so that the past seems almost as real as the present. However, do not let yourself become mired in nostalgia. If you feel slightly under the weather, you could be running a temperature; it would be worthwhile checking. If you are coming down with something, cancel any social event that is lined up. Instead, get an early night. While it is fine to devote yourself to household chores, do not ignore an equally real need to relax. You can draw inspiration from art or music.

3. SUNDAY. Good. Catch up on your phone calls or letter writing. This is an ideal time for getting back in contact with friends who have been absent from your life recently. If you have time to go over your accounts, you may find that you have more spare cash than expected. Certainly you can think of ways to put your money to better use by investing. Turning a small profit is better than none at all. Focus on your fitness, or lack of it, at the moment. This is an ideal time to begin building yourself up for the colder months ahead. Exercising outdoors might not be very appealing, but you can practice yoga or aerobics in the warmth and comfort of your own home.

4. MONDAY. Challenging. The workweek is likely to begin with a bang, so be prepared for a busy day. Fortunately there is movement in several of the areas of your life which you have been feeling dissatisfied with lately. For a start, relationships at home may improve markedly, particularly if you are prepared to act as peacemaker between warring parties. Romance contains a paradox: although you may think you want to end a partnership, this might not happen when you come to do it. Even discussing the differences between you and that special person in your life can draw you closer together once again. Keep all of your options open for as long as possible.

5. TUESDAY. Uneven. Seeking to confuse other people or put them off the scent is not a positive action, even if you persuade yourself that you have their best interests at heart. There is always some tactful way to tell the truth, if you think long and hard enough. Cancer people who are taking care of youngsters should keep a close eye on them, especially when out in public places. Children may show an almost uncanny ability to slip out of sight; you might find them talking to someone who is a complete stranger. It is very important to listen closely to instructions for a new work project so that you do not get the wrong impression of what you are supposed to contribute to it.

6. WEDNESDAY. Happy. The ordinary matters of life may seem attractively odd and offbeat at the moment. It is almost as if you had just opened your eyes and could see through surface appearances to a deeper reality. This is a promising day to buy or sell property, especially if you allow your good Cancer instincts to guide you. However, that does not mean you should not be quite hard-headed about the practicalities. A glamorous person might enter your life, perhaps through an introduction by a relative or close friend. You are almost bound to be enchanted. The good news is that as you get to know this person better, the fascination will grow between you.

7. THURSDAY. Fair. Having a sense of order in your life is more important than you might realize. Allow your affairs to become chaotic and you are piling up unnecessary work to eventually sort them out. The secret is to keep up every day with what needs to be done. A determination to finish some tiresome work before the end of the workweek will enable you to clear your desk with comparative ease. In fact, co-workers may be amazed as you even refuse to be distracted by pleasure. Try to remember that your mind needs exercise just as much as your body. A challenging book or some stimulating conversation will get your mental wheels turning.

8. FRIDAY. Changeable. The morning hours may drag a little, so that the hands of the clock hardly seem to move. Try to discipline yourself not to watch, but to concentrate closely on the work at hand. Money might be a worry at the moment; the prospect of a loan that must be repaid soon could be a burden. However, if you cut back on frivolous spending it should be possible to accumulate the required funds quite quickly. This afternoon includes the possibility of a romantic encounter close to your home or work base. Your hand may brush against a customer as you reach for items in a store, giving you a wonderful excuse to stop and talk.

9. SATURDAY. Disconcerting. If you make someone a promise, there should be no question of you not keeping it unless circumstances forbid. Even if it might be inconvenient, the other person's comfort should be your first concern. Bear in mind that personal ambitions need to be kept within the bounds of reason. While it is time to dream of grand achievements, you will ultimately only be fulfilled if you are actually able to realize these dreams. A friend's generosity might be so out of proportion to the services you render that it is embarrassing. They probably want to thank you just for being yourself and being their friend.

10. SUNDAY. Satisfactory. All efforts to get physically fit are favored. You will probably prefer exercising alone to being on a team. In that way you can go at your own pace and choose exactly the kind of activities that will be most helpful. As a Cancer you are excellent at recycling clothes and household items, making a virtue out of the necessity of using what is old. Today is a promising time to create your own unique style from items that have been in your possession for ages. Even though a passionate longing for that special person may not find expression, there are subtle ways of letting your mate or steady date know how much and how deeply you care.

11. MONDAY. Cautious. There is little to keep you from getting into a work project with almost wild abandon. Just make sure not to sacrifice judgment for enthusiasm. Cancers who are looking for a new and better career might receive a useful tip from an unexpected source. Do not waste time getting your job application faxed or in the mail. Sometimes it is more impressive to preserve a dignified silence than to run the risk of saying too much. This is particularly true when you are in the presence of someone for whom you have a great deal of respect. A quiet demeanor can give the impression of deep thought, even if that is not the case.

12. TUESDAY. Pleasant. Allow yourself to be carried away by inspiration this morning, so that new ways of approaching old problems spring from your unconscious. It is a matter of opening your mind to forces that are within, rather than trying to always keep conscious control. Today is good for buying communications equipment, whether you are thinking of a new phone or of upgrading your computer. You will probably be fascinated by many of the various gadgets on sale. The outlook for romance is rosy. You might even find that all you have to do to get a date is to be at the right place at the right time, and with the right person.

13. WEDNESDAY. Calm. This low-keyed day offers breathing space which is bound to be welcome in the midst of your busy life. It should be possible to regain a sense of the fun and playfulness that is often lost among the pressures of work and family. You can look sensational in daring new clothes, especially if you have the courage to be quite bold with color. You have the ability to turn heads, so make the most of it. Today is ideal for thinking about creative expression. Your uniqueness can come out in the arts or simply by living in an imaginative and stylish fashion. Turn down an invitation to go out with the friend of a friend.

14. THURSDAY. Useful. Your eloquence knows no bounds at the moment. As long as you are talking about a subject which you know something about, it is fine. Simply seeking to impress other people is another matter; you might reveal some ignorance. Youngsters can benefit from your teaching skills, even if you have not received any formal training. In addition, new colleagues will be certain to enjoy an informal induction, which you could enliven with a humorous touch. If you are strongly attracted to someone, there is no reason you should not tell them so. Just do not come on too strong; the person might be alarmed if you seem too intense and passionate.

15. FRIDAY. Variable. Finish the workweek with a flourish by getting a matter completed in record time. All that you do to enhance your reputation for efficiency is bound to count in your favor. Unfortunately wrong choices can sometimes be made in romantic matters. You might be wondering what you have gotten yourself into. If you are not happy in a personal relationship, there is no compulsion to stay in it. Socializing can be expensive. If you are more concerned with saving than with going out, let friends know. They will not realize the reason for your reluctance otherwise, so be honest and do not let them change your mind.

16. SATURDAY. Disquieting. Youngsters are likely to require quite a lot of your time, seeming to be particularly restless and hard to amuse. Lining up a variety of entertainment for them will help because they will not have to focus too long on any one activity. Your mood may swing remarkably during the course of the day, surprising not only loved ones but yourself. Try to stand back impartially and analyze your feelings, so that you are not fully identified with and overwhelmed by them. A trip might be quite tense. Not everyone will agree about what they want to do. Do your best to keep the peace without giving in to the person who talks the most or the loudest.

17. SUNDAY. Deceptive. If you consider that you know better than anyone else on any issue, you are wide open for accusations of arrogance and even stupidity. It is far more attractive to presume that there are always people who are better informed than you. In that way you are open to the possibility of learning from them. At this time of year it pays to check your plumbing; you might be able to identify weak spots before trouble develops. A peaceful evening at home will set you up for the workweek ahead. It would be ideal to settle down with loved ones for watching a good movie on television or a rented video. Do what you can to get everything ready for tomorrow.

18. MONDAY. Confusing. You might wake up with a start this morning, to find that the alarm failed to go off. Rather than trying to make up for lost time, get up without panicking. In that way your head will clear rather than leaving you unable to think properly. This is not the time to insist on having your own way in the face of strong opposition from family members. Their reasons may be based on instinct rather than logic, but they do have your best interests at heart. Where romance is concerned, it is not fair to keep someone guessing about your feelings. If you are unsure of them yourself, explain that you need some more time to settle into the relationship. You do not have to make a lifelong commitment right now.

19. TUESDAY. Demanding. Work is apt to be so demanding that you have hardly any time to relax at home. This is bound to take a toll on your nerves; if it starts to bother you a lot, ask for some assistance. Someone you have respected for a long time could be revealed as less principled than you presumed. This can be a useful lesson not to set up a mere human being as an example of perfection. Today marks the start of a period when you become aware of new opportunities to make money, perhaps by writing or using other communications skills. It would be foolish to pass up any such chance, even if you have to work without compensation for a while.

20. WEDNESDAY. Mixed. The day will divide into two fairly distinct halves. This morning marks a crisis point in a close relationship. You may have to choose between putting yourself first or the other person. There ought to be little question of which way to go. Later in the day the more imaginative and even magical atmosphere favors creative work of all kinds. Inspiration will be coming to you from a source deep within yourself, and all you have to do is sit passively and receive it. Try not to allow anger to skew your judgment during an argument between friends. Keep in mind that it is really their affair and should not upset you a great deal. Just remain as neutral as possible.

21. THURSDAY. Good. After a long period during which you thought a special person had no interest in you, they may clearly indicate that a date is just what they would like. Do not become so rattled that you fail to arrange an evening out together as soon as possible. Your finances might receive a welcome boost in the form of a small gift of money that can be used for current expenses. Thanks are in order, but do not go overboard. Some caution is necessary when exercising so that you do not pull a muscle or strain your back. It is better to do too little than too much; you can always work up to more demanding exertion later.

22. FRIDAY. Promising. Completing overdue work will give you the sensation of a heavy burden being lifted from your shoulders. Now all you have to do is tie up a few loose ends, then look forward to being paid with money or at least with compliments. There is more emphasis at the moment on finding out what it takes to make you secure. This requires examining whether you primarily need material goods or loving relationships in order to feel protected. If you are prepared to work hard during the day, reap a reward this evening by going out for a delightful evening with friends. Let your hair down and celebrate all that is good.

23. SATURDAY. Buoyant. You are ready to launch into the weekend with plenty of energy and enthusiasm. The good news is that loved ones also are eager to go out and have fun, so all is set for success. Today is also excellent for getting chores out of the way. Joint effort will speed the work. Health matters look promising. You might realize that a former chronic problem has faded away with time. If you stop to think about it, this is probably due to the better care you have been taking of yourself. Abstract ideas about life and its meaning are apt to have a strong appeal for you. As a Cancer you tend to be a sensitive thinker; try to come to grips with an important subject about the nature of love and life.

24. SUNDAY. Easygoing. This more domestic day will suit your mood, but it is unlikely to be dull in any way. Puttering around the house can have interesting results as your mind becomes free to think creatively. There is also a possibility of finding an object you had given up for lost quite a long time ago. If youngsters show signs of wanting to write or draw for their own delight, encourage them. All indications of an active imagination should be given special focus or they may fade quite quickly. In-laws or other older relatives will probably tax your patience, but try to be as polite and as understanding as possible.

25. MONDAY. Variable. In some ways it is quite natural to feel an attraction to someone who is superior to you at work, since the power they wield can be a compelling factor. However, do not delude yourself that such feelings are romantic; they probably have more to do with fantasies about what you would like to achieve for yourself. It would be a good idea to limit your spending at the moment since there are some expensive times ahead. Try saving coins on a daily basis, which will not leave you short of a luxury or two but will add up quite quickly. Compliments on your abilities are bound to come your way and will do your self-esteem a world of good. Be sure to accept them graciously.

26. TUESDAY. Excellent. If you are looking for a better job, just the one you want might be advertised in a special journal. Try to hone your resume to perfection, and then adapt it even further to fit each job description in a more individualized fashion. Do not neglect your health because of current work or home pressure, particularly to look after people who are capable of caring for themselves. Guard against making yourself a martyr; in the end, doing so does no one any good. The sky is the limit where personal ambitions are concerned. Aim high, and decide that you will not give up till you reach your chosen goal.

27. WEDNESDAY. Sensitive. Quiet changes are afoot, in your mind as much as in the world outside. Your ideals and expectations concerning love and other people are beginning to alter in the light of experience. Give some thought to your joint finances. With a little extra effort from you and your mate or partner it ought to be possible to improve your position significantly. You may decide to obtain professional advice concerning investments. A friend or relative who is having a hard time would appreciate a helping hand. Treat them as you would wish to be treated if in similar circumstances. Keep in mind the saying that what goes around, comes around.

28. THURSDAY. Manageable. To falter now in a work project when the end is so close would be a shame. Summon up your mental and physical strength for a final burst of energy to complete the task on time and within budget. Then you can rest with a clear conscience. This is not the ideal time for borrowing money because your prospects for being able to pay it back are not too good. Somehow making do with what you now have would be preferable. Social groups and clubs may make you feel less of an individual by submerging your skills and personality in a crowd of people, so that true self-expression is difficult. You might find more happiness in solitude or just staying home with loved ones.

29. FRIDAY. Mixed. It could be quite an effort to rouse yourself to action this morning. Once you are up and out, however, enthusiasm is almost sure to develop. Dealing with older friends can be a little tricky at the moment. They may not seem responsive to the same pleasurable activities as those you enjoy. It would be a good idea to settle down to a long, serious talk so that you can better judge what is going on in your relationship. Your talents should not be hidden away just because you feel they are not very special. Have the courage to put them on display, then sit back and enjoy some well-deserved praise.

30. SATURDAY. Cautious. A shopping trip could put you in a now-or-never situation with an opportunity to buy expensive items at a deep discount. However, they will still cost more than you can comfortably afford. You will have to choose whether to go without, or to forget the cost and treat yourself royally. When youngsters retreat into silence, you need to find out if they are concealing a problem. Some quiet talk might tell you all you need to set about helping them find a solution. Even though you are in good spirits, you may prefer not to go out on the town tonight. A quiet but luxurious meal at home or in a favorite local restaurant would be a perfect substitute.

December 2002

1. SUNDAY. Excellent. On this busy day you should have plenty of energy to cope with all that occurs. Not that there are many tasks to be done; the accent is on pleasure. New confidence allows you to put more effort into getting fit physically and looking great. This is a good chance to go through your wardrobe and note what clothes need to be replaced. If you are wondering whether to seek a date with that special someone, events might provide the perfect opportunity. Be bold, but also turn on the Cancer charm. Your true feelings will shine through, so that the other person will almost certainly want to get to know you better.

2. MONDAY. Disconcerting. You may have to deal with an awkward situation this morning, having little alternative but to take the blame for mistakes that are not yours. Try not to be a martyr about it. Today is not the most promising time to put your house or car on the market; you are likely to wait a long time for a sale. However if it has to be done, be sure to write up the particulars with reasonable accuracy. There may be trouble with the plumbing either at work or at home, necessitating some expensive repairs. Unless you are absolutely confident of how to fix it, do not attempt to do the work yourself.

3. TUESDAY. Unsettling. Today's tense atmosphere may lead to upsets during the first hour or two, but try not to leave home with an argument either started or brewing. Use some patience and you can avoid a fight with your mate or partner by being especially tolerant. Your parents might not approve of your latest efforts toward self-development, but be aware that your path is very different from theirs. However, it would be wise not to confide in them if you know it will only upset them. Your home computer might crash, so be sure to save all your work as you go along. It may be boring to read the technical manual, but in a crisis situation it can be a real lifesaver.

4. WEDNESDAY. Fortunate. The middle of the week brings opportunities for a new start in the area of personal finances. This time of the year is always expensive, so try your best to keep track of what you are spending. It may even be possible to put aside some cash to cover unusual expenses. All attempts to improve your physical fitness should be worthwhile. Today is ideal for resolving to exercise regularly. Do not let inclement weather put you off track; work out indoors if necessary. You may sense that your career has taken a turn for the worse, but actually you are probably stepping back in preparation for a big leap forward right after the end of the month.

5. THURSDAY. Exciting. Unusual and even quirky ideas for redecorating your home may pop into your mind. Act on them without delay. There is a lot to be said for recycling old furniture or saving money by buying secondhand; in fact, this can be a way of adding special character to your surroundings. Youngsters may need to be reminded that they cannot have new clothes and computer games on a regular basis. If they are made to wait a little while, they will probably forget all about their request. Try to think of ways of making money by taking on extra work which can be done in your current leisure hours, if only as a temporary measure during this costly time of the year.

6. FRIDAY. Disquieting. The best way to deal with the day is to take it easy in the realm of friendship. It would not be wise to press a close acquaintance to commit to social engagements for which they clearly have little enthusiasm, even if it means missing out yourself. Try to get a written report finished by the end of the afternoon so that you can begin the weekend with a well-earned sense of achievement. This might mean that you have to work through lunchtime. Stocks may not be performing too well at the moment. You could benefit from some professional advice. It would not be smart to sell on a whim. Nor should you buy more as the price plummets.

7. SATURDAY. Good. Allow yourself some time to think and reflect. Today is an ideal time for mulling over the happiness brought by old friends. Tap into the strength you get from your memories. Shopping is highlighted, with a good possibility of finding some intriguing items. If you are searching for a gift, this ought to be a particularly successful day. The later part of the afternoon and early evening favor settling down at home. You are likely to be fairly reluctant to go out. Loved ones will be eager to spend time together with you, not doing anything except relaxing peacefully. Make the most of this serene atmosphere, which should be relished as you contemplate the week ahead.

8. SUNDAY. Sensitive. The emphasis today is on local trips, whether this means a healthy jog around the block or a visit to a park or other recreational facilities. Youngsters will probably demand a lot of your time and attention, and may ask some awkward questions. They will know instinctively if you bluff in answering so be honest and admit your ignorance if necessary. Check around the house to see if water is dripping from a tap or a leak is developing in a pipe. The cold winter weather can play havoc with pipes, and it is better to be safe than sorry. Your mate or partner will appreciate an extra hug and a real show of affection this evening. Turn on your Cancer charm to make it a night to remember.

9. MONDAY. Difficult. Money matters are at the top of the agenda at the moment. You may have gotten into a bit of a bind with excessive personal spending. Turning a blind eye to your predicament is not going to help, so face up to it and see what can be done in the way of scaling back. Although it is a good idea to keep physically fit, as a Cancer you can sometimes be a little too soft on yourself. Try to take the middle ground between the extremes of laziness and obsessive exercise. A boss or colleague might attempt to misuse their authority, but do not let them walk all over you or take credit for your accomplishments.

10. TUESDAY. Buoyant. You brighter, more optimistic mood should carry you through today's quite challenging situation. Actually, the day will go fairly smoothly if you stay calm. There may be interesting opportunities if you are eager to further your career, with a lucrative position becoming available. Even if you think you may be overextending yourself, there is no harm sending in an application. Parents are apt to be particularly supportive of a personal project that you have been working on for quite some time. They want you to be successful and happy just as much as you do and will help if you need a hand.

11. WEDNESDAY. Mixed. If you prepare properly ahead of time, the events of the day can be a very positive test of your best Cancer qualities. However, indulging in self-pity when events do not go your way will only alienate potential supporters and sap your ability to cope. Brace up and be strong. Romantic matters may not be developing as you wish. If you cannot seem to win the love of that special person, it might be best to retreat for a while. This does not mean that you cannot try again later; just give them some space now. No matter how tempting it can seem to gamble, try to resist. Your chances of winning are slimmer than you may think.

12. THURSDAY. Frustrating. When a secret becomes known to you, it is natural to feel an urge to tell other people about it. However, it would be neither fair nor kind to do so. Promises of future financial security may be alluring. Indeed, it is never too early to start thinking ahead. However, be sure you do not take on an every-month commitment that might become a burden if you have less money free at some point. Today is not the ideal time for taking an examination because you are apt to be a little tired and even sluggish. However, if you can rouse yourself to concentrate, there is no reason you should not do reasonably well.

13. FRIDAY. Challenging. Set aside superstitious feelings about this date and determine to make the most of a day that offers both opportunities and challenges. This morning there may be a few misunderstandings between you and a friend unless you both strive to make yourselves clear. There is no point dropping hints that will just spark someone's imagination. It should be possible to easily finish a work project so that you look forward to the weekend with nothing pressing on your mind. If you are running short of time, enlist the help of a colleague. The pleasure of being out with friends might tempt you into drinking a little too much, so limit yourself at the start of the evening.

14. SATURDAY. Fair. Although you may not enjoy actually fitting in with the way other people do things, this can be good discipline. It jolts you out of your comfortable and familiar routine, making you more alert. Buying items for your home ought to be approached cautiously because your judgment is not as sound as usual. Do not allow yourself to be talked into anything you do not want, no matter how persuasive the salesperson might be. A difficult romantic situation that is not giving you what you want is at least offering what you need to learn. You will relate all the better in the future if you profit by the lessons you are currently being offered.

15. SUNDAY. Tense. There are bound to be clashes within your family, although they might be disguised as friendly teasing but with a cruel edge. Try not to take sides unless it is necessary to keep the situation from getting out of hand. Today is not ideal for entertaining friends because you are not eager to get organized. It would be better to offer only simple refreshments rather than botch up an elaborate meal. Happily, a good talk with the person who is closest to your heart can clear up a minor misunderstanding. It is important that you listen closely to each other rather than just propounding your own point of view.

16. MONDAY. Rewarding. If you are handling money at work, this could be a good chance to win a reputation for efficiency and honesty. Be sure to complete all required paperwork, and do not skimp on the details. A sudden turn of events later today could switch the course of your life where romance is concerned. You might find yourself relating in an entirely new way, one that is very satisfying to your profoundly emotional Cancer character. A breakthrough in family relations could improve the way you get along with your parents or in-laws, but this will take extra effort on your part and some degree of sacrifice. Also be especially considerate of school-age children.

17. TUESDAY. Manageable. You may not know whether to stick to the tried-and-true way of doing things or be bold and employ your own original ideas. Let your good Cancer intuition guide you, then watch colleagues closely for their reactions. Your sense of personal achievement should receive a boost when you are complimented by a relative who clearly appreciates you for who you are. It would be nice to return the compliment in some way. Money matters need close attention at this time of year. It would not be wise to splurge a large amount when there are major bills coming to you right after the holiday period.

18. WEDNESDAY. Fortunate. Cancers who have been hoping to advance in career matters might receive good news. A position that seems to have been tailor-made for you could open up. Do not delay in applying for it. It may be surprising to learn that someone you have always admired wants to get to know you better. After a few initially awkward moments you will probably get along extremely well. Your health should stay reasonably good as long as you bear in mind that body and emotions are closely linked. Stress and unhappiness can erupt as physical symptoms unless they are recognized and alleviated as soon as possible. Pamper yourself by going to bed early tonight.

19. THURSDAY. Variable. Matters relating to money are reaching a crisis point. You have to make a choice between being able to spend freely now and putting aside funds for the future. The ideal way is to compromise, so that you save but also leave yourself a little extra cash for current needs. A personal ambition could come closer to fulfillment if you are brave enough to overcome recent difficulties by backing down and finding a new approach. This is part of achieving your aim, so do not hold back. Memories of the past may have a tight grip on you, but it would be foolish to get lost in regrets about what is over and done. Your life would not necessarily have been better if you had taken a different course.

20. FRIDAY. Exciting. You will need all the positive action you can muster in order to breeze through this busy day. Luckily, this attitude suits your mood, so much so that you can inspire other people as well. Try to find a moment to sit quietly and count your blessings. Include in these your personal qualities which ensure that you are loved and appreciated. If you are going away for the festive season, try to get loved ones to agree to an early start. Do not worry too much about packing; it will not be difficult to purchase minor items that you might forget in your rush. Just be sure to take along packages destined for other people.

21. SATURDAY. Good. Hearing from friends and relatives who live at a distance can be a particular pleasure at this time of year. Do not wait for them to get in touch; pick up the phone and give them a pleasant surprise. You have more need than usual for beautiful surroundings and the finer things in life to inspire you. It would be good to take time to listen to favorite music or to read a chapter in a book that has special meaning for you. Children are likely to be a real handful; the best way to deal with them is to keep them thoroughly occupied. They will also appreciate being told stories or taken on an outing.

22. SUNDAY. Deceptive. There is bound to be some tension at home. It is better to acknowledge it rather than try to pretend it does not exist. If you can persuade the family to express their feelings, much can be resolved. Today is ideal for getting out in the neighborhood. You may need to visit friends, or just be eager for some exercise. A brisk walk would blow away the cobwebs and clear your mind. The focus is on relationships with brothers and sisters, so do not be surprised if they seem eager to stay in close touch. Their loving support can be invaluable in the months ahead. Be sure to call an older relative who is celebrating a birthday or anniversary.

23. MONDAY. Tricky. You have to watch yourself this morning since cutting remarks could spring to mind all too easily. Take a few deep breaths and try to regain a sense of perspective. What seems so irritating at the moment will be forgotten in an hour or two. Your romantic relationship might be under a strain, but there is a lot you can do to ease the situation. For starters, do not pretend to be superior or all-knowing. Your mate or partner's point of view is just as valid as your own. A more optimistic mood pervades the afternoon. That is a time when you can accept the generosity of friends and also give kindness in great measure to a needy person or charity.

24. TUESDAY. Enjoyable. A mixture of organization and spontaneous flair should make you successful on this enjoyable but rather eventful day. Keep your cool, even when everyone around you is losing theirs. Quickly check your finances, especially if you have some big spending still to do. You may be pleased to find that recent efforts to save have had better effect than you realized. There is a little need for caution when dealing with electrical items at home. If you are replacing light bulbs or doing minor repairs, make double-sure that everything is switched off first. This is a fine evening for a quiet get-together with friends just to celebrate your relationship.

25. WEDNESDAY. Merry Christmas! Even if you usually make little fuss about this time of year, you may be surprised to find the atmosphere especially warm and loving today. Get into the spirit of goodwill by relaxing and letting your hair down a bit. There may be a special surprise from friends or loved ones to show how deeply you are loved and appreciated. In return, make sure to give a helping hand with the work side of the day whenever and wherever help is needed. The only problem you are likely to encounter is excessive partying that leads to over-indulgence in good food and drink. However, there is no harm in going over the top once in a while providing you do not drive.

26. THURSDAY. Low-keyed. Getting over the excitement of the past few days can be quite difficult for youngsters, who look forward to this period for such a long time. Cheer them up by inviting a few of their friends to spend the day, but do not go to great lengths to provide a real party atmosphere. Loved ones will be grateful to walk away from household chores and go out for a drive or a jog. This will also give you time together for some quiet and affectionate talk. If a friend or relative is likely to be spending the day alone, it would be kind to drop by for a visit or to pick them up to shop. An evening around the fire would be ideal.

27. FRIDAY. Useful. If you are driving this morning watch out for carelessness by other people on the road. It is fine to relax, but be alert at the same time. Memories of the past may flood your mind when you are in the middle of routine tasks and minor chores. Some of these are bound to be pleasant, and may even prompt you to get back in touch with people you used to know. Thoughtfulness toward those less well-off than you should be the keynote of the day. There are several ways you can help a friend or a relative, but it would be wrong to act simply for the sake of receiving their gratitude.

28. SATURDAY. Changeable. Getting on the scale this morning might give you a slight shock, but it is hardly surprising if you have gained a few pounds over recent days. Just do not go all out trying to diet; a slow, steady approach to reducing will be far more effective. A friend who holds a position of some importance may prove quite boring with their self-centered stories and anecdotes. If they begin to really get on your nerves, find an excuse to leave the room or at least change the subject. This evening is a promising time to resolve to leave behind negative behavior patterns such as self-doubt. Let yourself shine as you are meant to.

29. SUNDAY. Stressful. When you have made a promise to a family member, there is no good alternative but to keep it. Do not try to slide out of it, even if you must miss some preferable entertainment. A rather absentminded mood may have a hold on you at the moment, causing a few problems unless you make an effort to wake up. For instance, you could start running the bath water and then wander off and forget all about it. At this time of the year it is natural to look ahead and come up with a plan to improve your life. While optimism is a natural Cancer outlook, you will do better to set realistic goals that can be reached.

30. MONDAY. Variable. This morning promises to be quite a passionate time for Cancers who are just beginning a new romantic relationship. It is likely that you will take the initiative to get an affair off the ground. Today is ideal for overhauling the way you look. Think about adopting a different hairstyle or mode of dressing. You can carry off dramatic fashions that would look silly on most other people. Your temper might get the better of you unless you are very careful. It can help to remember that loved ones are not deliberately setting out to annoy you, and that they will be quite shocked if you let off steam at them. Also be more considerate of pets.

31. TUESDAY. Tranquil. Allow yourself some peace and quiet in order to reflect on all of the events of the year now coming to a close. This very valuable breathing space will enable you to leave the past behind and prepare for the promise of the future. If you are having friends or relatives to your house tonight, keep the arrangements fairly informal. As long as you create a relaxed and welcoming atmosphere, it should be very successful. Check your personal money situation. Ideas for improving your income could come to mind, although you will have to wait a while to see if they really work out. Meanwhile, tighter budgeting can help you pay off holiday bills.

WHAT DOES YOUR FUTURE HOLD...?

DISCOVER IT IN *ASTROANALYSIS*—

COMPLETELY REVISED TO THE YEAR 2015, THESE GUIDES INCLUDE
COLOR-CODED CHARTS FOR TOTAL ASTROLOGICAL EVALUATION,
PLANET TABLES AND CUSP CHARTS, AND STREAMLINED INFORMA-
TION FOR ANYONE WHO HAS EVER LOOKED TO THE STARS AND
WONDERED....

__ARIES	0-425-17558-8/$12.95
__TAURUS	0-425-17559-6/$12.95
__GEMINI	0-425-17560-X/$12.95
__CANCER	0-425-17561-8/$12.95
__LEO	0-425-17562-6/$12.95
__VIRGO	0-425-17563-4/$12.95
__LIBRA	0-425-17564-2/$12.95
__SCORPIO	0-425-17565-0/$12.95
__SAGITTARIUS	0-425-17566-9/$12.95
__CAPRICORN	0-425-17567-7/$12.95
__AQUARIUS	0-425-17568-5/$12.95
__PISCES	0-425-17569-3/$12.95

Prices slightly higher in Canada

Payable by Visa, MC or AMEX only ($10.00 min.), No cash, checks or COD. Shipping & handling:
US/Can. $2.75 for one book, $1.00 for each add'l book; Int'l $5.00 for one book, $1.00 for each
add'l. Call (800) 788-6262 or (201) 933-9292, fax (201) 896-8569 or mail your orders to:

Penguin Putnam Inc.
P.O. Box 12289, Dept. B
Newark, NJ 07101-5289
Please allow 4-6 weeks for delivery.
Foreign and Canadian delivery 6-8 weeks.

Bill my: ❑ Visa ❑ MasterCard ❑ Amex _____(expires)
Card# _____
Signature _____

Bill to:
Name _____
Address _____City _____
State/ZIP _____Daytime Phone # _____
Ship to:
Name _____Book Total $ _____
Address _____Applicable Sales Tax $ _____
City _____Postage & Handling $ _____
State/ZIP _____Total Amount Due $ _____

This offer subject to change without notice.   Ad # 893 (3/00)

Are you Lucky in LOVE?

Will he call?
Does he love me?
Is he cheating on me?

All calls $4.99/Min
Visa/MC/Amex/Disc/Checks

Call NOW!
1-888-
241-LUCK
5 8 2 5

Wonder what he's doing now?

Find out!

Call **1-900-484-3888**

All calls $4.99/Min Billed to your phone!
YOU Must be over 18
For entertainment purposes only!

All NEW! - NO Credit Card PSYCHIC SERVICE
Dial 10-10-288-011-245-293-675
or
Dial 10-10-288-011-245-293-883

Int'l LD
Rates Apply!

100% LIVE 1-2-1 EXPERT PSYCHICS
1-664-492-5799
Int'l rates apply   18+

PSYCHIC EXPRESS ®
Call for your free sample reading
1-900-255-0606
Billed to your phone
1-800-796-LIFE
5 4 3 3
$3.99/min.   VISA   AMERICAN EXPRESS   MasterCard   DISCOVER   18+

BEST LIVE PSYCHICS
"We'll unlock the door to your future"
1-800-596-4897
18+ $3.99/min.

LOVE, HAPPINESS, WEALTH, SUCCESS.
Will come to you
Powerful Psychics
1-800-756-4SEE
4 7 3 3
from $3.99/min.
18+ credit card

INSTANT ANSWERS FROM MASTERFUL PSYCHICS!
1-900-255-0505
1-664-492-5799
18+ 900# $3.99/min.   1-664# Int'l Rates Apply

You're In Love... But Is He?
Hear from a live clairvoyant
1-800-826-TELL
8 3 5 5
18+   800# $3.99/min.

PSYCHICS 4 LESS ®
BILLED TO YOUR PHONE
1-664-492-5799
ALL MAJOR CREDIT CARDS ACCEPTED
1-800-568-6363
From $3.99 /min.   Be 18+

GET BACK ON TRACK!
Your road to true freedom can begin now with just one phone call!
Gifted psychics available 24hrs/day
1-664-492-5792
18+   1-664# Int'l Rates Appy

Live psychics devoted to serving
CANADIANS
seeking love, happiness, wealth & success.
1-900-451-3885
1-664-492-7844
900# $3.99/min. 1-644# Int'l Rates Apply 18+
SHOC3-2003

You Don't Have To Be Alone.
Talk to a psychic love specialist
1-800-692-LOVE
5 6 8 3
18+ From $3.99/min.